Praise for
Until We All Come Home

"UNTIL WE ALL COME HOME is a page-turner! This true-life story is so captivating the reader is fully emotionally engaged from the beginning to the end. Kim de Blecourt has done an extraordinary job of relating the gripping impact of saying 'yes' to God's leading in the life of her family. The tenacity, passion, and relentless cry of this mother's heart will make a lasting imprint on your life."
—Carol Kent, speaker and author of *When I Lay My Isaac Down* and *Between a Rock and a Grace Place*

"From its opening words to its last, UNTIL WE ALL COME HOME takes readers on a heart-pounding journey that combines the intrigue of a political spy novel with the warmth of a mother's diary. Kim de Blecourt's book is that rare true-to-life tale that combines warmth, perspective, and wisdom with a message for everyone: We are all orphans in search of a relentless love that fulfills the promise to bring us home."
—Shelly Beach, award-winning author of *The Silent Seduction of Self-Talk*

"UNTIL WE ALL COME HOME reads like a spy thriller, but with the reality that a child's life and livelihood are at stake. It's a terribly beautiful story of a family's love for a child, a corrupt bureaucracy, and the painful lessons we learn when we follow God wherever he leads. I loved this page-turning, God-breathed book."
—Mary DeMuth, author of *Everything: What You Give and What You Gain to Become Like Jesus*

"UNTIL WE ALL COME HOME is one woman's true story that will draw you in from the very first sentence. It's a story of love, intrigue, harrowing fear, and absolute faith in the One who protects and provides in the midst of great darkness. I literally could not put this book down."
—Kristine McGuire, author of *Escaping the Cauldron: Exposing Occult Influences in Everday Life*

"Wow! That is probably the word I used the most while reading this wonderful book! From the opening chapter to the last word and everything in between—it is a wild, page-turning ride that pulls the reader in and doesn't let go. Bravo, Kim de Blecourt, bravo!"
—Wanda L. Sanchez, producer, Salem Radio Network, San Francisco

"Watching God work in the lives of people is always intriguing, and sometimes very unique. UNTIL WE ALL COME HOME is a story of hope when every turn of events appeared to be hopeless. This is an open and honest review of God's faithfulness and one person's struggle in recognizing it."
—Dean Parham, pastor of Immanuel Church of Holland, MI

"I can describe this book in one word: captivating. It details the heart-wrenching excitement of running and hiding from one of the scariest government agencies in the world, and it is absolutely magnetic. I don't know how this family survived such a horrendous ordeal other than through God's intervention and favor. This is a must-read that you will be talking about for years to come, and a reference manual on the positive results that come from having a tenacious, never-quit attitude."
—Gary VanDyke, president of Food for Orphans

UNTIL WE ALL COME HOME

A Harrowing Journey, a Mother's Courage,
a Race to Freedom

Kim de Blecourt

with GINGER KOLBABA

New York Boston Nashville

Copyright © 2012 by Kim de Blecourt
All rights reserved. In accordance with the U.S. Copyright Act of 1976, the scanning, uploading, and electronic sharing of any part of this book without the permission of the publisher is unlawful piracy and theft of the author's intellectual property. If you would like to use material from the book (other than for review purposes), prior written permission must be obtained by contacting the publisher at permissions@hbgusa.com. Thank you for your support of the author's rights.

Scripture quotations are from The Holy Bible, New International Version® NIV®. Copyright © 1973, 1978, 1984 by Biblica, Inc. TM. Used by permission. All rights reserved worldwide.

FaithWords
Hachette Book Group
237 Park Avenue
New York, NY 10017

www.faithwords.com

Printed in the United States of America

RRD-C

First Edition: November 2012
10 9 8 7 6 5 4 3 2 1

FaithWords is a division of Hachette Book Group, Inc.
The FaithWords name and logo are trademarks of Hachette Book Group, Inc.

The Hachette Speakers Bureau provides a wide range of authors for speaking events. To find out more, go to www.hachettespeakersbureau.com or call (866) 376-6591.

The publisher is not responsible for websites (or their content) that are not owned by the publisher.

Library of Congress Cataloging-in-Publication Data

Blecourt, Kim de.
Until we all come home : a harrowing journey, a mother's courage, a race to freedom / Kim de Blecourt with Ginger Kolbaba. -- 1st ed.
    p. cm.
Summary: "De Blecourt's riveting first-person account of her battle to free her adopted son from a corrupt regime reveals the abiding power of God's protective care"--Provided by the publisher.
    ISBN 978-1-4555-1510-3
1. Blecourt, Kim de. 2. Blecourt, Kim de—Family. 3. Adoptive parents—United States—Biography. 4. Adopted children—Ukraine—Biography. 5. Intercountry adoption—Political aspects—Ukraine. 6. Intercountry adoption—Ukraine. 7. Intercountry adoption—United States. 8. Adoption—Religious aspects—Christianity. I. Kolbaba, Ginger. II. Title.
HV875.5.B53 2012
362.734092--dc23
    [B]   2012014124

To my heavenly Father,
to my husband, Jahn,
to my children, Jacey and Jake,
and to the remaining unloved children of the world.

Author's profits from the sale of this book will go to
Food for Orphans (www.foodfororphans.org).

Contents

UNTIL WE ALL COME HOME

Prologue

Imagine you're visiting a place where there's little to no English spoken and you wake up one day to find that the group you went with has all gone home and you are left there alone. You are stranded in a culture where you can't trust many, you don't fully understand the language, and you can't read the signs—and at the same time you try not to let on that you can't do those things. Then add to that a constant fear that you're being watched, followed, and that at any moment you might be arrested.

That was my experience—all because my husband, daughter, and I grew to love a small orphan boy.

While this book describes my journey, it is really God's story, because there is no other logical explanation for how things ultimately worked out except by God's hand. I don't know what God will choose to do with what happened or how he will use it—but I know he *will* use it... if in no other way than to change me, because I *have* been changed. God has grown within me a heart for those who have been abandoned.

That is my purpose in writing this story: to show how important the fatherless are to our heavenly Father. As a community, culture, and church, we've lost the urgency of caring for orphans, but I've learned firsthand how important these forgotten ones are to him.

Many people involved in this story made huge sacrifices to help my family. As I tell their roles throughout these pages, I could do them great harm if I didn't do everything to protect their identities. So I have changed many of the names and certain locations or time frames in order to protect the brave men and women who helped us get home.

Ukraine has become like a second home to me—the place where the one true God became my Abba Father, the homeland of so many dear friends, and the birthplace of my son. And so this book is in no way intended to make people shy away from international adoption—if anything, I've come away from this experience believing even more strongly in adoption of all kinds, foster care, and vulnerable child protection. We, who have so much, need to reach out to the orphans of this world and show them the care, hope, and love they deserve.

Ultimately, this is a story of an orphan who found a forever home. This is also a story of a mother who, alongside her husband and daughter, felt a call to adopt a child and remained resolute to make that a reality. But more important, this is the story of a God who will move mountains for one abandoned child, who will stop at nothing to show how much he loves and cares for the orphan, and who knows each one by name.

Soli Deo Gloria.

I

April 2010

THE CROSSING

Fear gripped me as my children and I arrived at the Ukraine-Moldova border crossing. It was busy for a Sunday afternoon. Guards were everywhere, automatic weapons tucked at their sides, snarling dogs at their feet. The guards looked irritable, as though the amount of traffic was bothersome.

I'd passed through this border dozens of times in the past year—a wedge of Moldova encroaches into Ukraine between Odessa and Izmail, directly over the road I had to take back and forth on adoption business. But the passengers jamming the buses I rode had always shielded me. Today, I couldn't hide among the sea of faces.

Breathe, I told myself. *Act normal.*

But I was anxious. Had the prosecutor gotten word to the border control that I was leaving with my Ukrainian son? Would they have a copy of the outdated warrant with my young son's name on it?

I stole a glance at our driver, Sasha. En route to the border, he had tried to reassure me that everything would be fine; he would take care of us and get us into Moldova. I sought reassurance from him now, but found that his easygoing smile was gone. In its place was a stern, intimidating look. His chiseled jaw was clenched and the muscles along his jawline twitched. His tan arms were grasping the steering wheel so tightly that I could see the outline of every muscle there.

God, please take care of us, I prayed. *Please get us out of here. You are faithful.*

Even though I knew Sasha was a man of faith, how well did I really know him? I had met him barely two hours earlier. Friends who'd introduced us had told me few details about him other than that he was a quick thinker, a skilled kick-boxer, and a competitive knife fighter who refused to flinch in the face of danger. Could I trust that he would be true to his word to help us? I thought so. I hoped so.

As we pulled to a stop I could feel my muscles tensing and quivering uncontrollably.

My eyes scanned the line of silver, black, and white cars ahead of us. A soldier in fatigues interrogated passengers as he stood at the driver's side window of a car at the front of the line. He shifted his weight and casually slung his machine gun over his shoulder, a constant reminder of who held power.

I took in the other soldiers patrolling the congested checkpoint. A few were clustered together chatting casually. Others were interrogating the drivers and passengers. About a half dozen officers kept a firm grip on German shepherds that tugged at their heavy chain-link collars, sniffing and growling every so often. With every move the guard dogs seemed eager to tear at something...or someone.

My fear mixed with resentment. For the past eleven months, I had lived in a constant state of unknowing, dread, and apprehension. But today it was magnified; my life and the lives of my children were on the line.

The officer ahead of us finally waved the driver on. We slowly inched forward, closer to the moment of truth. *One car down; three more to go.*

The conversation Sasha had tried to keep going on the drive here was gone now. He kept his eyes fixed on the soldiers, watching their every move.

An officer shouted at the passengers in one of the cars parked off to the side of the line, as another soldier motioned for the next car to pull forward. One more car sat ahead of us. As Sasha again crept forward, I forced myself not to look at my watch, not to panic.

"Please shield us, God," I whispered. "Don't let them recognize us."

I forced my gaze back inside our vehicle and toward the backseat of our cramped compact car. My children, Jacey and Jake, were huddled together in the center of the seat, transfixed by a Disney movie they were watching on the portable DVD player I'd brought from Michigan. Our bulky green suitcase took up most of the space on the seat next to the children, and even though Jacey was only nine and Jake four and tiny for his age, the two children sat hip to hip. Jake's head was tipped against Jacey's shoulder, and her hand rested lightly on his arm. Thank God they were distracted from the scene around them, didn't know a fraction of what had taken place over the past eleven months, and had no idea of what could occur within a matter of moments.

"Kim."

The now familiar, heavily Ukrainian-accented English reminded me again that I was a stranger in this land. I was fighting against forces bigger than I'd imagined when I first entered this country.

Sasha cleared his throat as he inched the car forward again toward the security gate. He muttered something under his breath in Ukrainian, and then slipped the car into neutral as he turned to face me. His steely blue eyes penetrated mine.

"Kim, it's important that you do everything I say, no matter what it may be. This will be important for *all* of you. Do you understand?"

Sasha's words hung in the air, the implications and uncertainty cutting at my heart. His eyes flicked toward my children. His voice was barely a whisper when he spoke again.

"The people at your embassy spoke to you about the realities of prison and how their hands are tied to help you if authorities take you, yes?"

The last conversation I'd had with the deputy consul general of the American embassy in Kiev came flooding back into my mind: *"If authorities arrest you, drink the water, and eat a little food. You don't want to get dehydrated since you don't know how long you'll be in prison. We can do nothing to help you if you're taken into custody. As delegates of the American embassy, we're guests in this nation too."*

Sasha waited for an answer, but I didn't want to give him one. I was afraid I'd end up admitting to the hopelessness I'd worked so hard to push away. He raised his eyebrows, appealing for my response.

Slowly I nodded. "Yes," I stammered, "the officials at the embassy were . . . quite clear."

I glanced again at the guard ahead of us, and then back toward Jacey and Jake. They were giggling, and Jake was pointing at something on the DVD screen.

Protect them, God, from sensing the danger here, from seeing where they truly sit in this moment.

Suddenly, every bone in my body ached. I was weary of fighting this battle on my own. Yes, my husband, Jahn, was supporting me at home in the States in every way he could. My church family and friends had been praying for me. But I'd been the one forced to hide for weeks when the warrant had been issued. I was the one who'd learned the art of disguise and deception, who'd braved a secret meeting with the Ukrainian mafia to secure the information I'd need to finally get out of the country. I was the one who'd worked to learn the language and banged my head against a culture that often seemed impossible to understand. I'd forced weariness from my bones day after day for love of the child our family could not abandon.

Jake's laughter rose from the seat behind me, and I felt the strength flow back into my soul.

Jake. The four-year-old child who had awakened the sleeping giant of the Ukrainian judicial system and brought down its wrath upon his head... and mine.

"I—" I cleared my dry throat. "I'll try to do whatever you ask, Sasha. Just tell me what you need. But warrant or no warrant, I will never abandon the child who is legally my son. I love this child. I am *not* leaving Ukraine without him."

Sasha's eyes narrowed and the muscles in his jaw twitched slightly. "You have made your choice clear."

His unspoken message was unmistakable: *You, a mere woman—and an American woman at that—have publicly opposed powerful leaders who do not believe Ukrainian orphans should any longer be allowed to leave their homeland. You have made these leaders uncomfortable and angry. They will not make things easy for you if you are arrested. You have caused much trouble for yourself and now potentially for me. The government does not like to be defied... ever.*

Sasha inclined his head slightly toward the backseat. The children's voices had stopped, and I became painfully aware that Jacey hung on every word Sasha spoke.

"I understand," I said.

"If we are questioned," he continued, "you must be polite and submissive, no matter what is said to you. This is not a culture where strong women are admired. Do not speak unless you are spoken to.

When you are asked a question, answer with as few details as possible. And most important, pray that news of the warrant's annulment has reached this border crossing. No matter how many times you may have prayed for this miracle, pray for it again. We will need it."

I pulled my eyes from Sasha and to the scene near a bus where several guards had gathered. No matter how important or true his words were, I wanted him to stop talking about what *might* happen. My job was to keep pressing through the next moment—to keep doing what needed to be done. It was the way I'd survived for the past eleven months. To keep one step ahead of the authorities and to keep pushing forward—no matter what the odds against me or Jake.

"Mom?"

I turned to see Jacey looking out the side window. Her wide eyes were staring at an armed guard thirty yards from us. He was working to control a dog that was barking viciously at a young man who was being removed from a vehicle.

Dear God, protect us. Let us just be faces in the crowd today. Please!

"Mom, why are they taking that man out of his car?" She turned her frightened eyes upon me. "They're not going to make you get out of the car, are they? They aren't going to take you away from us, are they, Mom?"

My mouth went dry. No matter what the danger, I'd never lied to my children. God had always given me the right words at the right time—even on days when we were hiding in plain sight from the police and I'd tried to make our secretive existence a game. But now I fought for an answer that wouldn't cause her alarm.

"Mom?" Jacey's voice caught in her throat.

A loud thud startled us. A guard had slammed his fist on our car's hood, signaling for us to move forward toward the first crossing gate.

I reached for the zipper on the lightweight jacket I wore that morning and pulled it up with a jerk. "Everything's going to be okay, Jacey. I've passed through this checkpoint dozens of times and never had a problem. This time, we've even got Sasha in case we need someone to help us with the language. You and Jake just need to sit quietly. No need to worry." I prayed my daughter wouldn't sense the tension I felt gripping my stomach as I spoke the words.

Sasha pulled to the first crossing gate; another guard leaned part-way into the window and peered inside. I kept my gaze lowered. I knew that to look him in the eye would have appeared confrontational.

My eleven months in Ukraine had familiarized me with much of the language. I'd learned to navigate my world speaking Russian, and now I schooled my face to passivity as I strained to understand the nuances of the exchange.

Sasha spoke to the guard, who eventually nodded and directed us toward the border security office.

Why couldn't we just show him our passports and go through?...This must be standard protocol, I reassured myself. *They do this with everyone leaving the country. It's nothing.*

As soon as Sasha parked in front of the building, I unbuckled my seat belt to get out of the car.

"No, no," Sasha told me. "This is what we are going to do. Give me your passports. I will take care of them. There may be some trouble with Jacob because he has a Ukrainian passport and you're an American taking him. But I will explain everything to them. It's for the best."

"Mom?" Jacey's voice came in barely a whisper.

Without turning around, I said, "It's okay. They just need to look at some papers."

"You're not going to leave us, right, Mom?" Her voice betrayed a slight quiver.

"I'm here, Jacey. It's okay."

"Don't leave the car," Sasha said. "And don't speak to anyone. Pretend you don't understand if you must." A cold resolution had settled into Sasha's voice. The muscles in his neck were working in a quick rhythm, and his eyes narrowed.

I nodded.

"We both believe in God, Kim, and he's given us jobs right now. Mine is to speak. Yours is to pray and to trust me." In one quick motion, Sasha opened the car door, slipped out, and disappeared into the grim, gray building before us.

The minutes dragged on like hours as we waited in silence. Jacey and Jake sat motionless in the backseat.

Just as a guard and his dog passed close to our car, Jacey tried to reposition herself and accidentally hit the door, making a loud thump. Immediately the dog thrust himself at her window, barking and baring his teeth.

Jacey's body went stiff and Jake began to cry loudly.

"Shhh," I said quickly. "The dog won't get you. It's okay." Even as I said the words, I knew I didn't believe them.

Please, God, please, I begged. *We're almost free. Please get us out of here!*

I glanced at my watch. Thirty minutes had passed.

Come on, Sasha, I silently commanded him.

Finally, the battered door of the security building opened, and Sasha emerged.

Although his face was impassive, the set of his shoulders told me everything. And he no longer had our passports. Something had gone wrong. I clutched my stomach, willing it to stop churning.

Sasha opened the driver's door and slid in beside me.

"Kim," he said quietly and calmly. "You must go inside with me, and you must leave the children here."

"Not happening."

"Kim, you don't understand. There's a problem with your passport."

"My passport?"

"You're going to get out of the car calmly, you're going to walk into that building with me, and you're going to leave the children here."

"Why?" Panic rose inside me. "Why can't someone come out and talk to me here? If I go inside, the children come with me. I'm not leaving them here alone."

"No, they must stay here. They will be a distraction, and these people are not in a good mood."

"Mommy," Jacey said.

I could feel my heart pounding in my ears and my face flush. "Sasha, I can't leave my kids out here *alone* while you and I go inside. No. *No.*"

"Yes, you can, and you will," he said, still sounding calm and re-assuring. "We're taking too long. We must leave."

Before I could fight him anymore, Sasha stepped out of the car and motioned to a guard.

"Mom, you aren't going in there, are you?" Jacey asked. "You aren't going to leave us?"

Sensing Jacey's panic, Jake started to whimper and sniffle.

"It's okay," I reassured them. "If we need to go inside, you will both come with me."

A guard approached the car and spoke to Sasha for a moment, then leaned casually on the front fender and rested his gun on the ground.

Sasha ducked his head into the car and said, "Kim, this guard is going to stay with the kids. He will not leave. They will be fine."

I opened my mouth to protest, but Sasha cut me off.

"Kim." All calm and politeness were gone from his tone and face. "You will get out of this car and come with me *now.*"

I understood. Before he had spoken to me with such politeness that I thought I had a say in the matter. Now I realized I had no choice. My going with him alone was not up for discussion.

"Explain to your children that they will be safe," Sasha said. "I will keep them safe for you. I pledge this to you as a father and a fellow believer."

My hands started to tremble. I clasped them tight into balls.

"Assure them," he said. "Then come with me. The guards won't wait long for us before they come and take you."

God. It was all I could pray. The urge to vomit overwhelmed me.

I forced myself to turn toward my children. Jacey had curled as close against the large suitcase as she could get and was holding Jake tightly in her arms. Tears clung to Jake's eyelashes. He kept sniffing loudly. It had taken him months to bond to me. I had barely let him out of my sight since the day he'd been released from the orphanage and into my custody as his mother. Now I had to willingly walk away from him.

"Don't go with Sasha, Mom!" Jacey cried. "Please don't go!"

I took a deep breath and forced calm into my voice. "You're both going to be okay. Sasha has asked a guard to stand next to the car to protect you while I'm inside. He will not allow anyone to harm you. We're going to lock the doors so no one can get to you."

"But, Mom—"

"Honey, you can't go in with me because you won't be safe."

"Mommy—"

"I know you don't want to walk by those dogs." I tried to think of anything to help them not want to come with me.

"But *you're* going past the dog!"

"I'll have Sasha to protect me. I have to go. The sooner I go in, the sooner I can explain things to the men inside and come back to you." I paused for a split second. "Remember, Jacey, the most important thing is that God is with us. Don't forget that, okay?"

Jacey still looked worried, but she nodded slightly. I felt the clock start to tick against me.

"Mommy loves you very much." I turned back in my seat and forced myself from the car. As my feet hit the dirt, they felt as though they'd been covered with cement. My brain scrambled to find some escape. *What if I run to the driver's side and speed away?*

I wanted to scream. I wanted to cry and throw my fists at the men.

I held still for a moment to allow my legs, weak and rubbery, to gain some strength. I knew I had to move purposefully, confidently. My children would watch me depart into the building; they needed to see a calm front from me so they would remain calm themselves.

"Mommy! Mommy!" Jacey's pleading, terrified voice shot through me. Jake's wails echoed around me.

I knew if I glanced back, I would collapse, and Sasha would have to carry me. I forced my eyes straight ahead and willed my feet to move.

My heart pounded against my chest so hard, I feared it would explode. I was walking away from my children. Something I swore I would never do.

Sasha took my arm and began to walk with me. I could feel him holding me up, with each step moving me closer to the building and farther from my babies. He escorted me up the few steps and through the door he had exited just moments before. Inside, the stench of body odor greeted me with force.

Don't throw up, I ordered myself.

We walked into a large inner office, sparsely furnished, in which three men stood. Two wore the military fatigues of the guards outside. The third wore a black wool hat and coat of an officer. His black eyes swept over me, head to foot, cataloging every detail. His face held deep-set lines around his eyes and mouth—as though he was in a constant state of anger.

He directed a question to Sasha in Ukrainian, nodding his head toward me. I assumed he was verifying my identity. I stood silently next to Sasha, my eyes downcast, trying not to meet the officer's stony gaze.

I forced myself to keep my gaze lowered until the officer directed his question to me.

"What is your name?" he asked harshly, switching to Russian.

I prayed I'd remember every word of Russian I'd worked so hard to learn since I had been in this country. "My name is Kimberly de Blecourt. I understand there may be a problem with my passport."

A look of disgust flashed through the officer's eyes. Then he laughed a hollow, wretched laugh.

"You have been misinformed, Mrs. de Blecourt. There is no *problem*." He sneered. "*You* are under arrest."

2

September 2007

THE BEGINNING

"Welcome!" the agency's spokesperson said with a kind and enthusiastic voice. "And congratulations on your decision to adopt. You are the answer, the forever family to an orphaned child."

I squeezed Jahn's hand as we exchanged excited glances. It was finally happening. We had been through almost a year of disappointment as we navigated the U.S. domestic adoption system, and now our dreams of adding to our family were within our grasp.

The spokesperson gave a brief overview of the agency's history and how delighted they were to offer adoption options on the international front. Tonight, their informational meeting focused on Ethiopia, Kazakhstan, and Ukraine.

I glanced around the room at the other couples. There were less than a dozen, but all appeared as hopeful as Jahn and I.

When her time was finished, the spokesperson turned the meeting over to the Ethiopian representative. Jahn and I were there to hear about Ukraine, so as the woman spoke, my mind drifted back over the journey that had led us to this Christian adoption agency.

Jahn and I were in our midthirties when we met and married in 1997. After a few rocky attempts, I became pregnant with our daughter, Jacey. I turned thirty-eight within a few days of her birth in 2000. And wanting at least one additional child, we began to attempt another pregnancy. But after two years of struggling with secondary infertility, we realized we would probably be the parents of only one child.

A deep sadness came over me as I gave away Jacey's baby things. I settled in to being the best mother I could and living out God's call on my life to also pursue other interests, which included short-term mission trips. Our church had been working with churches in Ukraine for many years. Although I couldn't explain it, I felt a strong pull on my heart to join a trip there.

The experience developed a sense of compassion within me, just seeing how people live in oppressive societies—especially the children. Hundreds of street kids roaming with no home, no family, no love. Hundreds of orphans kept in stark orphanages. Although I couldn't help every child, I could help one. I could save one child from a loveless place and a hopeless future. And with that realization, the seed of adoption planted itself in my heart.

But I arrived home and life took over. Although I took another mission trip, this time to Thailand, and again felt drawn to consider adoption, I didn't do anything to pursue it. Even though I was now in my forties, I still held out the faintest hope that somehow, some way, I would miraculously become pregnant.

But by 2006, the hope for a miracle was dead. A surgical procedure over some health issues ended once and for all the possibility that I could overcome secondary infertility.

The idea of adoption resurfaced, and this time I listened. I began to do preliminary research. The first place I checked: Ukraine. The faces of those homeless children tore at my heart. But Ukraine was closed to international adoption at the time, so I began to investigate domestic adoption.

One night in October 2006, while we were preparing for bed, I broached the subject with Jahn. "What would you say about us adopting a child?"

"Absolutely, Kim," Jahn said. "Actually I've been thinking and praying about that too. We should check into it."

I was surprised and overwhelmed by his immediate agreement and enthusiasm.

"You know," I continued, now feeling more confident, "initially I thought about adopting a baby from Ukraine, but they're closed. So maybe we can try here in the States?"

"That sounds good. It would be great to have a son."

I had never thought about a son. And I never knew it had been in Jahn's heart and on his mind, but it made sense: I had a daughter; Jahn was the only boy in his family, and he needed someone to pal around with. It made me determined now.

Within the week, I contacted an established adoption agency in our area and began the tedious job of filling out the preapplication and other paperwork. The agency kept us posted on several birth moms who were interested in us and wanted to have interviews to see if we would be what they considered a good fit for their babies.

The application process was slow for us, though, and by the time we were ready to pay the fees, they had gone up—a fact that my money-conscious husband was not happy about. That was blow number one.

The second blow came for my husband when he found out that many mothers wanted open adoptions. They wanted letters, photos, and visits. Although I tried to explain how many children are better able to reconcile their adoption issues when they have access to their birth mothers, I also understood Jahn's position: "The mother either raises a child, or we do. She can meet the child, yes. But stay in his life, no. You don't halfway give up a child."

Fortunately, in March 2007, not too long after our decision not to adopt domestically, one of the case workers from the agency contacted us with good news: Ukraine was getting ready to reopen its doors with a new international adoption policy. They would be ready before the end of the year, possibly even as early as June or July.

With that information in mind, I began to do more research to see if the agency we were with was the best one to handle the new Ukraine adoption policy. Soon I found what I believed was the best agency for us. It was thirty minutes from our home and was starting a program to concentrate exclusively on Ukrainian adoptions— with a native Ukrainian on staff, who would also be the first person from the agency to go through the adoption process herself. They also boasted a native on the ground in Ukraine to help facilitate the adoptions handled by this organization. It seemed like a win-win for us.

Financially, it was a little less than the amount we would be spending with the first agency, so that was an incentive for Jahn. They had their nationals, who would know the legal system, culture, and language, working with us—an incentive for me.

I contacted them to start the process and found out that an informational session would take place in September. In July, Ukraine announced it was officially open and receptive to internationals coming to adopt their child citizens.

Now here Jahn and I sat at their agency on a warm September evening. As we quietly listened to the Ethiopian representative share the wonders of adopting a child from that African country, I eagerly awaited the next woman's talk on Ukraine.

Finally a petite blond-haired woman stood and introduced herself.

"Hello," she said in a heavy accent. "My name is Alexandria. I'll be working with those of you who are interested in adopting a child from Ukraine. Ukraine is my home country. I met and married an American and live here now, but I am pleased that I'm able to work with such loving couples who want to adopt and care for Ukraine's children. In fact, my husband and I just recently adopted a child from there. Her name is Maria."

Alexandria proceeded to tell us about how smoothly her adoption had gone just a few months before.

"I can speak from experience that you've made a wonderful decision toward adoption," she continued. "Since I've been through it now, I know firsthand all the changes to their new policy, so I can help walk you through the complexities of the adoption process."

Then she got to the logistics. "We aren't sure yet about the timing of the adoption process since they just reopened. It takes a lot of diligence, so the sooner you get through the paperwork—and there is a lot of it—the better prepared you will be.

"You also need to have multiple clearances—local, state, federal, Homeland Security. These all take time. On average, the paperwork and approval from the U.S. government will take between three and six months," she told us. "Then we send that documentation to the Ukrainian government and wait to hear from them. The fastest time for the entire adoption process is nine months from start to finish. But you should expect twelve to sixteen months."

Twelve to sixteen months! I thought, and groaned inwardly. *But I'm ready now. We've already waited seven years to add to our family.*

She continued, "Once you receive your appointment date, you'll be able to travel there. Typically people do the adoption in two trips. During the first trip you go and select the child you want. Then it takes about four weeks for the courts to finalize the paperwork, during which time you can return home and wait, then fly back over to pick up your son or daughter once the final court date has been set.

But you could just stay there. It may be *cheaper* to stay than to pay another round-trip airfare!"

The group chuckled.

I could feel the butterflies twirling in my stomach with excitement, and I looked again at Jahn and smiled.

Next she touted the guy on the ground there. "Boris is wonderful. Very capable. He has been an adoption facilitator in Ukraine for more than ten years now. He will work with you night and day while you're there, to make sure your experience is smooth and enjoyable."

She finished her time with an invitation to visit the table at the back of the room where she would answer any questions we had.

I was ready! *Sign us up. Let's go.* I wanted to get started on the paperwork and get everything rolling. Despite the past year of domestic adoption heartache and the expenses attached with bringing another child into our family, we were finally moving toward our new child.

3

May 2008

HOLDING PATTERN

"*Kim, I have* some bad news," Alexandria, our Ukrainian representative at the agency, said over the phone.

"Was our dossier refused?" I asked, putting my coffee cup into the kitchen sink. We'd submitted the last of the paperwork in February and our agency had put together the official dossier and sent it to Ukraine in April.

"Not exactly." Alexandria's voice sounded tight, anxious. "They have the dossier, but they aren't accepting dossiers for review or giving out any numbers."

My eyes narrowed as I listened.

"Ukraine has decided that this year they want to encourage women to keep their children. They're going to pay them for up to two years to keep and raise their babies. And they're going to give financial incentives to Ukrainian couples, as well, to try to get them to adopt."

All that work had taken a toll—financially, emotionally. All of those months of waiting to bring home our child. Was it all for nothing?

"Kim, for Ukraine, this is a good thing. You know?" Alexandria said. "If we can help children stay with their parents, isn't that something we should do?"

"Yes, of course it is," I admitted. If a little bit of money could entice a mother to keep her babies, if Ukrainians were willing to adopt and care for these orphaned children, I should be glad about it, not selfishly upset.

But all I could think about was the possibility that our child was still in the system and would be there longer, perhaps neglected, and being raised by somebody else.

"Do you think this will be a permanent change? Will we still be able to adopt from Ukraine?" I asked.

"I don't know. No one really knows right now. We may not find out if your dossier has been accepted until the end of this year or possibly the beginning of next year. They have it, but we haven't had official word of its acceptance yet because all the dossiers are on hold."

"Okay, well, let me know if anything changes. And please, stay in touch."

"Of course," Alexandria said. "As soon as I hear something, anything, I'll call you right away."

Another obstacle.

"What's going on, God?" I asked, frustrated. "We've felt your call on our family for this adoption. How long do we have to wait?"

A small inner voice reminded me, *God's got this. Maybe our child isn't available yet. Maybe the timing isn't right.*

My head knew the truth behind those thoughts. But the ache of empty arms stayed with me. And I wasn't sure when they would be filled by our future adopted child.

4

May 2009

A CHILD FOR US

I felt tired after the more than twenty-one hours of travel and the seven-hour time difference, but I was filled with anticipation as our plane landed in Kiev, the capital of Ukraine. After a year and a half of waiting and working toward this moment, it had finally arrived.

Just a month earlier, Jahn and I had been sitting in Alexandria's office at the adoption agency. We were there to make our final payment and to go over last-minute details before we left for Ukraine in May. We had waited almost a year from the time we learned that Ukraine had closed its doors to international adoption once again.

Ukraine re-reopened its doors in late 2008. We waited to hear that the Ukrainian government had accepted our dossier and that we had been issued a visitation number to the State Department of Adoption and Children's Rights (SDA). As soon as we had our number and appointment date, I rushed to make our travel arrangements—thrilled, but anxious that the government would change its mind again.

Alexandria was now telling us more specifics about our facilitator and interpreter in Ukraine. "Boris is very good and will give you as much assistance and time as you need," she reassured us. "I think you'll like him and find him very helpful."

I breathed a sigh of relief. I was glad that a native Ukrainian would be there to represent us and handle all the details while we were there.

"By the way," she said before Jahn or I could respond, "Boris has told me about a little boy he thinks you will be interested in considering. His name is Dmitry, he's from an orphanage in Izmail, and he's eighteen months old."

This new information caught my attention immediately. I didn't think we were allowed to know about any of the children until we had our official appointment. And I didn't think a facilitator was supposed to refer any of the children.

"Typically, we wouldn't pass on this type of information to any adoptive parents," Alexandria said, as though reading my mind. "But in this case, we're simply offering it as a possibility. This boy, Dmitry, he looks like your daughter, Jacey. He's blond with blue-green eyes. Boris saw the boy himself and said there appeared to be nothing wrong with him."

My eyes flickered across my husband's face. Maybe this was the child we were supposed to adopt.

I felt tingles flow down my back. Everything looked like it was finally falling into place.

Our appointment to meet the officials and discuss available children was subsequently scheduled for May 14 at 9 a.m. at the SDA office in Kiev.

Now, at long last, Jahn, Jacey, my father-in-law, Jacob, and I were ready to disembark from the plane and enter the land where our child was waiting.

FIRST SHADES OF GRAY

As soon as we got through customs, we immediately felt slapped with a somber, oppressive atmosphere covering the country, like being forced into an old, heavy coat. I could see the oppression in the people: their shoulders were stooped, their heads bowed. No one looked you in the eye. No one smiled.

I had learned a few things during my first trip to Ukraine: for instance, don't smile. If you're overly friendly, they think you're soft in the head, perhaps mentally unstable. How different from midwestern America, where most everyone offers a ready smile and a friendly hello.

We made our way to baggage claim, where I saw a thirtysomething man dressed in black from head to foot. He was square-jawed with close-cropped black hair and eyes the color of coal. He stood tall and serious and appeared to be looking for someone.

"Are you de Blecourt?" he asked my husband.

"Yes, I'm Jahn," my husband replied, offering a handshake.

"Welcome to Ukraine," the man said with a thick accent. "I am Boris. I will be your facilitator and interpreter."

Boris appeared surprised by the handshake, especially from me. But he seemed friendly enough as he helped us with our mounds of luggage.

"I have taken the liberty of renting you a flat here in Kiev," he informed us. "Since you don't know how long you will be here, it is less expensive than a hotel, especially in Kiev."

"Thank you," Jahn said. "Inexpensive sounds good."

It was late afternoon and the sun shone brightly over the sprawling city of almost three million people. It appeared to have a westernized flavor, with billboards advertising products from Coke to Nokia, yet I noticed large tenement buildings and run-down areas, reminders of the communism that had infested this once proud country until 1991, when it regained its independence. The biggest surprise was the number of stray dogs and cats roaming the streets. They were everywhere.

As we drove, Boris told us about what to expect during our appointment with the SDA.

Soon we arrived at our flat, a simple two-bedroom apartment, which was sparsely decorated but clean. We unloaded our bags and dragged them up the eight flights of stairs. Our building had no elevator.

"Tomorrow I will pick you up for a day of sightseeing around the town. Then the next day, Thursday, we will be ready for your appointment, yes?" Boris asked.

"That sounds wonderful," I told him. "Thank you, Boris."

Within a few hours we took to our beds. The seven-hour time difference meant it was still late morning for our bodies, but we knew we needed to get as acclimated to this time zone as quickly possible.

"We're finally here, Jahn," I said as we got into bed.

With happy thoughts I forced myself to drift off to sleep.

♦

Early Thursday morning, Jahn, Jacob, Jacey, and I were dressed, eager to get going to make this adoption happen.

"Today's the day you could get a little brother or sister," I told Jacey as I fixed her hair and gave her a kiss on the head.

"I know!" she replied excitedly. "I can't wait." A moment passed as her eyes narrowed. I could tell something serious was on her mind. "Mom," she said finally, "what does an orphan look like?"

I hesitated, surprised by her question. "They look the same as everyone else, honey. We may adopt a child who looks a lot like you do!" I touched her honey-golden locks of hair. "Or we may adopt a child who is dark-haired, or maybe a child who has darker skin or is more Asian-looking. We don't know yet. But it's not the outside that's important. It's the inside of a person, isn't it?"

"Yeah," she said. My answer seemed to satisfy her for the moment, or at least keep her busy with her thoughts.

Jahn walked into the room. He seemed filled with nervous energy as he paced back and forth. "How about we pray for this appointment?" he said.

I agreed immediately. We both recognized that although this appointment was filled with excitement and promise, it was also a life-changing time. Jahn asked God for guidance and direction regarding our adoption, and concluded by asking for a sense of peace over any decision we would make.

Boris arrived around eight o'clock. He was dressed rather casually, I thought, in a T-shirt and jeans. Together we left the flat and went to the curb, where Boris hailed a cab.

The taxi moved up a steep cobblestone incline toward the SDA.

"Look at that!" Jacob pointed to a beautiful teal- and white-columned baroque cathedral.

"Wow!" Jacey said.

"That's St. Andrew's Church. It's very famous," said Boris uninterestedly. "It was built in the 1700s. It is one of four architectural landmarks of Ukraine that is listed as a treasure of the country. Actually, this hill we're on is an historic site as well. This is the Andriyivska Hill. It is a major tourist attraction."

Before we could ask any more questions, the cab driver pulled in front of a communist-style building that housed the SDA offices. It was situated beside St. Andrew's. The exterior was brick on the bottom, with a rough, nondescript concrete stucco on the top. It looked plain with its dull gray coloring—especially in contrast to St. Andrew's. It had two stories and what appeared to be a semi-basement. We walked to the side of the building, toward the cathedral, where there was a gated courtyard.

"Kim, Boris wants to know if we're interested in that little boy Alexandria told us about," Jahn said.

Boris interrupted. "He's a good boy. He looks like your daughter—blond hair. The other couple who was going to adopt him, they left right after they met the child. Got on a plane and left the country. They didn't even try to see if another child would be right for them," he stated in a tone of disgust. "He would be a good boy for you. There's nothing wrong with him. His name is Dmitry."

I don't know why, but all of a sudden I felt bothered about the way this was being handled. Although I wasn't sure I trusted Boris, I pushed aside the uncertainty. Of course, we would consider Dmitry—along with the other children. I would be fair.

Boris was pulling out some last-minute paperwork for us to go over when out of the corner of my eye I noticed Jacey approaching a mother dog with her pups near a den in the Andriyivska hillside.

Jacey, lover of all things animal, grew excited. "Hi, doggie," she said and began to approach it. She pulled out a crust of the morning roll she had brought with her from breakfast and held it out toward the dog.

The indistinguishable shepherd slowly lowered on her haunches, every muscle in her body tense and poised to lunge.

"Jacey! Get back!" I yelled. But she didn't hear me. The dog bared her teeth menacingly.

I raced to Jacey's side, grabbed her hand, and drew her into my arms. Together, we slowly backed away.

"Jacey, you *can't* get close to her. She could attack you. She's protecting her babies."

Jacey looked at me in disbelief from the dog's frightening response to her food offering. Her sea-green eyes darkened with disappointment as she sighed and dropped the bread crust to the ground. "But she's hungry, Mom. I know she's *hungry.*"

The pain in her eyes tugged at my heart. "I know, baby." I sighed and pulled my daughter away from the dirt hummock the shepherd had hollowed out in the hillside between the cathedral and the SDA. "But we can't trust her. I need you to be careful and stay away from all the strays, okay? Your dad and I would never forgive ourselves if you got hurt."

I squeezed Jacey's shoulders, and then tucked her under my arm as we rejoined Jahn, Boris, and "Opa," her grandfather Jacob.

Finally, the building opened and we were set to enter and begin looking at the folders of available children. Jacob turned to Jacey and held out his hand.

"Are you ready to go shopping, honey?"

Jacey smiled and nodded and put her hand in his.

"Good luck," he said. "I know you'll make the right decision."

"Thanks, Dad," Jahn said.

As we turned to enter the building, Jacob led Jacey down the street to do some souvenir shopping in the market square nearby.

"Mom!" Jacey yelled as she pointed back at the shepherd. "She found the crust and ate it."

"I'm glad she did, sweetheart. Have fun with Opa."

My thoughts again turned toward Dmitry. I didn't want to feel confused. I wanted the adoption process to feel black and white, edged in certainty and conviction. Instead, I feared that the foreboding that had swept over me would paint the days ahead in shades of gray.

OUR FIRST SDA APPOINTMENT

Boris ushered Jahn and me into an office with once-white walls that had aged to dirty beige. An attractive brunette seated us side by side on a worn brown loveseat. My six-foot-one husband carefully maneuvered his legs to fit behind the glass-topped coffee table in front of us.

Boris sat to Jahn's right in a worn wooden chair, and the woman seated herself across the coffee table from us. Her expression told me she'd conducted this interview a hundred times. I glanced around the room. In an office nearly twenty feet by twenty, I saw nothing that gave a clue to anyone's personal life—no family photos or mementos on desks, not even a sweater thrown over the back of a chair. There were only filing cabinets, office furniture, and neat piles of manila folders meticulously stacked on a table against one wall.

The brunette SDA representative laid twelve or so manila file folders on the table in front of her—one file folder for each child. As she opened each folder, she read from paperwork about that child, including age, sex, any known medical or psychological conditions he or she had, and what was known about the family, if anything. Boris interpreted as she read. It seemed odd to us that she appeared to be reading a lot more than he was translating.

Paper-clipped to the top of each folder was a photo. The photos didn't appear current. The children's clothing looked old and worn. None of the children were smiling. Most had deadened eyes and an all too serious look for babies who were less than five years old.

Jahn and I carefully considered each file. We asked questions, especially regarding any known medical issues. This seemed to irritate Boris, although we couldn't figure out why.

As I looked at Dmitry's photo, he appeared healthy enough. Boris was right; Dmitry did resemble Jacey, with his blond hair and blue-green eyes. He had a tiny, upturned nose and a slight smile.

Dear God, help us see the things we're supposed to see, not just faces and facts. Give us your eyes and your heart, I prayed.

As we continued the review of file after file, I became painfully aware of the eyes taking in our every movement from across the table as both Boris and the SDA worker sat and listened.

Less than an hour later, we had made our way through the pile of folders, which were now neatly restacked. The only folder that remained on our side of the table was Dmitry's.

Jahn gestured to Dmitry's file. "Would you translate this again for us?" he asked Boris.

"It just says that he tested HIV positive for his first test. There's nothing wrong with this boy."

"But what else does it say?"

"I'm not going to sit and translate this whole thing," Boris said. "But I can tell you, there is nothing wrong with him. He is a good choice."

"Why won't he translate all of Dmitry's paperwork?" I asked Jahn quietly. Our agency had told us he would translate anything we wanted him to.

"I don't know. But Dmitry does look like the best choice," Jahn said.

I agreed.

It was decided. We were going to visit Dmitry.

I took comfort in the fact that Jahn and I had contributed to the University of Minnesota's International Adoption Medicine Program and Clinic before we left for Ukraine. Their specialty department, under their pediatrics section, offered a service that included long-distance diagnosis of common abnormalities in intercountry adoptions. They were aware that we intended to adopt from Eastern Europe, and they sent us information about what we could expect and even a few things to be aware of. During our decision-making process, we were to email them information, including photos, about the children we met. If we had questions about medical issues, they would assist us in making any such determinations.

Boris picked up the file, handed it to the SDA representative, and said a few words.

She told us she would process the paperwork and prepare a letter for the orphanage. The letter basically told the orphanage that we had permission to see and spend time with Dmitry—and only Dmitry.

Their system wouldn't allow us to walk into the orphanage to visit at will because a few of the children still had family. For various reasons, families who didn't have the ability to care for their children placed them in orphanages. Not all the children were available for adoption, let alone intercountry adoption, which only happened after each child had been available to Ukrainians for at least one year.

While we waited for the letter, Boris and Jahn went to the train station to purchase tickets for the night train that would take us to Odessa. From there we would ride to Izmail, located in southern Ukraine, and the Special Baby House where we would meet Dmitry the following day. I was excited about meeting Dmitry, but something still felt odd about the situation, especially as I saw a self-satisfied smile cross Boris's face.

We took a nine-hour overnight train from Kiev to Odessa, the administrative center of the Odessa Oblast, the southernmost and largest oblast (or province) in Ukraine. In Odessa, we spent some time resting at Boris's house before we took two cars and traveled five more grueling hours to Izmail to visit Dmitry.

The roads were horribly bumpy, with large potholes everywhere. The intense jerking made my teeth grind into one another and set my jaw so hard that it began to throb. I could find no comfortable position to make my body stop aching from the way the car interacted with the pavement.

About halfway to Izmail, we stopped at a gas station and convenience store to refuel and use the restroom facilities. The restroom doors were outside along the side of the building. An "attendant" sat nearby with toilet paper. She appeared to be waiting to hand some to everyone.

Although Jahn shook his head as he approached her, she persistently stopped him from proceeding into the men's restroom and kept repeating something that sounded angry.

He looked at Boris. "Would you please explain that I don't need toilet paper?"

"It's not the toilet paper. You have to pay to use the restroom," Boris said, pulling out a few coins and plopping them into the woman's jar.

"What?" Jahn said exasperatedly.

"You have to pay to use the restroom, whether you use toilet paper or not," Boris explained.

We all paid the few hryvni, the Ukrainian currency, and Jacey and I took our toilet paper and entered the dimly lit room.

"Ewww," Jacey wailed and pinched her nose shut. "Mom, this is disgusting."

"Just go quickly so we can get out of here." There were no flush toilets, no sinks with running water to wash your hands, nothing sanitary anywhere. In each stall was a squat toilet, a rectangular hole employed by squatting rather than sitting.

Jacey and I raced back out into the sunshine and fresh air to find Jahn standing by the car looking pale. "Dad, our bathroom was gross!" Jacey said, running over to him.

"Mine too," he said.

Such a pleasant trip we're having, I thought as I climbed back into the car to suffer a few more hours on the neglected roads.

♦

We arrived in Izmail by midafternoon and went directly to our hotel and got settled in. Fortunately, it was a new hotel that was western-ized, meaning flush toilets at least.

"Wow, Mom, this is gorgeous!" called Jacey as she ran around the room taking in all the décor. I chuckled silently. Jacey loves anything that looks or feels princessy. A satin comforter covered the two beds and the pile of pillows. The drapes were big and puffy and shiny.

I fell onto one of the beds and breathed in deeply. The orphanage visiting hours were two hours in the morning and two hours in the afternoon. The afternoon visiting hours were already over, which meant more waiting. Boris arranged an appointment for us first thing the following morning as soon as the doors were opened to vis-itors. But until then, we would rest, eat, and freshen up. I went to bed early, hoping that would make the time pass quickly.

◆

The next morning, we arrived at the Izmail Special Baby House, where approximately one hundred and fifty children aged five and under lived. Around the perimeter stood a towering cement wall about ten feet tall. We had to walk through a door next to a large wrought-iron gate. We passed a haggard-looking guard who looked as though he lived in the guard office, and went down another paved driveway to get to the main building. It was surrounded by concrete and a large plain dirt field with overgrown weeds scattered about. A few pieces of severely rusted playground equipment from Soviet times were still standing. Ragged metal pipes protruded from the ground where other playground equipment had once stood. There was little green, little living, little celebrating life or creation—just blandness, drabness, dryness, and death.

Children were running wild, chasing one another, hitting and yelling.

Babies were tucked five and six in large buggy-like prams. They all looked at us with deep, fixed gazes as we passed them.

The urge to sob overwhelmed me. No matter how hard I'd tried to steel my emotions for this day, the moment I laid my eyes on the bleak, crowded conditions at the orphanage and looked into the eyes of the children for the first time, my feelings crumbled. I could only hope it would be better inside.

As we entered the building, I noticed it felt constrictive and dark, almost oppressive. There were no screens to keep insects out; ragged lace curtains covered the windows and doors.

Love certainly doesn't live here.

One of the administrators escorted us into a large room that appeared to be the doctors' office. She informed us through Boris that we were to wait here and they would bring Dmitry to us. A group of doctors stood around, but made no effort to introduce themselves or welcome us.

I tucked Jacey into the crook of my arm. She and I sat next to Jahn and Jacob on a scarred sofa that leaned against a faded green wall.

A moment later, the door swung open and a young girl, one of the caregivers, stepped into the room. She was holding both hands of a tiny boy with a lopsided smile. He wore a denim sailor's hat, denim overalls, and a striped shirt.

"Hello, Dmitry!" one of the doctors said. "Come and meet Mama and Papa!"

I had no idea what the doctors were saying—until I heard "Mama and Papa." My eyes widened. I may not have known Ukrainian, but those names were somewhat universal.

I wanted to stand and say, *Hold on there a minute. We haven't made our final decision yet. This is just our first meeting with the child!* Instead I asked Boris, "Why are they calling us that?"

"It's what they do. While you're here, all the children will call you that."

This isn't right, I thought. I felt manipulated, which made me angry.

But I looked at this small child now standing in front of us. I couldn't deny how innocent and lovely he was. I smiled and said hello. Perhaps things would be okay.

His eyes looked past me—almost as if he didn't see people in front of him—then they came to rest briefly on my face before drifting away. Something in my heart plummeted as my eyes read the vacant look on Dmitry's face.

He was adorable. As we sat and tried to connect with him, though, he kept fading off into a vacant stare and started to drool slightly. Something was wrong with this beautiful child.

For the next three days, we returned twice daily to visit Dmitry. Jacey especially had fun playing with him and showering him with the little gifts we'd brought with us.

He would be fine, and then he would look off into the distance, glaze over, and usually begin to drool.

"Where did you go, Dmitry?" I would say softly and gently. "Come back."

Whenever we would see him, he would scramble to meet us. Although he couldn't walk unassisted, he could scoot.

Each day, Jahn and I questioned the doctors about Dmitry's health. We went down the list of questions the University of Minnesota's team had provided us. And each day a different doctor—all of whom seemed frustrated by our barrage of questions and concerns—would insist he was fine, perhaps a few months delayed for his age, but a healthy child who would catch up with other children his age once he'd adjusted to his new life in America. Each day as we walked along the crowded streets of Izmail, the heaviness in my heart grew.

Something *was* wrong with Dmitry, no matter what the doctors said. Even Jacey noticed how slow he was to respond when she played with him.

Although he was almost two, Dmitry could barely maintain eye contact with Jahn or me for more than a few minutes before he drifted away into a vacant stare. His body was out of proportion—his legs were too short for his torso. When I held him, his frame seemed misshapen. Jahn and I expressed our concerns to each other as we waited for the results of our email and photos of Dmitry to come back from the International Adoption Clinic.

"We both know something is wrong with Dmitry," Jahn said, "something that his paperwork didn't mention."

"I know," I said.

"I know we all care for him, but we have to carefully consider this choice."

I nodded, but said nothing.

Whatever decisions we made about the child we decided to adopt, Jacey would have to live with them beyond our lives, especially since we're older parents. We had determined boundaries before we left the United States. We had defined what we could and could not accept. We could accept something like tuberculosis; we could accept HIV; we could accept a surgically correctable condition. None of those things would deter us. But we could not accept a condition that required lifelong care from another individual—ongoing care for the rest of our daughter's life.

It was difficult to be that honest with ourselves, but we had to be because of Jacey. An important goal in this adoption was to protect and respect her.

Now Jahn was reminding me of our agreement. He could see that I had already grown attached to this little boy.

I hated that we were in this place, having to make this decision. I hated that one hundred and fifty children were without love and comfort and compassion. I hated the thought of leaving Dmitry in that orphanage.

I blinked hard to keep from crying, and then I slowly nodded again. "You're right."

The next day, we pulled aside yet another doctor and expressed our concerns once again.

The doctor crossed her arms and said, "Why do you ask so many questions? You want to take the child to America to sell him for body parts, don't you? That's why you ask so many questions about his health, isn't it?"

The doctor's words came like a slap. I was flabbergasted that anyone would even think that, let alone say it.

I turned to Boris. "Why would she say that?"

"It's an unfortunate rumor that has been going around for a while, that Americans are adopting children from other countries to sell their organs. It's ridiculous."

"But where would they get that outrageous idea?"

"It ... has happened," Boris said haltingly.

"From America?"

He shook his head.

"From where, Boris?" I demanded.

He looked away.

Silence.

"Boris, can I speak to you for a moment?" Jahn said.

Boris looked grateful that Jahn might be changing the subject. "Of course," he said.

They disappeared together into the hallway. After a few moments they reappeared and Jahn walked to my side. He reached for my hand and said softly, "I've asked Boris to speak to their one male doctor and the orphanage director on our behalf about what we discussed last night. I think it's time for us to step out into the hallway."

Tears welled in my eyes. "Are you sure ...?"

"We've been talking about this, Kim. It won't be easier tomorrow. Boris needs to ask a few more questions and speak on our behalf."

After about fifteen minutes, Boris opened the door of the office and stepped toward us. He shook his head. "It took a little coercing, but the doctor finally admitted something is wrong with the boy. The doctor doubts that Dmitry will ever be able to operate above a three-year-old level. I told the doctor and the director that you would be unable to adopt this child."

I began to weep. We had to say no. We would have to look for another child. And I knew it was going to be painful for that sweet little boy.

Just hold it together until you get out of here, I thought. But I couldn't.

"Stop that!" Boris reprimanded me. "Not in public. Stop crying!"

We went back to the hotel and checked out, then immediately left for Odessa. From there we would head back to Kiev, back to choose another child, back to square one.

I was unprepared for the wave of despair that swept over me on the five-hour drive from Izmail to Odessa. I couldn't talk to anyone or I knew the floodgate of tears would open again. I simply looked out the window at the dull countryside, bouncing and being jostled on the road, trying to hold my emotions in check.

"That one didn't work out," Boris said with no emotion, as though he were commenting on the clouds outside. "But the good news is that I have learned about a three-year-old boy named Alexander who will be available for adoption within the coming weeks. He is from this same orphanage and the doctor told me he is healthy."

I couldn't bear the thought that now I was being asked to possibly give my heart to another child. In my despair, I poured out my heart to God on Dmitry's behalf, for his future family to come soon, and that I would somehow learn of his eventual adoption.

5

June 2009

CULTURE SHOCK

From Izmail, we returned to Odessa and stayed with Boris and his family until closer to the appointment date at the SDA. Staying in a stranger's home, unable to truly relax, and with nerves frayed by the stress of worrying about this next decision, we grew tense. We realized that the four weeks we had anticipated it would take to adopt our child were now turning into six weeks or more. Both Jahn's employer at Visser Brothers, Inc., a commercial construction firm, and my employer at Avalon School of the Arts were understanding and knew this could be a possibility. Yet Jahn and I both felt the pressure of not wanting to take advantage of our employers' generosity.

Jahn was doing his best to keep from worrying about his job. He was project manager over several construction jobs and they were in the height of their busy season.

I became plagued with thoughts: *What if this one doesn't work out? What's going to happen to our jobs? How are we going to afford spending more time here? And if this child doesn't work, what about the third one? What happens if that one doesn't work for our family either? What if we've spent all this time and money without adopting a child?*

I found myself thinking about the day before we left for Ukraine. It was Mother's Day, May 10, 2009. Our church home, Immanuel Church of Holland, Michigan, celebrates each Mother's Day with a parent/child dedication service. Not only does this special service include parents declaring their desire to raise their children in a godly way, but we wrap ourselves around the family, as a greater church family, dedicated to helping them in their walk with God.

During this service, church members are invited to come to the front of the sanctuary to pray with each family involved in the dedication. Our pastor asked if Jahn, Jacey, and I would also come up front. He explained to the congregation that we would be leaving the next day for Ukraine to adopt a new child. He felt it fitting that church members would pray for our adoption, that we would find the child God had chosen for us, and that God would watch over our family while we were out of the country. It was a special time of prayer with our many friends there. Just thinking about it renewed my strength.

Now, in Ukraine, we did our best to adjust to life more as natives than tourists, but I could tell it was taking a toll on Jahn and Jacey as culture shock set in. Jahn was used to travel, but although he had traveled internationally a great deal, it was always as a tourist. He stayed in nice hotels, in the good parts of each country. This was different. We weren't tourists. We were on a mission, which included being in areas that didn't particularly cater to tourists—especially Americans.

Jahn was unusually cranky. Jacey was incredibly whiny.

The culture, the environment felt so foreign to us that it took intense energy just to keep everything straight.

We couldn't make sense of anything anymore. When we thought we were doing something right, we were told it was wrong. We were constantly being corrected. We didn't understand the language. We couldn't read anything or watch any TV shows or movies. There was little we could do to pass the time. There was nothing familiar we could recognize or connect with. Our minds just couldn't normalize our conditions. Our brains went on overload.

I found myself irritable and fighting to hold back biting comments. Jahn started to experience insomnia. Jacey became clingy and never satisfied with anything. No amount of love, attention, food, toys—nothing—could satisfy her.

Fortunately, I recognized the symptoms of culture shock and knew what was happening to my family. We had become depressed and extremely homesick, the new culture no longer something to embrace or explore. We were clearly in the distress stage, and I felt the need to bring some familiarity to all of us.

I knew just what to do when we returned to Kiev.

◆

We arrived back in the capital a day before our appointment. Everyone was feeling particularly snippy.

"Look," I said finally. "Let's walk over to Independence Square to the McDonald's there. It's a long, safe walk. We'll have an early lunch, walk around the square, and just do some touristy things to take our minds off everything. Okay?"

Jacey perked up immediately. "Yes! Let's go."

Jahn, however, wasn't as excited. "Kim, you know we don't have a lot of money."

"It's McDonald's. Come on. The walk will do us good."

"Come on, Daddy," Jacey chimed in.

Reluctantly, he agreed.

Independence Square was filled with hundreds of people. Everything seemed alive and bustling. Across from us were six fountains and a waterfall. In the center at the end of the square was a huge building with a tower and chimes. And not too far from where we stood, we caught sight of the Golden Arches. Jacey yelled with delight and started to race toward the flight of stairs leading up to the McDonald's.

I grabbed at her arm and pulled her to my right side. "Hold on, Jacey," I said, concerned about the number of people.

Jahn was walking several steps ahead of us, about to open the restaurant door at the top of the cement stairs.

Suddenly I noticed an elderly woman walking across the stairs toward us. A faded floral scarf covered her head and shoulders, and her clothing looked worn and threadbare. Her gait was steady, but she was holding her right arm funny.

Her eyes locked on mine, and her face hardened. Something wicked emanated from her. It made the hairs on the back of my neck rise. I froze as she quickened her pace.

Without thinking, I took Jacey by the shoulders and moved her to the other side of my body, away from this woman.

The woman muttered something as she neared and seemed to want an answer from me. I replied with one of the few Russian phrases I knew: "I don't understand."

The blow to my skull snapped my head back, and my knees threatened to buckle beneath me. A bolt of pain exploded through my head and down my neck. Intense nausea filled me as I felt the world start to go black.

THE BIRTH OF FEAR

"Mom!" A terrified high-pitched voice called out from what seemed miles away.

"Mommy!"

Through the pain and fog, I recognized Jacey's voice.

"Oooh," I groaned as I slowly regained my sight.

"Mommy, are you okay?" Jacey's words sounded worried and scared.

I blinked and closed my eyes again. Bursts of red were surrounded by blackness. Everything was spinning and the pain in my head felt as though my skull was about to crack open. A dim memory of the woman flashed through my mind and panic joined pain.

"Jacey?" I forced my eyes open again. "Jacey, are you all right?"

"Mommy!" Jacey sobbed. I looked at her hugging me fiercely around the waist. She was safe.

Thank you, God, that I moved her out of the way in time, I thought. *This could have been her.*

"I'm okay, Jacey," I said and tried to take another step up the flight of cement stairs. A second jolt of pain tore through my head, and I lurched forward. It was Jacey's arms around my waist that stabilized me.

Jacey was shouting, "Where is that woman? We need to tell the police. Why did she hit you? Are you sure you're okay, Mommy?" She began to whimper.

"Jacey, I'm all right. I just need to get inside McDonald's and sit down. Can you help Mommy get inside?"

"Kim, what happened? What's wrong?" Jahn slid an arm around my shoulders.

I worked to separate the throbbing from my thoughts, to make sense of it all. "It happened so fast, Jahn. Did you see her? Is she still here? She could come after—" A wave of fresh terror tore through me, and I feebly struggled to free myself from Jahn's arms.

"She *hit* you, Mom! Why did that lady want to hurt you?" Jacey began to sob.

I caressed her arm. "She's probably just sick and confused."

"What are you talking about?" Jahn said, the concern in his voice rising. "Who hit you? What woman?"

My head now felt as if someone had smashed an egg on it and the yolk was dripping down through my hair.

"Am I bleeding?" I asked weakly.

"I don't see any blood," Jahn said. He gently searched through the right side of my head.

I slowly looked around to see if I could find her and stopped at the place where she had hit me. I was only a few feet from the edge of the cement stairs we had just ascended. Beneath us, the square spread out in a wide expanse of concrete, the climactic setting of Ukraine's Orange Revolution in 2005.

I swallowed hard. If Jacey hadn't grabbed me around my waist, the woman's strike would have sent me careening down those steps. I could have been seriously injured.

"Did she say anything to you?" Jahn asked. "Anything that would make you think she knew who you were?"

"I'm not sure. She was muttering something in Russian, I think, but I didn't understand the words. She was looking right at me. Her eyes locked on mine, and then she hammered me with her cast. She hit me with her casted arm, Jahn. Who would do that?"

Jahn glanced toward the staircase. His face went ashen. He too realized the seriousness of what could have happened to me.

"You're okay, Kim," Jahn said and lightly held my head to his shoulder. "She was probably mentally ill..."

I wanted to believe him. "Jahn, she disappeared into thin air. Look around you. There's nowhere for her to go." I dropped my head to Jahn's chest. "You really didn't see her?" Somehow knowing my husband had seen the woman who'd attacked me in broad daylight would have validated the reality of my fears.

"I'm sorry, Kim." Jahn ran his fingers over the growing goose egg on my head. I cringed at his touch. "She obviously hit you very hard. Do you want to go to a hospital?"

"No, I'll be fine. I just need to sit down."

Jahn didn't seem convinced. He sighed heavily.

"Okay. But I want you and Jacey to sit at a booth where I can see you, and then we're going to head straight back. I'm not letting you out of my sight." Jahn herded Jacey and me protectively through the door of the McDonald's and sat us at a table near the counter while he ordered.

Apprehension was still running through me, and my eyes were searching the faces of everyone who passed.

Jacey watched me intently, still afraid that her mother wasn't okay.

The woman had probably asked me for money and I had not replied in the way she wanted. It was that simple, wasn't it? But the fresh fear inside me spoke something else. What about the evil I felt from her? Could there be more to it? It felt like a spiritual attack. We sat in silence until Jahn returned and took us back to the apartment.

The throbbing in my head slowly died down to a dull ache, but the alarm I sensed at first seeing that woman didn't diminish. Instead I felt as though fear was now to be my constant companion.

OUR SECOND SDA APPOINTMENT

Boris opted not to escort us to the SDA office this second time.

"The representative is a little upset with me, because I pushed for you to get this appointment faster than they normally allow," he told us before we left for the office. "It would be better if I don't go in with you. So I'm sending one of my colleagues, Fedor. He will be good for you. Alexander is not available yet—the little boy from the Izmail orphanage—but maybe you will find another child for your family."

Fedor met us at the SDA, introduced himself, and ushered us into the same plain office. Jahn and I walked over to the same couch and took a seat. A new pile of folders lay in front of us. More decisions. More children to reject. More heartbreak.

I sighed sadly as the SDA representative picked up the first folder, then the second, then the third. Absentmindedly, my hand went to the bump on my skull where the woman had attacked me and met a sharp pain when I touched it. I cringed. Was it worth it? Were we doing the right thing? We were judging these children with a flip of a manila folder and then moving to the next one as though they were commodities. God saw each precious baby as a beautiful diamond in the rough.

We arrived at one folder that seemed to interest Fedor. "*This* boy," he said, "this boy is a good boy. You take him. He's a good boy."

The photo showed a child with an unusually small head and very large features all pressed together. I noticed he was from close to Chernobyl. We had heard that many babies born in that region had birth defects.

Our hesitation made Fedor press harder. "There is nothing wrong with this boy. His report says he is fine."

I looked at the photo again. Oh, there was definitely something wrong. And I knew I didn't want to believe what anyone said otherwise, because they had told us the same thing about Dmitry! *Burn me once*, I thought, *but not again.*

"Well, what isn't in his paperwork?" I asked. "We had this issue with Dmitry, about whom you all said everything was fine, and he clearly wasn't. You know, we're here to find the right child for our family."

Reluctantly Fedor translated my comments. The SDA representative stiffened her back and responded. Fedor translated her comment to us.

"She said, 'We are not in business to find you the right child. We are to find homes for these children.'"

An uncomfortable silence filled the office.

"Let's keep looking," Jahn said. The next folder said this boy's name was Isaak and he was three years old. He had light brown hair and dark brown eyes and lived in Donetsk, on the far eastern side of Ukraine.

"This boy is fine, except he has one foot that is turned out a *little* bit," the SDA representative said and pinched her forefinger and thumb together to show us how "little." "It makes it hard for him to walk. And...he also had to have surgery shortly after birth."

My eyes widened.

"But he's fine now," she said quickly. "They fixed everything."

"Well, is he going to be okay?" Jahn asked. "Was it serious?"

"No, no, he's fine now. It was nothing really."

Fedor interrupted, obviously irritated. "Stop looking at that boy! You don't want him. Take this one," he said and pushed forward the boy from northern Ukraine.

I looked at Jahn and pointed to Isaak. Jahn nodded.

Although the mention of surgery concerned us, we felt Isaak was the best candidate for our family. Since the young boy Boris had learned of in Izmail—Alexander, or Sasha as they called him—wasn't available for international adoption yet, we handed Isaak's file to Fedor and asked for the letter to the orphanage to be prepared.

His curt nod and downturned lips assured us he did not agree with our choice, but the decision was made. We were headed to Donetsk to meet young Isaak.

ROBBED

"What do you mean you didn't get first class?" I asked as I looked at the second-class tickets Jahn held in his hand.

"These were half the price of first-class tickets, and they were the only second-class tickets left," Jahn said. "I hate this idea of being separated too, but Boris said they were fine and that we would be safe."

I thought back to a conversation I'd had on the flight over to Ukraine. While flying the last leg from Amsterdam to Kiev, I'd conversed with two pastors who said, "Always stay in first class when riding the trains. They're the only place you're truly safe. Pickpockets and thugs hang out in the second and third classes looking for trouble. You don't want to mess with them."

Now my husband set us up with sleeping arrangements in second class, and we weren't even all together. Jahn and Boris were in one compartment, and Jacey and I were in another—with people we didn't know.

So the four of us boarded the overnight train and separated. Our plan was to go to Odessa, where we would drop off Jacey to remain with Opa, then Jahn, Boris, and I would continue to Donetsk.

The train compartment where Jacey and I stayed was compact. A small table sat at the far end of the compartment next to a dirty window. Two foldout beds were at eye level and two benches that converted to beds were below.

A young man and woman were in the compartment and had already claimed the lower berths. They appeared to be strangers to each other as well. The woman, in her early twenties, wore her blond hair parted down the center with barrettes on each side. She looked like a schoolgirl wearing that fashion, and she appeared to be upset about something. I wondered if she was leaving behind her family or a boyfriend.

The man was in his late twenties or early thirties. He had sandy blond, wiry hair and wore wire-rimmed glasses that made him look nerdy. Although they both appeared innocent enough, I was still concerned about our safety, given the pastors' warnings.

Both of them barely acknowledged us.

Jacey and I took the upper beds and placed our belongings next to us.

I hardly slept that night with the rickety train rolling back and forth. I was mentally exhausted—dealing with seeing the conditions these children lived in, trying to keep Jahn and Jacey calm, and concerned we might never find the child God had called us to adopt.

The next morning, we didn't have much time to dress and get ready before the train rolled into Odessa. Moments before it arrived, the man made gestures to us that we needed to give him some privacy so he could change clothes. He made such a fuss trying to communicate with us that Jacey, the other female passenger, and I quickly exited to wait in the hall.

He shut and locked the door behind us before I realized I had left my purse and wallet in the compartment with him.

Surely it will be all right. He won't find it since I left it in the upper bunk, I rationalized to myself. I patted my stomach, where I had my passport in a concealed pocket.

He seemed to take a long time to change. Too long. When I heard what sounded like him climbing into my bunk, I banged on the door.

"Mister, we need to get in there," I yelled. The train had come to a halt and we needed our things.

Suddenly, the door flew open and the young man rushed past us and fled the train. I walked into the compartment and discovered my purse was still there. I breathed a sigh of relief. Jacey and I gathered our things and waited for Jahn and Boris to pick us up at our compartment.

We all walked onto the train platform and I pulled out my purse. I nonchalantly put my hand in to grab my wallet. The purse felt emptier than I'd remembered it. Suddenly a sick feeling poured over me. I looked down and started to push items around. My wallet was gone. My cash, credit card, and driver's license—they were all gone.

"He stole my wallet!" I blurted out. "The man in my compartment took it!" My stomach felt sick. I looked around to try to locate the man, but he'd disappeared.

"I'll find the conductor," Boris said quickly and ran off.

Jahn's face went pale. "Are you sure it isn't there?" he asked. "Did you maybe put it somewhere else? In one of the other bags?"

"No. It was in my purse, where it always is. It's gone."

My mind started going over everything in the wallet that I would now have to cancel.

Within minutes Boris returned with the conductor. I repeated the story and everything I could remember about the man—white short-sleeved shirt, glasses, hair, height, weight. The conductor wrote it all down, but shook his head.

"Unfortunately, he's long gone by now. And realistically we won't find him. We will search your compartment again."

The search turned up nothing.

"I'm sorry, but there's nothing more we can do," the conductor explained to Boris.

I couldn't believe how violated, helpless, and afraid I felt. All I could do was turn on Jahn. I felt my face flush with anger. "Please, don't you ever," I said quietly, "put us in that position again, Jahn. Don't ever allow saving money to put us in danger." Tears streamed down my cheeks.

Once again I wanted to go home, without my wallet and, more important, without our child.

NOT QUITE AS EXPECTED

We arrived on June 2 at Donetsk and headed to the Liverpool Hotel. Boris went to the orphanage to present the letter requesting an appointment to meet and possibly adopt Isaak.

The Liverpool was a former youth hostel that had been transformed into a chic hotel dedicated to all things Beatles. Beatles music played throughout the lobby and hallways. Beatles photos and memorabilia hung from every wall. Behind the registration desk was a large photograph of the hotel owner smiling widely and standing next to Paul McCartney.

Boris returned about an hour later. "We go tomorrow morning."

The next morning we arose and grabbed breakfast in the cafeteria connected to the hotel. Jahn and I ate a meal of eggs and toast as we listened to "Yellow Submarine" over the hotel speakers. We managed small talk, but mostly kept to our own thoughts and insecurities about what this day held for us.

I prepared myself for the same experience of seeing the orphanage as I had had in Izmail, but I was surprised when we stopped in front of a more open and inviting compound. Although the building was still surrounded by a fence, it wasn't as tall or foreboding. The gates were wide and open, almost like arms welcoming us in. And this building had color, not the drab gray and aged white of the previous orphanage. It was practically singing with blues and reds and yellows. It wasn't the lap of luxury, but neither was it an oppressive prison.

The orphanage worker escorted us to a visiting room with toys strewn about. "You'll wait here and we'll bring Isaak to you," she informed us.

"Nice," Jahn said. "They didn't have a visiting room in Izmail."

"Too bad," I agreed. "They definitely needed one."

Within moments the door opened and another worker walked in carrying a precious little boy—who had both feet and legs turned out completely at ninety-degree angles.

She put him down not far from us and stepped back. He slowly and what seemed torturously got up and hobbled toward us. With each few steps he would fall and repeat the process—work himself into a standing position, hobble a few steps, and fall.

But his face shone with joy at us, his visitors, his mama and papa. He immediately gravitated toward me and didn't show any interest in Jahn.

We got down on the floor beside him and started to play with him. He squealed with delight as he and I played together, but would turn his back slightly toward Jahn.

"I'm not sure about this boy," Jahn said seriously.

"What do you mean?" I asked. Although I was disturbed that the "one foot that is turned a *little* bit" was actually both feet turned out at ninety-degree angles, I was sure we could work with that disability and make him part of our family.

"There are other issues here," Jahn said. "I can just tell."

"Really?" I couldn't grasp how Jahn could sense that. I was typically the one with stronger discernment gifts.

He nodded. "Really."

♦

For two days we visited Isaak and got to know him. But Jahn was proving to be right. Isaak adored spending time with me and making sure I gave him my sole attention. But when Jahn tried to get involved with him, he would shun him. I began to see what Jahn saw: Isaak wanted me all to himself and Jahn was a threat to that relationship. Isaak would push Jahn away or shake his head vigorously if Jahn wanted to participate in our playtime. He would pull on my arms and try to get my attention if I talked, sat next to, or even looked at Jahn.

But other indications began to surface of potential problems. During one visit, Jahn picked up Isaak and Isaak urinated all over him. From the look on Isaak's face, we could not be sure if he knew what he had done or not.

"Why did Isaak do this?" Jahn demanded of the caregiver.

She shrugged. "I do not know. I thought he was toilet trained."

Her answer didn't sit right with us, so we demanded answers from the orphanage doctor.

"Isaak was born with a heart murmur, not unheard of with newborns, and surgery did take care of it," the doctor admitted. "But he was also born with spina bifida."

The words sent a chill down my arms. Spina bifida is a congenital disorder in which some vertebrae overlap the spinal cord, which instead of forming normally remains unfused and open. While doctors can surgically treat the open part of the spine to close it up, they can't restore normal function. Isaak was incontinent, and undoubtedly would remain so.

"That was part of the surgery he had, then?" Jahn said.

The doctor nodded.

That night, we contacted the University of Minnesota adoption staff and gave them the report.

"I cannot recommend you adopt this child," the University of Minnesota doctor said. "This is an adoption risk for your family. There is no healthy outcome for him, and your family may not be prepared for the kind of care he is going to require. Most remain incontinent their entire lives."

In my heart, I knew he was right.

"That poor child." The doctor's voice grew soft and sad. "How long will it be before his caregivers understand this is something he can't control?"

"I can only imagine," I said.

"No, I don't think you can—or would want to," he replied.

I couldn't listen anymore.

The next day we entered the orphanage and headed straight for the doctor's office to explain our decision not to adopt this child. I felt a sense of déjà vu—the same heartbreaking scene repeating itself.

Boris explained the situation to the doctor, a nurse, and the administrator.

"Oh!" the nurse said, genuinely surprised. "We thought you had bonded to him. He really took to you. He will be disappointed."

Tears sprang to my eyes. I had bonded with him, too. Now he

would be left abandoned, lonely, crying out for someone to love him. And we were purposefully walking away from him.

As we were leaving the orphanage, I heard Isaak crying from the stairwell and a nurse trying to comfort him.

As we reached the long hallway to the main entrance, I heard him scream, "Mama!" I crumpled into Jahn as Boris led us to the waiting taxi.

WAITING . . . AGAIN

"No more," I told Jahn.

We were seated on the overnight train from Donetsk to Odessa to pick up Jacey and Jacob before heading back to Kiev.

I couldn't get the cries of Dmitry and Isaak out of my head. I felt as though we had led them to believe we were going to adopt them. We had bonded with them so quickly. Now we were possibly going to do the same to a third child. I wanted to go home.

"I can't handle any more, Jahn. I just can't. I don't want to go to the SDA anymore," I said forcefully. "I don't know what we're doing here anymore."

"Kim, God called us here. If we quit now, then we're not giving God the opportunity to show up!" Jahn said. He paused. "We're going to visit a third child. Maybe it will be that boy, Alexander, the one Boris told us about. We're going to wait the two weeks to get our next appointment, visit him, and then we're all going home."

Was he right? What if he wasn't? What if all this trouble, stress, and heartache—what if the assault from the old woman, which still caused me pain where she hit me on the head, the robbery, this whole trip—had been for nothing? What if after all we'd been through, we still left with empty arms and Jacey without a sibling?

I just wasn't sure I wanted to push through to see this situation out and have Jahn be wrong and my greatest fears be proved right.

God, I need you, I prayed desperately.

◆

The next two weeks were agonizingly long. To make up for it, Boris insisted that we stay with his family in Odessa. So for those weeks we made a schedule for ourselves to help us get through each day without losing our minds. We got up early, got ready for the day, and then left. Typically, we would walk the two miles to the nearest McDonald's and hang out there as long as we could. The McDonald's had Wi-Fi, so I was able to connect to the Internet and keep our family and friends up to date on our life in Ukraine.

Jacob announced that his return flight was scheduled for June 13 and he would be on it.

"You're not going to stay?" I said. "But our appointment is just a few days after that. Can't you wait a little longer?"

"No, no," he said decisively. "I'm going. I've had enough of this country." He took my hands and held them tenderly. "If you find you need anything, let me know, Kim...I really hope this next boy is your son."

From your lips to God's ears, I thought.

OUR FINAL SDA APPOINTMENT

Although I was still upset about the robbery, I was no longer angry with Jahn. He had apologized profusely and I could tell he felt terrible. He'd made a mistake—and I realized it was a mistake encouraged by Boris.

Fortunately, I had written down all our credit card numbers, so I was able to contact our creditors and have them cancel everything.

During this visit to Kiev, we settled into the apartment of Boris's coworker Alla. Alla was an excellent English speaker and a delight to be around. She was single and lived with her parents in a nice flat on the outskirts of Kiev. We paid them for their hospitality. It was a relief to be in such a nice flat for a fraction of what the Kiev hotels cost. As I gazed toward the one church spire I could see from their windows, I thought about the great traditions of our faith, which teach that God is intimately involved in our lives. I felt renewed: my family had been brought here for a reason, and I couldn't quit now, especially when we were so close to meeting our third and last child.

Within two days we received our next appointment, for June 19, when we returned again to the same SDA office.

"Good news," Boris told us. "It looks like that boy from the orphanage in Izmail is available."

"And he's healthy?" I asked, feeling suspicious. We had already been through this scenario twice before. I didn't believe the SDA or the orphanage doctors—and I wasn't entirely sure I believed Boris.

"Yes, yes," he said. "He tested positive for HIV, but his birth mother had it; he doesn't have it."

So again we viewed a new stack of manila folders with a listing of new children. But Alexander's file was not among them.

"Do you have the file for Alexander Mazurek?" Boris asked the SDA agent.

She looked in the stack and at a few other folders on a desk and shook her head. "No, I don't have that file."

Boris's eyes gave a little squint. "Hmmm," he said. "Why don't you look in that stack of folders over there." He pointed at a bookshelf off to the side of her desk that was not easily accessible.

"What are you saying to her?" I asked. I was now beginning to understand bits and pieces of Russian—very broken, but I was slowly picking it up.

He told me what he had said to her.

She flipped through several folders and then pulled one out. "Here it is." She walked it over to us and handed it to Boris, who opened it and scanned its contents quickly.

"Ah, good," he said, obviously pleased.

"Why was it over there?" I asked.

"This is good for you," Boris said. "It looks as if another facilitator knows about this child and has asked for the file to be put aside. That means he's a good boy."

"Great!" Jahn said, eager to hear what was in the folder.

I was surprised at Jahn's response. He seemed hopeful, almost excited about this child, whereas I felt more cautious and concerned.

"He looks good," Jahn said to me. The boy, Alexander, looked the most normal of the bunch. He appeared healthy but intensely sad. It was heartbreaking to see the misery in his eyes and face.

The medical concerns listed an initial positive test for HIV, but subsequent tests were negative. Boris translated the file and said it also listed a concern that Alexander had a misshapen head. I glanced at his photo again. His head looked fine to me.

"Is 'misshapen head' a real medical issue?" I whispered to Jahn.

He shook his head slightly. "I don't think so. It must be a Ukrainian thing."

"It also says," Boris continued, "he has kidney issues."

"What specifically?" I asked.

Boris glanced at the file. "It doesn't say." He read more of the file to himself. "It also says that he is small for his age."

Many of the children in that orphanage are, I thought.

"He was hospitalized for bronchitis once, for about a month," Boris continued.

That poor boy had probably been left alone in the hospital. He must have been terrified. I had already begun to feel something for this small boy I hadn't yet met.

Boris finished scanning the file. When he closed it, he looked satisfied.

"His Russian nickname is Sasha," Boris continued and smiled. "Sasha is a good name. A solid, manly name. Sasha definitely sounds like a good choice."

"I think he's the one, Kim," Jahn said, smiling.

I had to agree. But as promising as this child appeared, my stomach clenched at the thought of going back to Izmail—back to Dmitry's orphanage. Could I handle seeing him again? Would he recognize me? Would he cry out for me?

I nodded slowly. Jahn picked up on my concern.

"You're thinking about Dmitry, aren't you?" he asked. "I know how you're feeling—but right now we need to focus on this child and the possibilities he may have for our family. We already made the decision about Dmitry."

"I know you're right." I breathed in deeply and tried to present my best smile. "Sasha really does sound promising."

As we left the SDA, Boris saw another facilitator outside the building. He appeared to be younger than Boris, but with short, dark hair and dark eyes. Boris asked us to wait for him. He spoke to the other facilitator, and it wasn't long before it became obvious they didn't like each other. Several minutes into their conversation, the other man stormed away.

Boris returned to us with a smug look on his face.

"What was that all about?" Jahn asked him.

"I thought Mikhail might have been the facilitator who had Sasha's file folder put aside. I was right," Boris said.

I kept quiet, but wondered what it all meant.

♦

Later that afternoon the SDA agent contacted us with news about Alexander—Sasha, as we had begun to call him.

"There's an issue they neglected to tell us," Boris said after he finished his phone conversation. He seemed angry.

Here we go again, I thought. "What is it?"

"Sasha has two siblings."

"And...?"

"They weren't available for adoption until just today. So if you want to adopt Sasha, you also have to visit his two siblings and adopt them. They must go together as a family. So you will need three orphanage visitation letters. They are preparing the additional two letters for us to pick up in the morning."

"What?" Jahn said.

Boris gritted his teeth. "Nobody told me this! The director at the orphanage, he didn't tell me Sasha had siblings! This isn't right. You do not have to do this. I will *make* them show you other children again."

"It's okay, Boris," Jahn said calmly.

Boris wasn't persuaded. "I've never worked on a case that involved siblings. I don't know that we should visit this boy."

But this was our third visit to SDA—three strikes and we were out.

"Excuse us for a moment, Boris. Kim and I need to discuss this," Jahn said. Boris started to say something, then nodded and walked out of the flat.

"What should we do?" I asked.

"Well, I think we should visit them all," Jahn said. "Who knows how God is leading us and what he has in mind? We don't understand, but let's pursue this and see what happens."

I agreed and felt strangely at peace about it.

As soon as Boris returned, Jahn told him, "Pick up the other two letters. We came here for one child, but we'll visit them all."

♦

The next morning, armed with our bags and letters, we traveled back to Izmail to the orphanage. On the way we found out more about Sasha's two siblings.

The oldest, Svetlana, was sixteen and was living in an orphanage in Odessa.

"This is a good thing," Boris said. "She can choose whether or not she wants to be adopted."

Sasha's other sibling, Nikolay, was a seven-year-old boy living up the street and around the corner in a different orphanage compound. Sasha lived in the baby house, or *doma lutke*, which was home to children five years and under. The *internaat* was the home for children six and older and was close to where we would visit Sasha.

"Let's visit Sasha first," I said. "He's the one we heard about first. He's the reason we came here."

"While you're visiting Sasha," Boris said, "I will pay a visit to the internaat to see what I can find out about this other boy, Nikolay, and then to set up a time to meet him."

SASHA

On June 20, a little more than five weeks after arriving in Ukraine, we met our child.

After we sat for several minutes on the worn sofa in the orphanage doctors' office, a woman brought a small boy into the room. His large blue eyes were wide and his hair had been shaved. Although he appeared undernourished, he was utterly beautiful. Something within my soul leapt with excitement and joy.

"Mom," Jacey cooed, "he's adorable!"

Immediately Jahn, Jacey, and I got onto the floor to greet him at his level. He greeted us tentatively, cautiously. No smiles for the strangers.

We discovered that although he was three, he was in a class with five-year-olds.

"He's smart." Jahn smiled brightly.

Sasha seemed suspicious of us. But soon Jacey pulled out a toy car we had brought him as a gift and his eyes lit up. He began to jabber away in Russian baby talk, which nobody could understand. But he seemed to be saying he liked the toy car. He wasn't sure what exactly to do with it since none of the kids had toys of their own. But Jacey showed him how to play and he caught on quickly. We asked the doctors to tell him it was a present for him.

During that visit, we asked all the questions and looked him over like the University of Minnesota's facilitators had encouraged us to do. We took the photos they had requested. We found no signs of fetal alcohol syndrome or mental disability. We spent about an hour with him, walking around the grounds.

That afternoon as we headed back to the hotel, Jahn asked, "What do you think?"

"I think we've found our son," I said and genuinely smiled for the first time in weeks.

SASHA'S FAMILY

"I met the director of the internaat and I think there may be a problem with meeting Nikolay," Boris told us later that evening. "He's out at scout camp and we cannot visit him until after he returns. After that I think he is leaving right away for your country."

"Leaving?" I said. "How can he be leaving?"

"He's going to visit a family who may want to adopt him."

"What?" Jahn said.

"Why do they have us coming to visit a child who is already set to be adopted by another family?"

"I don't know. And it may be nothing. Sometimes families will take in a child for the summer to give them a vacation from the orphanage, with no intention of adopting. Maybe that is this situation. Do you want me still to try to see if we can meet this boy?"

"I don't know how I feel about this." I felt confused and frustrated.

◆

The next day, after we returned from visiting Sasha, Boris and Jahn went to the internaat and returned with more information.

In January, Nikolay had met a woman who was visiting the orphanage on a fund-raising trip. Her family was one of the investors in a fifty-thousand-dollar playground to be built for the internaat. Nikolay took to her immediately and stayed close to her during her visit, so she arranged for him to go to her house in America for the rest of the summer.

"I didn't think you could do that," Jahn said.

"Technically, no; however, some organizations have permission to arrange these trips to encourage the adoption of older children..."

"The director asked us if we intended to adopt Nikolay," Jahn said.

"What did you tell her?" I asked.

"That we didn't know. We wanted to meet him first and get to know him."

"Jahn, it sounds like this boy actually got to choose his own family, doesn't it? Now he's going to spend more than a month with them in America?"

Everyone was silent for a while.

"Let's visit Nikolay next. He will be at that camp for a few more days, but he will be right around the corner," Boris said, unconcerned. "That's the thing to do. We will visit Sasha's half sister last."

◆

The following Monday, we arrived at the internaat to visit Nikolay before he left for America, and were told he was gone.

"He's gone?" I asked. "But you said last week that he was going to be at scout camp all week and that he leaves for America tomorrow."

"Yes, but the group had to travel to Kiev first to pick up their visas for travel. The bus we hired went directly to the scout camp and picked him up there. So you will not be able to meet him." The director smiled.

Something wasn't sitting right. She knew we were in town. She knew we had a letter from the SDA to see him. Yet she still allowed him to be taken away without giving us a chance to meet him.

"This is unacceptable!" Boris roared.

"She had no intention of allowing us to meet Nikolay, did she?" I asked, already knowing the answer. I prayed that if another family were adopting him, any burden of separating half siblings would be eased.

◆

The following day we traveled the five hours back to Odessa to meet Sasha's sister, Svetlana. Before we could meet her, however, we needed to be presented at the central Odessa SDA office. Boris explained that the office was newly positioned in between the four smaller district SDA offices in Odessa. He also remarked that he didn't think the people in the other four offices were happy about another office being put between them and the headquarters in Kiev.

As Boris explained our desire to meet Svetlana, he described us as "a loving, Christian family." That was obviously the wrong thing to say to the newly hired manager.

"We've heard many accusations from older children who have returned from visiting families in America. They tell us of their being forced to attend church on Sunday mornings and having to pray before they eat. Such terrible treatment of children."

I couldn't even reply, while Boris hastily tried to change the subject. The manager regarded us coldly from that time forward. I knew we might need their assistance in the near future and hoped our faith wouldn't be used against us. She begrudgingly accompanied us to visit Svetlana.

It happened to be Svetlana's high school graduation day. She walked into the room where we waited. She was beautiful, petite and thin, with light brown hair and the same facial features as Sasha.

Without any greeting, she stated in Russian, "I don't wish to be adopted."

By now I understood enough Russian to catch what she'd said, and I physically registered my surprise.

Boris's face registered surprise as well. Then he looked at me as if to say, *Why do you look taken aback? How do you know what she is saying?*

I had made a decision not to let Boris know I'd been slowly picking up Russian. Although it was getting easier for me to understand, I was still struggling to speak the language. I didn't want him to know, because I wanted to make sure he was translating everything and then telling us the whole story rather than cherry-picking or changing something. Every piece of information was crucial. My ability to trust was shrinking.

After a few pleasantries she said, "It's nice to meet you. I have never met my half brothers. I want them to be adopted; it would be good for them. But I don't want to be adopted." Even though she was speaking to Boris, I could tell what she was saying. "I have my friends and my life here. I don't want to leave."

"What did she say?" I said quickly to dismiss his suspicion. "You look shocked."

"What do I need to do?" Svetlana interrupted. "I can write a letter right now. I have a graduation party to go to with my friends." She grabbed some paper and sat down, pen poised in hand, looking expectantly at Boris.

I noticed a horrible scar that ran the length of her right shin. She caught me looking at it.

"My mother dropped a pot of boiling water and it landed on my leg," she explained.

"Actually," Boris whispered, "her files stated she had a problem with her leg bone, which required surgery. She never had plastic surgery to correct the scars."

"Oh." I wondered why she had made up the story about the boiling water. Or had she made it up? I didn't know what to believe.

Svetlana turned and looked at Boris again.

"You need to write two letters," he explained. "Since your mother is deceased, you are now the head of the family. You need to write one letter that gives permission for either or both brothers to be adopted by this family." He gestured toward Jahn and me. "The other letter states that you are sixteen, you do not wish to be adopted, and you are asserting your right to make that decision."

Svetlana's orphanage director was present and seated at the opposite end of the table. She moved closer to Svetlana and proceeded to watch her write the two letters.

We had come to Ukraine to adopt one child, and then we were told we might be able to adopt three, but now we were down to one again. Svetlana's letters would be presented in court to enable us to adopt Sasha.

Svetlana wrote both letters, signed them, and handed them to Boris. He looked at them quickly, nodded his okay, and placed them inside a clear plastic protective sheet. Then Svetlana stood, nodded to us, turned, and walked out to meet her friends who were waiting outside.

"Well, that's done," Boris said easily. "Now you should be good to proceed with adopting little Sasha."

It finally looked as though things were on our side and would move smoothly. We could adopt Sasha as our own within a couple of weeks and go home. I breathed a sigh of relief. I was pleased, yet still unexplainably sad. Something within me ached for Svetlana.

THE ORPHANAGE

We returned to Izmail to spend time with Sasha while we waited for our court date to be set. Since Boris wasn't translating Sasha's words and we didn't really have anything official for him to do while we waited, he decided to return to his home in Odessa to work with another adoptive family. I knew just enough broken Russian for us to get by. Although it was difficult, we encouraged one another by saying, "We'll be home in two more weeks!"

In the meantime, our lives fell into an easy rhythm. We explored the city—visiting a turtle pond or a wonderful bakery we'd discovered. And we attended church in Kiliya, about an hour from Izmail, where I reconnected with friends who were surprised that we were still in the country and still dealing with adoption issues. But most of the time we visited Sasha. We were not allowed to remove him from the orphanage grounds, so twice a day we visited him there during orphanage visiting hours. Each day we would get there at about 10 a.m. and wait for him. Once he arrived, we would take him to find a spot to play. This orphanage had no visiting rooms, so we had to make do and get creative about where we would go.

At first, because the visiting hours were the same as the children's outdoor playtime, Sasha wanted to play with the other kids. So we would let him, but would always make sure he was within our view. I wanted him to feel secure. I was always concerned about his feelings, realizing we were strangers to him and we needed to try to see things from his point of view.

So our visits were filled with lavishing attention and affection on him, giving him gifts, and playing with him. When he wanted to go back with the other kids, we gave him our blessing and let him. We agreed that we never wanted Sasha to feel that our time with him was drudgery.

When Sasha did stick around with us, Jahn loved playing with him and getting to know him. He would blow bubbles with him or swing him on the one working swing or take his hand and run him down the rusted slide on the sparse playground.

Sasha was most excited about Jacey, though—and she about him. They took to each other immediately and loved being together and playing. She seldom strayed more than a few steps from his side. And when Sasha wanted to join the other children, he would often grab her hand and lead her over to the group. She would push him around in the large baby strollers or on one of the few tricycles. The kids loved playing Wolf and Rabbit with her, based on a popular Russian children's cartoon. She would be the wolf and chase all the rabbit kids around. I could hear the squeals of laughter as they all played together.

While I was glad that Jacey was able to play with the children and bring a bit of joy into their lives, it disturbed Jahn and me to see one hundred and fifty kids being warehoused in this place. Every day we heard a lot of crying babies whose cries weren't being answered. And my heart broke for the children who weren't receiving the same care or compassion as Sasha was now. These children just wanted to be held. They wanted love.

I wanted to shower all of them with affection. But I knew I could help only one: Sasha. More than anything, I wanted him to experience not only love, but safety, security, and peace.

Sasha was intelligent for his age. He was three and a half years old in a group where all the other kids were five. But he learned quickly how to throw a punch even at that young age. This place was a miniature *Lord of the Flies*. It was all about survival. When the children were outside playing, the two caregivers for the fifteen kids would sit on a log and chat or talk on their cell phones and pay no attention to the kids. The kids would run wild in an untamed field with sharp remnants of Soviet play equipment still sticking up dangerously.

There was no compassion. If a child clearly hit another child, one of the adults might come up and smack him across the back of the head. There was lots of yelling and threats, with little or no discipline.

Outside, the children ran wild. Inside, they were extremely restricted. They had to walk and sit a certain way. There could be no loud noises, no laughter, and no talking.

Since Sasha was so young in his group, he became an easy target. We would arrive for a visit only to discover some bruise or cut on him. The other kids would take the toys we had brought for him. They would pour dirt on his head or shove him around.

Jahn and I would complain to the caretakers, who would listen, but clearly had no intention of doing anything to stop the aggression.

Slowly, Sasha began to trust us and became less wary of our funny language and clothes. He still didn't seem to understand why he was being pulled away from the other kids—especially during their playtime—and yet he would greet us at each visit with a warm smile and eventually a hug, and then chat easily about what we would do. Or at least I assume that's what he chatted about!

Although we enjoyed playing with him, trying to communicate was still a struggle. Jacey and I were picking up the language, but communicating with a three-year-old has its own set of challenges. So we had to make do as best we could.

HELP ARRIVES

Our second week there, as we were walking around the orphanage with Sasha, a young woman in her twenties with black hair and bangs rounded the corner and began to walk toward us.

I knew her. My mind quickly turned over where, how, and why I had met her before.

"Katya?" I blurted out.

"Kim!" she said, her eyes widening in joy.

We both shouted, laughed, and grasped each other in a strong Ukrainian hug that left little room to breathe.

"What are you doing here?"

"I work as a teacher and an interpreter now!" she said in perfect English. "I live here in Izmail. I am married and have a young daughter, who is almost three years old."

I shook my head in disbelief and wonder at the timing of this meeting. I laughed as I introduced her to Jahn. "This is Katya. When I came on the mission trip in 2003, I stayed with a church family in Kiliya. The teenage girl in that family had friends who were also in the youth group, one of them being Katya! Katya's father was the youth pastor and her mother was the Sunday school director at the New Kiliya Church."

"What a small world," Jahn said.

"Yes!" Katya agreed.

"What are you doing here?" I asked again.

"The family you stayed with when you were here before told me you were still in the country and having trouble with your adoption. They also mentioned you were having trouble with your facilitator not translating everything you need. So I've come to offer my services. Would you like to hire me for a small amount of American money and I will interpret for your son? I can teach him English. I have all the flash cards with pictures that have Russian and English on them. I can show him all the animals. I can teach him his letters and colors and numbers. And I can explain to him what is going on and who you are and why you talk so differently. Plus my daughter is almost three, so I can understand baby talk, too. I'm teaching her English now."

"Yes!" Jahn and I both said.

"Oh, Katya, you are an answer to our prayers," I said. "We would love to hire you. How soon can you start?"

"Right now." She smiled.

I felt overwhelmed by seeing God's hand at work. We had visited the New Kiliya Church when we were in Izmail to meet Dmitry and again when we returned to meet Sasha. God used those trips to answer our prayer for an interpreter. Again, I felt that everything was falling into place. Now we just needed the court date that would make our adoption official.

6

July 2009

MY FAMILY LEAVES

It was the Fourth of July.

"Kim, take a look at this." Jahn was sitting on the bed in our hotel room with his left pajama pant leg pulled up. A round red splotch about the size of a quarter sat halfway up his calf. It looked painful.

"Oh no," I said as I walked to investigate closer. "That doesn't look good."

"I think it's a bite. A spider maybe."

"Let's keep an eye on it." Inwardly I groaned, not just because of the bite, which looked scary enough, but also because it was the last thing Jahn needed in his already overextended mental state. I prayed it would go away quickly and uneventfully.

As the morning wore on, though, it got only worse until I knew it was infected. I was concerned the bite might go septic. Jahn cringed if anything accidentally hit it, and it had become more swollen, with pus seeping out around the edges. We couldn't wait any longer, simply hoping it would heal itself. But I didn't trust the doctors to know how to fix it.

I called Katya and asked for her help.

"Go to the drugstore and tell them you need medicine for Jahn's leg. Have him show them. They will get it for you."

"But it's really infected, Katya. I think we may have let it go a little too long. He's going to need prescription medication. Don't we need to see a doctor? Won't we need a prescription?"

"No," she said. "Everything is over the counter here. The pharmacist will give him whatever he needs. No prescription is needed."

Well, that's good, I thought, halfway impressed and halfway shocked. I was concerned about not seeing a doctor at first, but relieved that we could get Jahn some help right away. Katya met us and we immediately took a taxi to Izmail's largest pharmacy. The pharmacist came out from around the counter, took a good look at Jahn's leg, and asked us a few questions through Katya. A few minutes later, he handed us both oral and topical antibiotics with directions that Jahn was to take two pills right away.

Jahn's leg had started to throb whenever it wasn't elevated, so after getting him back to the hotel, covering his bite with the topical medicine, and setting pain relievers and a bottle of water within reach, I could relax.

"Mom, it's the Fourth of July. Aren't we going to do something?" Jacey said.

"Why don't you two go find something fun to do?" Jahn said. "You've wanted to check out the new pool over at that park by the marina. You and Jacey should take your suits and towels, just in case, and go check it out. I'll stay here and sleep."

"Can we, Mom? Please?" Jacey pleaded.

It was hot outside, and Jacey had been patient with our orphanage visitation schedule. I wanted to do this for her.

"You look so pale, Jahn. I'm afraid to leave you alone," I said.

"I want to sleep, Kim. Please, take Jacey and have a good time. I'll be okay. I'll call you if I have to. I'll probably sleep the entire time you two are gone. Go have fun," Jahn said. He managed a weak smile.

Jacey and I walked to the main road and flagged a taxi to the small amusement park, near the Danube River shipping area. The pool was brand-new and I could actually smell chlorine. It was a wonderful break from what had become long, repetitive days.

When we returned to the room, Jahn was still asleep.

◆

Things grew worse.

Our friends Don and Linda Wilson emailed us about a flood in our hometown. They checked on our house for us and our basement floor was covered with water. They spent the better part of two days mopping it up and sanitizing the area.

The flooding only added to Jahn's stress. Being away from his job for more than eight weeks made him concerned. He tried to stay in touch with his boss through Internet phone calls with the MagicJack I brought with me. His boss was growing concerned over Jahn's extended absence: they were in the middle of two major construction projects, which he had bid on and on which he was supposed to act as the project manager.

"When is this court date going to be set?" Jahn would demand.

"I don't know," I said. "Boris is trying to keep us posted, but he hasn't heard anything yet."

"Well, if it doesn't happen soon, I'm going to have to leave beforehand."

"I know, I know."

The bills were piling up. When we left the States, we hadn't anticipated being gone so long, so we hadn't set up any electronic payments to handle our household bills. Even though we had paid a month ahead, they would soon be overdue.

"I sure hope we still have a house to go home to," Jahn said, sharing my concern.

Finally, on July 8, Boris called with news.

"No court date yet," he began. "But all your paperwork goes to the Izmail judge tomorrow. So we should get a quick date set."

"Good. I don't know how much longer Jahn can wait." I hung up and prayed that the court date would come...fast.

◆

As another week went by and no court date was set, Jahn and I discussed the reality of his leaving.

"I hate leaving you here by yourself with no court date set yet," Jahn complained. Fortunately, the medication for his spider bite had helped and he wasn't dealing any longer with the pain from that. But the anxiety over his job and the slow adoption process was wearing on his nerves.

"I know," I said. "But we agreed you and Jacey would return before I did anyway. We agreed that I would remain to finalize everything and bring Sasha home."

"Yes, I know. But that was also before we knew what a mess this process would be. That was when we both thought we'd have a quick court date to get everything finalized."

"It's going to be okay, Jahn. You need to get back home and get back to work. I'll be fine. Boris submitted the paperwork. Plus, I have Katya to help me translate. It's not like I'm going to be here for long."

◆

"What would the ramifications be if I weren't at the court date?" Jahn asked Boris during our next visit with him. "I really need to get back to my job, and unfortunately, I can't stay here waiting indefinitely."

Boris nodded his understanding. "I don't think it will be a problem at all. We'll get all the paperwork and your signed testimony taken care of before you leave so we can present that to the court. Izmail is a sailor town, so lots of times proxies are used and the court is especially understanding of this type of thing here. Don't worry about it. I will take care of everything for you. Plus, since Kim will still be here, the judge shouldn't see any problems."

On Boris's advice, we decided that Jahn and Jacey would leave Izmail on July 14 to travel to Kiev. On July 16, Jahn would go to the American embassy to sign off on paperwork giving his agreement to the adoption. The visit to the embassy was important because it dated our paperwork. According to the law, we had one year from that date to finalize the adoption. Otherwise, we would have to return to the States and start all over again. Not that we even considered that as a possibility. We knew the legal system was slow, but it couldn't possibly be that slow, we joked.

In the meantime, Boris proved true to his word. With each new visit, he either brought paperwork for Jahn to sign or took him to get paperwork notarized. We continued to visit Sasha—and we made a strong effort to let Jacey and Jahn spend more time with him than me, since they would be leaving soon.

We still had no word on a date. And the closer it got to July 14, the more I could sense Jahn's worry about leaving me alone.

"I hate this," he said one afternoon. He was so frustrated. He laid his head in his hands as he sat on the edge of the bed.

"What else can we do, Jahn?" I asked.

"I don't know. I'm so sick of this place. Yet I'm so uncomfortable leaving you here. I'm worried about your safety, being here alone. I'm worried about . . ."

"The money," I suggested. "We've been so focused so far. I can see the light. I know it will be soon."

"I hope so."

♦

"Good news!" Boris told us a few days before Jahn and Jacey's departure. "We have a date: August 5."

Jahn and I breathed a sigh of relief.

"That is good news!" I said. For a moment, I wished Jahn and Jacey could postpone their trip back to the States, but I realized it wouldn't work. That was still two weeks away. Then after the judge gave his approval for the adoption, we would still have to wait another ten days for any possible appeals, which were considered unlikely. Then another two weeks to get Sasha's passport, visa, and adoption papers in order. But we had the date—and that was definitely something to celebrate.

"Okay, now I feel better." Jahn turned to me and smiled brightly. "Now I can leave here and know you're going to be okay."

"I LOVE YOU"

The morning after Jahn and Jacey left, I woke to a deafening silence. I was completely alone.

Okay, I told myself. *Not the end of the world. You can do this. Actually, you may even enjoy the freedom a bit!* I felt a little guilty that I was appreciating the thought of silence and calm, that I wouldn't have to try to appease anybody out of a bad mood or make peace at every turn.

I had now been in the country more than two months and I knew enough of the basics of Russian to get by—I hoped.

I was also pleased that Jahn and Jacey were finally getting to leave their misery. They could go home to the familiar. Jahn could get back to work. Jacey could see her grandparents and friends.

DMITRY GOES HOME

My daily visits to Sasha now included Katya. She prepared lessons for Sasha. We would play a little first, he would have a lesson, and then we would play some more. Sasha wanted to play all the time, of course. But he soon adapted to the new routine and started to look forward to the games he would play and the songs he would sing with Katya.

Upon our arrival at the orphanage one morning, we met a young blond couple from France. They appeared to be in their late twenties, and their facilitator explained to Katya that they were there to pick up their son. We wished them congratulations and watched as they entered the building to process their new child out of the orphanage.

Sasha's group was running late that day for playtime, so we were still waiting outside when the young couple reemerged holding Dmitry. I immediately teared up. They looked happy as they headed toward their waiting taxi. Dmitry looked so nice in his new clothes. He looked happy.

Thank you, God, I prayed. *Thank you for giving Dmitry a family that loves and adores him. And thank you for allowing me to see Dmitry's Gotcha Day, his adoption day.* God had been faithful and had allowed me to witness how he cares for all the orphans.

♦

The more time I spent with Sasha the more in love I fell. He was smart as a whip and would sing his ABCs in English with Katya and me. His mind was picking up English quickly and he was asking all kinds of questions about the language and why I smelled so funny to him (it was my shampoo and perfume).

Now with each new visit, Sasha rushed through the door and bolted toward me, shouting, "Mama! Mama!" and giving me a hug and a big kiss on the cheek.

On Friday a few days after Jahn and Jacey left, as Sasha and I were visiting, he reached his little arms around me and squeezed.

"*Ya tebya lyublyu*," he whispered. *I love you.*

"*Ya tebya lyublyu*," I whispered back and held him tighter. My eyes filled with tears.

Thank you, God. You are so good.

♦

At the end of July, I took photos and an album with me to the orphanage. During my visit with Sasha, I planned to compile it to present to the judge in our case to show how we had bonded. While Sasha looked on, I showed him each photo, then slid it into the album.

When I got to our family photos that included him, he placed his hand on my arm. Then he pointed to himself in the photo.

"Who's that boy?" he asked.

At first I thought he was joking, so I started to laugh. "Who do you think it is?"

But his eyes were serious as he shook his head.

Sasha had never seen a photo of himself? I choked up.

"That's *you*, Sasha."

His eyes grew large and jumped to mine, then back to the photo. "That's *me*?"

"That's you! Aren't you handsome?"

He took the photo from me and held it closely to his face and stared at himself. He had never seen his face. There were no mirrors in the orphanage.

I took a hairbrush that had a mirror on it from my purse and held it up for him to see. "Who's that boy? That's you!" I said, trying not to cry.

That was my first real sense of the true deprivation of these children. To be almost four years old and never have seen his face in the mirror was unimaginable to me and felt so very wrong.

AMERICAN FRIENDS

Katya and I headed to the administration building to meet with Inna, the SDA worker representing the Izmail district. We were trying to figure out what we needed to do to prepare for the upcoming court hearing.

As we stepped out of the office and debriefed a bit, a woman approached me.

"You speak English?" she said, looking at me. "Are you an American?"

"Yes."

"Praise God, I found you! I have two American workers here who..." She tried to think of the English words. Finally she said, "Ugh!" and turned to Katya and began blurting out Ukrainian words so quickly that Katya began to laugh.

"This woman works with two attorneys from the USAID branch office. They work out of her office. They are very lonely," Katya translated. "One speaks Ukrainian, but not Russian. The other speaks neither. And she wants you to come see them."

"What?" I said. "Okay. Well, tell her I am alone too, that my husband and daughter just went back to America, so I would love to meet other Americans."

This woman became so excited as Katya translated my words that she threw her arms around me and squeezed me into a strong hug.

She reached into her purse and pulled out a business card. "Come see me, come see me!"

Katya took the card. "I know where this is. She's over by the courthouse and the police department."

"Tell her we'll come and we'll have dinner or something."

"Yes, yes, that's good!" the woman exclaimed and waved as she nearly skipped out of the building.

◆

The next day, Katya and I stopped by the woman's office to meet the two attorneys.

As soon as we walked into the office, I knew these two Americans would become special friends. They were a husband-and-wife team, Ilse and Carl Whisner. Both looked to be early retired and in their mid- to late fifties. They were quick to chat—and to smile, which was a welcome sign indeed.

"I understand you are attorneys for the USAID office?" I said.

"What?" said Ilse. "No, we work for the Peace Corps. I was formerly in public relations and journalism. Carl was in human resources for large corporations."

"Oh!" I laughed. "An example of Ukrainian 'lost in translation.' I would love to have you come to my hotel for dinner tonight. My treat. The restaurant there is pretty good."

"That sounds wonderful! The Peace Corps doesn't exactly pay high salaries," Carl added.

That evening, over a five-course meal, we traded our stories from America and our Ukrainian experiences. Ilse's family was originally from Ukraine, so that's how she was able to speak the language. They immigrated to the United States right after World War II and grew up in a tight-knit Ukrainian neighborhood in New Jersey that kept up the culture of their homeland.

Ilse met Carl in college when they were both taking journalism classes. They married after they graduated, settled down, and raised a family.

After they both retired from corporate life, they decided to do something more significant with their lives. They had considered becoming missionaries, but felt uncomfortable with the thought of raising the support.

"But then I saw a newspaper article about how the Peace Corps was recruiting baby boomers, because they were hard workers and more mature," Carl said. "It took a little coaxing, but I talked Ilse into it!"

Their job in Ukraine was to write grants to get different organizations in Izmail funding for projects, such as providing schools in the area with basic supplies.

They listened to my adoption experiences silently and shook their heads. "Wow, that's crazy," Carl said.

"We know a few people here who can probably help you if you run into any trouble," Ilse suggested. "Just in case. You never know with this country."

"How are you handling the culture shock?" I asked.

They both laughed and raised their wineglasses. "It's great, isn't it?"

"Well, I pretty much knew what to expect since I was raised with the Ukrainian culture," said Ilse. "But we both had culture training through the Peace Corps, so that helped."

"Still not crazy about this place, though," Carl admitted. "By the way, now that you're alone here, you need to take extra precautions for your safety. For instance, if you're ever stopped and in a situation that you aren't sure how to handle, you need to think, *How would a Ukrainian handle this situation?* Then try to do that. You can't think like an American, because it may end up getting you into more trouble. Watch how the Ukrainian women act and react in different situations and try to mimic them."

"Okay," I said, storing that bit of advice for future use—but hoping I would never need to recall it. "Thanks. I will do that."

We hit it off fabulously. Our visit ended up going late into the night, with laughter and promises to stay in touch and get together again the next week. As I watched them leave the hotel, I realized God had looked after me again. When I was most alone, he provided American friends who were Christians, great listeners, and wonderful storytellers. They smiled easily, put me at ease, and had connections. They were just the people God knew I needed in my life.

7

August 2009

FIRST POLICE ENCOUNTER

By the end of July, I had decided I needed to take better care of myself and began buying fresh fruits and vegetables for my small hotel fridge. I had been living on food from the hotel's restaurant and the local cafeterias. So one morning after I visited Sasha, I decided to go to the open-air bazaar on the other side of town. Instead of taking a taxi, since I was trying to conserve my spending, I decided to walk the two miles each way.

The bazaar was full of vendors with their wares spread out on blankets or small tables. Some had makeshift awnings to protect themselves from direct sunlight. I walked around until I found a vendor who sold fruits. I purchased a bunch of red grapes and plums that looked clean. I got a good deal on bottles of water—less than a third the price I had to pay at the hotel—so I stocked up on those, since bottled water was the only safe water to drink.

I headed back to the hotel carrying two heavy bags. Slowly I made my way to the main street, which was within two blocks of my hotel. As I crossed it, I noticed to my left two police officers talking to a Ukrainian man near his car. At first I didn't pay much attention, but as I got closer I realized I was going to have to pass them. I could go a different way, I knew, but ahead of me was an alley shortcut that took me back to the hotel faster. I was hot, my feet hurt, and the bags were heavy and slicing into my fingers.

I knew that Ukrainian police officers could stop and interrogate you for anything. They only needed a suspicion—perhaps a suspicion you had money they could relieve you of.

Oh no, I realized, looking down at my outfit. Because the day was around one hundred and ten degrees, I had worn my only pair of shorts, which didn't have pockets. I had had to leave my identification and passport back at the hotel. If the police stopped me for any reason, they could end up arresting me because I had no papers on me.

I really didn't want to take the long route, though, so I put my head down, quickened my pace, and began to walk toward the alley. I had turned into the alley when I heard the Russian for "Stop!"

I froze. I knew they were behind me, but I wasn't sure they were talking to me since my back was toward them. I turned slowly to see if they meant me.

"Come here!" one of the officers yelled at me.

"Me?"

"Yes! You." The officer had a small, black club and was smacking it against his hand.

Between his tone, the weapon, and my realization that I had no identification on me, I panicked. I stood for a moment in that alleyway and thought I was going to lose bladder control. I slowly stepped my way back toward them. I thought back to Carl's words about how to react in a situation like this. So once I was a few steps from them, I put down my bags and shrugged my shoulders like an irritated Ukrainian woman who's been bothered unnecessarily in the middle of her chores. I'd heard how Ukrainian women who were hot and annoyed spoke to people. So I put my hands on my hips, straightened my back, and put on a frown.

"Do you understand English? I'm an American," I said in my best Russian.

The officer frowned, but held a slight twinkle in his eye. "*Nyet*. You are an American *woman*," he stressed.

"Ah," I said. I'd used the male Russian term for American. "Yes, an American woman. Do you understand English?" I was grasping for any Russian words I could put together.

He cocked his head, but didn't say anything. Then he seemed to look at my clothes. I had recently purchased the lightweight, short-sleeved shirt from the Ukrainian bazaar. I could tell he wasn't sure if he could believe what I was saying.

Finally, I said loudly and irritably in English, "Look. I'm an American. Do you speak *English*?" I hoped my Ukrainian woman attitude would help make me more believable and they would let me go my way.

He took a step back, shocked. I knew he now believed I was who I said! I reverted to Russian again. "Do you understand English?"

"*Nyet, nyet*," was all he would say. And although he still held his billy club, it didn't seem so threatening to me anymore.

"Eh!" I shrugged harshly again, picked up my bags, and turned quickly around. It felt as though something invisible grabbed on to my shoulders, turned me, and then pushed me forward. I began to walk with my shoulders hunched, listening for footsteps, waiting for the officer to run up behind me. I kept walking but began to tremble. I couldn't believe I had just pulled off that scenario.

I walked all the way to the other end of the alleyway before I dared to turn around. The officers seemed as though they had forgotten all about me and were once again focused on the man by the car. I could only assume they had stopped me to act as a witness to whatever transaction they were about to start. I didn't want to stick around to find out—especially because my spirit warned me it was trouble.

I was so grateful to my new friends from the Peace Corps who had told me what to do. Their advice and God's strength helped me stay strong and act the way I needed to.

But the most shocking realization was that I had changed. That wasn't my personality. I was becoming a different person. And although I was relieved that it had helped me out of this particular circumstance, I wasn't sure I wanted that rougher personality to remain.

PUSHING AHEAD

Boris and Inna, the Izmail SDA worker, were both nervous as we sat in Inna's office going over the last-minute details before our court date on August 5, two days away. They kept glancing at each other with knowing looks—while leaving me out of the loop.

"What?" I finally demanded. "What is going on? Why are you both acting so fidgety?"

They exchanged glances again.

"I just hope this works out okay," Inna said. "I wish we had held off on the court date until the end of August. But I'm sure everything will be fine."

"Why wouldn't it be?" I said.

She sighed and looked to Boris for help.

"If we'd requested a later court date, then you could have met Nikolay, Sasha's brother. He could have said no to you, just like his sister, Svetlana, did, and that he wants the other family, not you, to adopt him. We could have gotten a letter from him stating he was okay with the separation."

By now, I had been in Ukraine by myself for three weeks. The last thing I wanted to do was stick around for another month. But I saw their reasoning and was willing to accommodate whatever they advised.

"Is that what we should do?" I asked. "Should we ask to reschedule the date so I can meet him?

Boris thought for a moment, and then shook his head. "No."

"Are you sure?" I didn't want anything to hold us up.

"I am sure," Boris said, more decisively. "It will be fine. We have the letter from his sister. We can tell the judge about his trip to America and his upcoming adoption with the host family. The judge will understand. I will make sure of it. No worries."

AUGUST 5: THE COURT HEARING

At midmorning, Katya, Boris, Inna, and I entered the Izmail courtroom and took our seats at the front right-hand side of the room. The room was fairly small with wood paneling, wooden chairs, and benches.

Within a few moments of our arrival, the prosecutor entered and took his place across from us at a table on the left. He seemed agitated. He appeared to be about twenty-eight years old. He wore a dark mop of hair that needed a good combing, and his short-sleeved shirt looked worn.

I hoped his agitation was more from something that had happened earlier or that perhaps he hadn't had his morning coffee. I hoped he wouldn't take out his aggression on my case.

I looked at Boris to see how he reacted to this prosecutor. Boris fidgeted with his jacket and kept his eyes downcast, as though he didn't want to see.

Uh-oh, I thought. Something moved in my spirit that suggested all would not be well, but I hushed it. *It's a simple adoption. They happen every day. There should be no problem. I'm just nervous and overreacting. That's all.*

The judge, along with two jurors who represented the people of Ukraine, walked in and settled themselves behind a high table. The judge was gray-haired, in his sixties, probably close to retirement. He wore tiny glasses on the tip of his nose. He looked impartial and fair, but he also seemed kind and wise. The two jurors, one woman and one man, appeared to be close to the same age.

"This hearing is to discuss the adoption of Alexander Mazurek by Jahn and Kimberly de Blecourt of the United States of America," the clerk announced.

The judge looked at me.

"You are Kimberly de Blecourt?" he asked, through Boris.

I answered, "Yes."

"Where is Jahn de Blecourt?"

"Your Honor, Jahn had to return to America, but he left a signed and notarized affidavit stating he approves of this adoption," Boris interjected.

"You realize the law has changed and both parents are supposed to be here?"

Boris cleared his throat. "I was not aware of that new ruling, sir."

The judge squinted slightly, then riffled through some paperwork and nodded.

"Your Honor," the prosecutor began passionately, "the state wishes to reject this file for adoption. The de Blecourts are trying to break up this boy's family. He has a brother and a sister, both in orphanages. This family should be kept together. I do not agree to breaking up a family."

I tried to keep up with the dialogue as best I could and relied on Boris's sketchy translation, but I could tell he wasn't translating everything. I wanted to know what I was missing.

"What is he saying, Boris?"

Boris shook his head.

"Boris, what is he saying? Why is he so angry?"

"There's a problem with you not adopting all the children," he whispered.

The prosecutor pointed to Svetlana's letter. "We understand the girl doesn't want to be adopted. But the de Blecourts never even visited Nikolay. And he is close in age to Alexander."

"They are willing to give you a pass on the girl," Boris continued. "But you have to adopt both boys."

"But tell them we couldn't meet with Nikolay," I insisted to Boris. "Tell them he was in the United States with another family."

Boris spoke to the judge.

The prosecutor sneered. "That's your fault you didn't meet him and proceed with the adoption."

"No, it's not our fault," I whispered in a panic. "We had no control over his leaving the country. The director allowed him to be taken before that could happen."

Boris tried to explain the situation to the judge.

The prosecutor remained unmoved. He refused to look over at us. "I strongly disagree with this move to break up a family," he spat out.

There was silence.

"Am I allowed to say anything?" I asked Boris.

He asked the judge if I could speak while he translated.

"What's your definition of family?" I asked pointedly. "Is it maternal blood ties between children who have never even met each other? Or is it love and spirit that ties people together in a family? People who cherish this child? Who will give him a loving and safe home?"

I knew my words were forceful, but I was panicked. I didn't care what this prosecutor's definition of *family* was. We were Sasha's family.

"Their mother was never married," I continued. "They all carry her maiden name but they all have different fathers. They've never lived together. They've never lived with her or one another, as she gave them up at birth. How can you call this a family?"

The prosecutor simply stiffened his back and ignored me.

"Thank you, Mrs. de Blecourt," the judge said after I had finished my appeal.

The prosecutor began again heatedly spouting off. "The de Blecourts' facilitator didn't even obtain the correct documentation! Where are the letters from the SDA offices in Odessa? Their absence proves the SDA does not support the separation of these two brothers."

Boris spoke up. "Your Honor, I tried to obtain those letters. The district Alexander was born in refused to offer a letter without one from the brother's district. When I went to obtain a letter from that district, they also said no. So when I went to Odessa's main SDA office to explain the back-and-forth situation we were dealing with, their office refused to get involved. You can see that everything else is in order. Both boys will be adopted. Ultimately, it is your decision, Your Honor. Not theirs."

Inna crossed her legs, which caught my attention. Her face was fiery red in anger. I couldn't understand why.

"Your Honor," Boris continued. "This family is willing to adopt a child that nobody in Ukraine is willing to adopt. He is an untouchable because of his initial positive HIV test."

The judge gasped audibly, as though this was the first he was hearing of it. No one wanted a child who potentially had HIV—even if the child tested negative every other time. One positive test was a sentence to live the remainder of your youth in an orphanage.

"But the de Blecourts love him and want to make him part of their family. It doesn't matter to them what his test revealed."

The judge's face softened and a slight smile touched his face. He was moved by Boris's plea on our behalf. The two jurors also listened intently and appeared sympathetic.

"Why do they do this?" the judge asked, nodding toward me.

"Because they are people of faith."

THE VERDICT

After Boris pled our case, we were dismissed to wait in the hallway while the judge and two jurors deliberated in the courtroom.

I filled Katya in on what had happened, since she had not been allowed to be in the courtroom with us.

While Boris went down the hall to find a restroom, Inna confirmed my suspicions about the letter situation. "He is so cheap," she said angrily. "If you lose this adoption hearing, it will be because Boris wouldn't pay to get those letters." Her outburst explained her anger in the courtroom.

I was beginning to understand the Ukrainian way.

After about thirty minutes, the clerk called us back into the courtroom to announce the judge's decision. This time Katya was able to join us. The prosecutor brushed past us and sat down at his place. I gripped my hands and prayed, *God, you've brought us this far for a reason. Show us your power and goodness. Give this child a home.*

"After deliberating all sides of this case, we find for the de Blecourts. I grant their adoption of Alexander."

I breathed out and whispered, "Thank you, God. You are so good!" A huge weight lifted off my shoulders.

Unfortunately, the prosecutor didn't have the same reaction. The muscles in his jaw twitched and his neck and face went scarlet. He grabbed his briefcase, slammed it onto the table, and flung his folders into it. Then he picked it up, turned on his heel, and stormed out of the courtroom.

"That's not good," Inna said.

"Kim, that prosecutor is upset," Katya said. "You know he can appeal."

"Appeal what?" I said. "This is an *adoption*! He would appeal an adoption? It doesn't make sense."

"It's seldom ever done," she continued. "Something is going on with him. It just doesn't look good."

"Well, I'm sure eventually he'll calm down and forget about it," Boris suggested.

"Yes, let's wait and see," Inna agreed. "He has ten days to appeal. Probably nothing will come of it."

Katya shook her head but remained silent.

I heard their words, but my heart was celebrating because it heard, "I grant their adoption of Alexander." Inside I was shouting, *Sasha is now legally our son! Thank you for being so faithful, God!*

READY TO LEAVE

Over the next several days, my mind was in a whirl. I had so much to do to prepare to take Sasha home. My checklist was long: get Sasha's birth certificate, Ukrainian passport, and United States visa; travel to Odessa to finalize my Extension of Stay paperwork at the OVIR office (Department of Citizenship, Immigration, and Registration of Physical Persons), since my visa was good for only three months and I needed more time, "just in case," as Boris said.

As soon as Sasha's adoption was declared legal, Jahn and I decided to change Sasha's name. We wanted to name him Jacob—after Jahn's father. Passing along family names was important to Jahn's family, but also because Jacob had done so much for us throughout the adoption and we wanted to honor him with this blessing.

I wanted to celebrate God's goodness and rejoice that finally our adoption was complete. Jacob and I would be going home soon!

But it seemed as though the others weren't as enthusiastic. Each time I met or talked with Boris, Inna, or Katya, they would speak more tentatively and even occasionally suggest holding off on any final procedures.

"The prosecutor could still appeal this adoption, Kim. It's rare, but not unheard of," they would say. "If he does appeal, your case will be lost. You'll need to return home without the boy. We're not in the clear yet; don't get your hopes up too high."

I heard their words but nothing sank in. *Of course the prosecutor won't appeal. Why would he? It's an adoption, for goodness' sake! It's not grand larceny or murder or arson! It's the loving adoption of a little boy whom nobody in this country will adopt! There's nothing to appeal.*

♦

The appeal was the last thing on my mind. I had other troubles to deal with. One morning when I went to visit Jacob, he ran to greet me as normal, but his left eye was covered with a large gauze bandage.

"What is this?" I asked the caregiver.

"It's nothing," she assured me.

I bent down and tried to lift the gauze. Sasha pulled away from me, not sure he wanted me to touch it. I smiled at him and motioned for him to come to me. Katya, who stayed in the background, now encouraged Sasha to show me his eye. He hesitated, and then stepped forward. I gently lifted one corner of the gauze to find a deep cut centered under his eye. It was red and swollen, with a bit of dried blood crusted along it. The cut appeared to be infected. Katya gasped.

"This cut is *nothing?*" I stood and faced the caregiver.

"One of the boys hit him quite a while ago. Perhaps a cut from that incident has become infected," Katya translated. The worker showed no hint of apology or concern.

"And you didn't try to stop him? Why hasn't his eye been treated with more than this covering?"

The woman merely shrugged as if to say, *What could I do?*

"That's it." I took Sasha's hand and the three of us marched to the doctors' office and pounded on the door.

"This is unacceptable," I said to the female doctor, who also acted as the assistant director of the orphanage. I showed her Sasha's eye. "My husband and I have brought these types of things to the workers' attention on multiple occasions, and they have done nothing to stop it. Now Sasha has a cut on his eye that appears infected. If left unmedicated, who knows what could happen? What are you going to do about this?"

She examined the cut. "This doesn't look good. His eye will need to be treated. We will contact the special eye clinic here in Izmail. They will tell us what needs to be done."

"Katya, please tell the doctor I can pay for this eye specialist."

"The doctor says it is an arrangement they have with this clinic. No need for you to pay. However, if special medicine is needed, the doctor says you will need to pay for it. Their medicine budget here is very limited."

"I'd like Sasha to be seen as soon as possible. His eye seems to bother him."

"I will take care of it," the doctor promised.

I could only hope she would be true to her word.

EARLY MORNING, AUGUST 12: THE VISITOR

Seven days into the ten-day appeal waiting period, I felt more and more confident. We had heard nothing from the prosecutor or his office, nor had we any indication of any trouble from the orphanage.

"We're going home soon, Jacob," I told him that day. "You'll have your own room with your own toys and you can play with Jacey as much as you want. You'll make new friends. You're going to love it there!"

I cuddled him on my lap and stroked his thin, brittle hair. "Are you excited to come home with me?"

"Yes, Mama. I want to be with you always."

My heart fluttered.

My son.

That night, I enjoyed a quiet meal at the hotel, then got ready for bed. I closed the thick, dark drapes so the sun wouldn't wake me the next morning—since it typically rose around 4:30 a.m. and shone brightest directly into my window. I turned off the lights and nestled into my bed. The last few nights I had finally enjoyed sleep and was hoping this would be another good night.

Sometime in the middle of the night, however, I was roused from sleep by an intensely bright light, which filled the room.

Ugh. I forgot to close the curtains again.

I was so tired and I didn't want to get out of bed to close them. But even with my eyes closed the light felt blinding, dazzling.

All of a sudden I heard a voice begin speaking to me. I had a visitor. I didn't know who, I only knew it was from God.

It was as if something inside, perhaps the Holy Spirit residing in me, began to have a sort of reunion with this visitor. I exploded with praise. I had no control of the words coming out of me.

Whenever I tried to open my eyes, I couldn't. The light in my room was simply too bright. I kept my eyes covered and continued to gush.

"God, I love you! You are so wonderful. Thank you for the way you work in my life and take care of me. God, how worthy you are to be praised! Oh, God, thank you for choosing me to be here with little Jacob. I want to be a light in this country for you. I love you, God. I love you."

My visitor spoke, but I couldn't stop uttering continuous phrases of praise. Then I heard the visitor say something strange: "Be patient."

For a split second I thought, *That's a crazy thing for him to say.*

"Of course I'll be patient, Lord. I *have* been patient and I'll continue to be. I'll do whatever you ask."

Immediately the light began to fade, eventually leaving the room in total blackness. I adjusted my eyes and looked around. The curtains were fully drawn, just as I'd left them when I went to bed.

My heart pounded with excitement, awe, and wonder. I had heard about people receiving a visit from an angel or from God's Spirit, but I had never actually known someone who'd had that experience, let alone have it be me.

Now I *knew* things were going to turn out okay. Jacob and I were going to be leaving soon. God had just sent someone to visit me who told me to be patient. He meant we might have a few delays but nothing major. Everything was going to be all right.

LATE MORNING, AUGUST 12: SET IN MOTION

I arose early and prayed, praising God and thanking him for how he had taken care of me throughout my time in Ukraine. I thanked him for the visitor. Then after a quick breakfast, I visited Jacob.

After visiting hours were over, I took the bus, as I had done every day, twice a day, back to the hotel to run errands and wait until my afternoon visit with him. I was walking from the bus stop to the hotel when my cell phone rang. Boris had given me his extra phone to use while I was waiting to go home. It was an old, beat-up one, but I didn't mind. It worked, and it allowed me not to feel so alone, and that's all that mattered to me.

It was Katya.

"Kim, I have bad news," she said.

"What is it?"

"I have heard that the prosecutor filed a letter of intent yesterday. He is going to appeal your adoption."

Appeal the adoption. No, this can't be true, I thought. Everything had been going so well.

"Are you sure?"

"Yes."

"How did you hear?"

"Inna mentioned it to me."

My heart caught in my throat. If Inna knew, if Katya knew, then Boris, my facilitator, had to know also.

"Does Boris know? He's the one who should be calling me. Why isn't he calling me?"

"I don't know, Kim. Maybe he does not want to give you bad news. My friend, I am so sorry. Do you want me to come be with you? Are you going to visit Sasha this afternoon?"

"I don't know what I'm going to do. I'll let you know. I…" My mind went blank. "I…I have to call Boris." I quickly hung up with her and dialed Boris's number.

One ring. Two rings. Three rings. *He's going to let it go to voice mail.*

After the fourth ring, Boris finally answered. His hello told me everything I needed to know. I stopped walking and faced my hotel across the street.

"Is it true?" I asked Boris when he answered. I still wanted to hear the words from him.

There was silence on the other end.

"Is it true, Boris? Did the prosecutor file for an appeal?"

Hesitantly, softly, Boris said, "Yes. He filed a letter of intent to appeal."

"Why didn't you call me?"

Silence.

"When did you find out, Boris? How long have you known?"

Silence.

"You found out about this yesterday, didn't you? Why didn't you call me?"

Silence. Then, "I didn't want to tell you."

"You didn't want to tell me? What were you thinking, Boris?"

"I don't know. I did not want to upset you." In a quieter tone, he asked, "What are you going to do?"

"How many days does he have to file the actual appeal?"

"Twenty."

"Twenty days from when? From now or from the court date?"

"Counting from when he filed the letter of intent, August 11, so August 30. He has to turn it in at the courthouse. He may turn it in early, but usually that doesn't happen."

My throat constricted and I gasped for air. Tears began to stream down my face. My own facilitator had known and had done nothing. He had gotten us into this mess perhaps from his greed and inexperience. And now my son could be taken from us.

"Nice job, Boris," I spat out and hung up.

I sank onto the filthy sidewalk across from the hotel and began to sob uncontrollably. I put a hand onto the ground to try to raise myself back up, but all my strength had gone.

The street was empty except for the guard at the hotel gate, who looked at me wide-eyed and then turned away.

I was devastated and angry and terrified. Boris should have called me first. He should have told me. And now all I could think of were Inna's and his words since the hearing: "*If the prosecutor files for an appeal, that will be very bad for you. You might as well just go home. The adoption won't go through then. You'll just need to forget about this boy."*

I took several deep breaths, picked up the phone again, and dialed Jahn's number. I didn't care that it was an international call and that the charges would be astronomical. I could barely register the numbers through the thick tears swimming in my eyes.

"Jahn! He's filed for an appeal," I blurted out as soon as he answered. I gasped again, starting to hyperventilate. My tears were uncontrollable.

Jahn expelled his breath heavily. "Why were we appealed? Are you sure?"

"Yes, and Boris didn't even have the guts to call me himself. Katya told me. What are we going to do?"

There was a stunned silence from Jahn for what seemed like more than a minute, as I quietly continued to sob.

Finally, Jahn said, "It's going to be okay, Kim. We'll just keep going. No matter what happens, we have to keep going and see this thing through."

I stopped crying. I looked down at the dirty, foul ground I was still half lying on. I had been reduced to this, and I snapped.

"That's really easy for you to say, Jahn! You're sitting at home in America with your job, in our home, with our daughter. I don't have any of those things! No matter how you look at it, I'm *here*. And I'm alone!" I snapped the phone shut before he could respond.

Time stopped as I sat on the sidewalk and continued to weep. Slowly, I tried again to lift myself from the sidewalk. Gradually I got to my feet and began to calm my sobs. I knew I needed to get myself into a more controlled state before I entered the hotel and walked past the hotel reception workers to get to my room.

Call Jahn back, I heard a small voice inside my head whisper. *Your attack against him wasn't fair*. I knew it wasn't fair. I knew he was just as upset and helpless and worried. I knew he felt terrible that I had to go through this. But I couldn't call him. I wanted to let my anger hold me. I wanted to punish someone for the pain I was experiencing, and, fair or not, I was going to punish Jahn.

I waited a few more minutes to pull myself together. I wiped my face, certain that I looked terrible, then crossed the street, keeping my head down, and walked past the guard without saying anything. I could feel everyone's eyes on me as I walked through the hotel lobby and past the reception desk.

Once in my room, I collapsed onto the bed and began to sob fresh tears that wouldn't stop. I didn't try to make them stop. I cried until I exhausted myself into sleep.

Forget about that boy. You should just go home. You did your best.

I couldn't imagine not adopting Sasha, my Jacob. I couldn't imagine having to stay here longer to fight. I was so tired. But I also couldn't imagine not being home with my husband and daughter.

I was going to lose, no matter what. I could see no win in my situation.

I woke to new tears and the voices telling me to quit and leave. Those voices even drowned out the visitation from earlier that morning. My rationale was gone. I could not function or get out of bed; I could only cry until I wore myself out again and fell into a fitful sleep. That became the pattern: sleep, wake, cry, sleep. I couldn't eat. I could barely breathe. I refused housekeeping. I refused to answer the phones. I felt like Job. I had failed my family and this darling little boy. I couldn't escape the oppression this time. I was suffocating and all I could do was cry.

AUGUST 13: A SOUND DECISION

I awoke twenty-one hours later feeling drained. I had no more tears left. My head ached, my lips were parched, and my stomach was nauseated. I felt hungover.

I weakly rolled over and looked at the clock on the bedside table for the first time. I had been in the room for a little less than twenty-four hours and had already missed two visits with Jacob. I wouldn't miss another.

I inched off the bed and grabbed a bottle of water to drink. Slowly, I walked into the bathroom to wash my face. A woman I didn't recognize stared back at me from the mirror. Her eyes were puffy and had black circles under them. Her cheeks were chapped from the continual stream of tears. I washed my face and looked at myself again, this time nose to nose with the woman in the mirror. My hair now had a shock of pure white about an inch and a half across the right side of my scalp.

My hand reached up, pulled back my hair, and touched the spot. I blinked and looked again, and then I shook my head to clear my thoughts.

"I never want to be that weak again," I swore to myself. "I will never lose control like that again." I looked up toward the ceiling. "God, please don't ever allow me to go there, to wherever that was, again. You love this little boy more than anybody else. If he's to be with us, fine. If he's to be someplace else, I will accept it. You will help me accept it. But don't ever let me go to that place of despair again, no matter what happens. My faith is in you, God, not a foreign judicial system. Help me remain hopeful and patient."

I stood up straight, pushed my shoulders back, and walked to my suitcase to get a fresh set of clothes.

I'm just going on, I thought as I threw on a blouse and pants. *I'm going to wait this out. Help me be strong, God...for Sasha.*

I picked up my room key, my wallet, and my cell phone. My first call would be to Jahn, to make things right between us. Then I headed back to the orphanage to visit my son.

THE VOICE ON THE OTHER END OF THE PHONE

Katya had been a huge help. Though I was learning to understand and speak the language, I still couldn't read it, so she helped me go to the market, translated papers for me, and encouraged me in my faith. I often wondered if God had me take the short-term mission trip here specifically to meet her those years ago, because she would be so instrumental in my experiences now.

Now I needed more help. The day after I heard about the letter of intent, I called Katya to tell her I needed to move into a flat. I knew I would be in the country for at least another month, and I couldn't afford to stay at the hotel any longer. I asked her to find me a cheap but livable apartment. Then I went to visit Ilse and Carl to tell them what had happened.

Ilse's face brightened. "We have a flat for rent right across the hall from us. You can move in there! The landlord has been working on it. It's really small, but I think you'll like it. Come home with us for supper and you can check it out."

It was a one-bedroom furnished apartment. I suspected it was roach-infested. But it would save me a lot of money and it was next door to Carl and Ilse, my closest support system. However, the landlord informed us that it wasn't available; someone else had it reserved.

"Oh well, thanks for the idea, Ilse. You tried. I'll see what Katya finds for me."

I kept looking for divine intervention, praying earnestly, and practicing patience. I wasn't good at the patience part. I wanted God to move on our behalf *now*. I had been in Ukraine more than ninety days. That seemed a lot like patience to me.

Every moment, it seemed I had to pray anew: *God, help me to be patient. Help me to remember you are working behind the scenes on our behalf—even though I can't always see it.*

Finally, I put out a fleece to God and asked if I should stay in Ukraine or return to the United States. "I'm leaving it to you, God. Just make it clear to me."

The next day, I received a call from Katya. "I've looked through three newspaper pages filled with flats for rent, but I think I found one that seems right for you." She began to describe the place and location.

"Wait a minute," I said. "I think I know where that is. I think that's the flat over at Ilse and Carl's. It's not available."

"Hmmm," Katya said. "I just spoke to the landlord, who said that it is now."

I was stunned. Could it be that God had just answered my prayer with a resounding "Stay!"?

That weekend I packed my bags and headed to the other side of town. That meant that instead of an eight-block walk from the hotel to the bus stop where I would catch a bus to the orphanage, I now had a two-mile walk to the bus stop each way. Four times a day—back and forth twice, to visit Jacob twice a day, every day.

"Eight miles of walking to visit Jacob," I told Carl and Ilse the night I moved in, "and that's not counting walking to the market or anywhere else. Well, that's one way to stay healthy and destress."

For the first time in a long time, I felt hope. I was close to my new friends. Sasha was learning English and bonding with me quickly. And I had God who remained close.

I tried to keep my thoughts focused on my divine visitor's message: *Be patient.*

◆

On Monday morning, August 17, I awoke early, ate breakfast in my flat, and went to the main Izmail bus station, where I met Boris, who had arrived from his home in Odessa. He looked terrible, gaunt, ill.

"Are you all right?"

"I've been so sick. I can't sleep. I have stomach trouble. It's been awful." He would barely look me in the eye.

Guilt? I wondered.

We walked to the courthouse, where a clerk informed us formally that a notice of intent to appeal had been filed on Tuesday, August 11. The prosecutor had twenty days from that to file the appeal with all the supporting documents—*before* August 31.

He handed a copy to Boris, who looked it over silently, then translated what seemed like just bits and pieces.

"Technically, according to this letter he needs to get the paperwork filed with the courthouse *before* the twentieth day, which means he has to have it in and stamped no later than Friday, August 28. Everything may not be lost," he said as we walked out into the sunshine and heat. "Sometimes they will file the letter but not file the appeal. We just have to wait."

"What if we just explain the situation to the other orphanage director and go see Sasha's brother to get his sign-off on everything? That will nip this whole appeal."

"No," Boris said. "You need a letter to see him. You can't just walk into the orphanage and request a visit. And your original letter to visit him has expired."

"Okay then, let's go back to Kiev to the SDA office and get another letter."

"No, it doesn't work that way. You have had your three visits to the SDA. You visited Sasha. They will not allow it. That—what do you say?—ship has already sailed? No. Let's wait and see what happens. Maybe he won't file the appeal." He gave me a halfhearted smile and then looked at his watch. "I need to catch the bus back to Odessa."

I glanced at my watch as well. Two hours had passed since he stepped off the bus. Two hours was all he could give me.

"I need to get going to see Sasha," I said and took a step in the opposite direction.

"Yes, yes. Well, enjoy your time with him." And with that he turned and left me alone again.

♦

"Can you help me? I received a letter of intent to appeal. I need help. Can somebody there help me? My facilitator is having trouble getting the job done." I explained our appeal situation.

The woman at the American consulate replied kindly, "Let me make some phone calls and I'll call you back."

A few hours later, I received a call from the woman. "You are going to get a call from a man named Viktor. He is a good man. He knows Ukrainian systems very well. He lives in New York, but he still comes over regularly. He just happens to be here right now working on another adoption. I've told him your situation, and he says he's willing to help you. He will call you."

"Thank you!" I said. "I appreciate your help."

I hung up the phone feeling more in control. Mentally, I decided now I really needed to spend more serious time learning Russian. I felt I couldn't trust Boris, so the more I could understand the language, the better I would be able to tackle whatever lay ahead.

I visited Jacob, or Jake as I had started to call him, and we put together puzzles and I taught him how to do a high five. Then we hung out at the main gate to the orphanage and watched the cars go by, something he loved to do. It was his only connection to the other side of the giant walls surrounding his home.

My phone rang. I didn't recognize the number so I assumed it was this Viktor.

"Hello?"

A deep voice responded in English, but with a Russian accent. "My name is Viktor. I understand you need some help."

"Yes!" I breathed a sigh of relief.

He began to ask me the details of the case. "Who is your facilitator?"

"Boris Romanov."

"Hmph. I've heard of him. I'm not impressed. And who is your SDA case worker there in Izmail?"

"Her name is Inna."

"Okay, I know her. I will give her a call. Just sit tight. I'll be in touch."

THE DEMAND FOR THE ADOPTION DECREE

Over the next several days, I kept myself busy by settling into my new flat and buying a few inexpensive items at the bazaar, like a couple of pans so I could cook, and a couple of new dishes. I enjoyed hanging out with Ilse and Carl or Katya when I wasn't visiting Jake.

Carl and Ilse suggested I talk with an attorney friend of theirs, nicknamed Akula. He had an office across from their office, which was situated in the building between the courthouse and the police station. Although he was a criminal attorney, not an adoption attorney, they felt it would be good at least to seek some advice, and Akula had a good reputation.

He listened to my story but offered little advice. I noted his name and expertise, hoping that I would never need to use him—not because I wasn't impressed, but because I just wanted out of the country.

I had no word from Boris. But Viktor called every few days to check up on me.

By Friday, August 28, I was at wit's end. I hadn't slept in days and I walked around almost in a daze. I was afraid to think of what would happen if the prosecutor did appeal. I kept a close eye on the time, which seemed to drag on at the pace of a funeral dirge.

The courthouse, which typically closed at five, closed at four on Fridays. The prosecutor had until four o'clock.

Four came and went. I tried to make sure I was acting as normal as possible while I visited Jake. I didn't want him to know anything unusual was going on.

At 4:20 my phone rang. It was Viktor informing me that the prosecutor had not filed an appeal.

"How could you possibly know that? You're in Kiev!"

"Kim. It's *Ukraine*. I will call you soon with more information. But you must go to the judge Monday morning and demand your decree. The prosecutor has missed his deadline. So you go this weekend and buy your son clothing. The orphanage will not give him to you with any clothing. Tell the workers you are going to come early next week to pick him up."

My head was spinning. The prosecutor had missed the deadline. Could it be that simple?

"Kim!" Viktor's voice was demanding and whipped my mind back into focus. "Kim, you must make sure you do this, do you understand?"

"Yes. I will."

"Monday morning. Do not be late."

I hung up and hugged Jake tightly. As soon as my time with him was over, I met with the assistant director and told her I would be picking up Jake to take him home either Monday or Tuesday, then I left in a hurry. I had a lot to do before Monday morning.

♦

I received another call from Viktor.

"I believe the prosecutor did prepare the appeal against your adoption. It was signed at approximately 4:35 p.m., but since he didn't get the appeal to the court before it closed, you might still have caught a break. Regardless, you still need to make sure you're at the courthouse Monday morning, okay?"

"Definitely!" I responded.

I called Jahn and we rejoiced together. Then I called Ilse and Carl.

"That's wonderful!" Ilse said. "We must take you shopping and then have dinner to celebrate."

On Saturday, Ilse and Carl went with me to the Izmail bazaar, where I bought clothes for Jake. That night she made a wonderful dinner of tortellini with jazzed-up sauce, followed by homemade berry blintzes with a cream-and-Baileys topping. I couldn't remember having a day so wonderful in a long time.

I called Boris. "We're getting the adoption decree and picking up Sasha on Monday. Can you come?"

"No, I can't be there. I am in Kiev with another family."

I couldn't believe what I was hearing from our facilitator. "Are you kidding me?" I said. "Now that I'm actually getting Sasha, something I've paid you for, you're not going to be there?"

"I cannot do anything about this. I will be there Tuesday, okay? I still do not feel well. You will pick up Sasha on Tuesday and I will be there."

I wanted to put my hands through the phone and strangle him. "Fine. Be here Tuesday."

Off and on that day and all of Sunday, as excited as I was, I had a feeling that I should sleep as much as possible and prepare for what could be a tough week. The Spirit was definitely talking to me, so much so that I actually mentioned this to Carl and Ilse: I felt I was being led to prepare myself physically for the upcoming week. I spent most of Sunday alone—resting, cleaning, listening to Dr. Charles Stanley over the Internet, and praying.

Although I didn't know what to expect, I knew I should expect *something*.

◆

Monday, August 31, Katya and I went to the courthouse. We went over the plan one more time before we entered the clerk's office.

"Kim, this is not America. You must be more...stoic."

Being stoic about it was what was going to make me worthy of getting their attention, she explained. It made no sense to me, and I wasn't in the mood for a lesson on being stoic to get your way. But I was in Ukraine, where their mentality about such things was the exact opposite of how Americans view them.

"Don't go in there crying," she persisted. "The judge is a lot more likely to blow you off and resist your request if you're emotional. Be strong and determined, but don't be emotional. Don't show you are weak."

We entered the clerk's office and Katya told him that we needed to see the judge for my case.

"He's not available," the clerk said, barely looking up from his work.

"Put all the blame on me," I told Katya. "Tell him that this crazy American woman is demanding time with the judge."

Katya's voice cracked as she said more sternly, "We must see him. This woman is demanding to see the judge."

The clerk looked at me for a moment, then nodded. "Just a moment."

Within a few minutes, he ushered us into the judge's chamber. Katya nervously wrung her hands as she asked to either see the appeal or have a copy of the judge's final ruling offically signed and stamped.

The judge looked startled. "You're right. The appeal was not filed by the deadline. Come back tomorrow and I will give you the decree."

"No, I want it today," I said. I got the sense that the judge really wanted to help me, but I also sensed that he didn't want to do anything wrong.

"That is not possible," he told me. "My clerk has to put everything together—all the paperwork. Tomorrow. Be here at 7:30 in the morning." His tone sounded kind, but final.

My muscles tensed and I felt my blood pressure rise. I was afraid that the prosecutor would manipulate things somehow to still be able to file the appeal. But I had no other recourse; I would return the following day.

♦

I went to visit Jake, and then called Boris to tell him what had happened. Our plan was to pick up the adoption decree and head over to process Jake out of the orphanage. Then, we would go immediately to Odessa to get his birth certificate, then we would head to Kiev to the American embassy to do his health exam and get his American visa, *then* we could go home. If everything went according to plan, we could be back on American soil within a week or so.

Viktor called again to find out how it went—although I was strangely suspicious he already knew. After I told him what had happened, he said, "This is important, Kim. As soon as you receive that decree, you go immediately to the orphanage and get your son out of there and out of the country. Quickly. Do you understand?"

"Why?" He was making me nervous. "I'm not doing anything illegal, am I? I won't do anything illegal, Viktor."

"No, you will have all the legal paperwork, won't you?" He liked to answer my questions with questions. It drove me crazy.

"Yes."

"Then get out as quickly as you can." Viktor paused before he continued. "Kim, you're in Ukraine now, you understand? A prosecutor in Ukraine can make life very difficult for you. They have connections. You must understand this."

This wasn't the first time I'd heard an explanation of corruption in Ukraine. Many of my Ukrainian and American friends alike had warned me. However, Viktor, who was generally in a hurry, took the time to try to explain it to me again, and it made me listen very closely.

"Yes, I think so."

"If a prosecutor can find you, things can be planted. Unpleasant items you don't want to be found with. You understand? They will plant them, come back with the press and find these items, then arrest you. If this prosecutor wants you imprisoned, he will make it happen. Don't make anything easy for him. Don't draw attention to yourself. Be quiet. Never be easy to find. And get your son home as soon as possible. Well, I must go. I will call again soon."

With that, Viktor hung up, and left me speechless.

8

September 2009

MORNING, SEPTEMBER 1: THE ADOPTION DECREE

I managed to sleep a few hours that night, but woke up feeling tired and nauseated. I kept dreaming a worst-case scenario of the judge telling me he couldn't give me the adoption decree because the prosecutor had paid him off; then they dragged me away screaming, leaving Jake at the orphanage gate crying and calling out, "Mama! Mama!"

"God, I need your strength today—whatever happens, if we get the judge's ruling or if we get the copy of the prosecutor's appeal, I need your strength to make it."

I applied some makeup and tried to look my best, but the previous four months had taken a toll on me, and it showed in the mirror. I looked haggard.

I met Katya and we took a taxi to the courthouse. We were there at 7:30 a.m., as requested, but the judge was not there. Neither was Boris.

Finally, more than a half hour later, the judge walked in and showed us to his chamber.

"I'm granting you the adoption. We have the paperwork. I just need to add some stamps and a signature."

"Thank you, Your Honor!" I was elated. I couldn't believe it was finally done. The clerk was finalizing the paperwork when Boris arrived. He greeted us, went in and spoke briefly to the judge, then returned and took the documentation from the clerk. He seemed uncomfortable, on edge. He kept shaking his legs and running his hand through his hair.

"Why is he acting so nervous?" I wondered to Katya. "We're just going to pick up Jake."

Boris looked over everything in the document very carefully to make sure there were no mistakes, and then handed it back to the clerk, pointing out several errors. They worked together to fix those on the clerk's computer, then the clerk printed it, made a dozen copies, wax-sealed and stamped them, and had the judge sign them all.

I held my breath. Could the prosecutor still pull strings? But then the clerk walked over to us with multiple copies of the ruling. We were done. Jake's adoption was official.

AFTERNOON, SEPTEMBER 1: THE LAST ORPHANAGE VISIT

We rushed out of the courthouse, clutching the documents and smiling. "I'm so happy for you, Kim!" Katya said. "God is so good. He has proved faithful."

"I know. He really has!" I laughed.

"While you collect Sasha, I'll go home to pack a small bag. I will accompany you to Odessa."

"Thank you, Katya, for all you have done for us. I can't tell you how much I appreciate it."

She gave me a quick hug and then headed toward her flat.

From the courthouse, Boris and I hired a taxi to take us to the orphanage. Once there, we presented our documentation to the orphanage's paralegal, Dominika, who looked everything over and began to process Jake out of the orphanage.

As she was processing the paperwork, she asked Boris a question that I couldn't understand. He responded in Ukrainian, which I also couldn't understand. But then she asked the same question a few more times. It seemed as though she was asking, "Where is she?" but that didn't make sense to me and I didn't pay much attention to it.

Finally, Dominika gave us all the paperwork we needed to take with us to Odessa. Since Jake was born in Odessa in the Malinovsky district, we had to go to the birth certificate office there to get his new birth certificate. It was the only office that could issue it.

Again Boris seemed nervous and cautiously went over every detail of Dominika's paperwork to make sure she gave us everything we would need. Once he was satisfied that everything was in proper order, we proceeded upstairs to Jake's wing. We presented the paperwork to one of the caregivers, who was shocked.

"How did you get the decree?" she asked. "How are you here with this? The prosecutor must not have appealed."

She escorted us to Jake's room and called all the other children to gather around to celebrate this happy day. As she stripped Jake of his clothes, I reached in my bag and pulled out the new outfit I had brought for him.

Where are his shoes? I rummaged around in the bottom of my bag, but came up empty-handed. *Oh no! Katya has them in her bag. I can't believe I don't have his shoes!*

I put the new clothes on him as we laughed and hugged. Jake was all smiles, but I was sure he didn't understand the significance of what was happening. All the other kids came around him and began to shout their goodbyes.

While I was excited and took a few photos, I also felt the pressure of the clock.

"We should go," I said finally as I picked Jake up—I wasn't about to allow him to walk in his new socks on the filthy ground. "We have a long ride to Odessa to complete everything."

On the way out, we passed a couple from America whom I had gotten to know briefly who were also in the process of adopting a child from the same orphanage. As soon as they saw us their faces brightened.

"Are you going home? The appeal didn't go through?"

Everyone knew about the appeal!

"Yes, the adoption was finalized!" I said as I kept walking. "Sorry, I don't have time to talk, we have to get out of here to get to Odessa before the birth certificate office closes."

"Congratulations!" they yelled.

Jake was snuggled up against my chest, still not quite sure what was going on, but enjoying all the attention and excitement. As we approached the gate and the taxi, his eyes widened with fear and he began to squirm and tear up.

I put him on the ground to have him get into the taxi. I wanted him to do that himself. As I encouraged him to get in, he stretched his arms and legs out spread-eagled over the opening and refused to go inside. He started screaming.

I dropped to my knees in the dirt and hugged him.

"It's okay." I stroked his head, which calmed him. He stopped screaming, but he continued to sniffle loudly.

A full minute later, still hugging him, I stood and slowly got into the backseat of the car with him wrapped around me. He tensed as

I closed the door. As the driver pulled the cab away from the gate, Jacob let go of my neck and stretched his arm past my shoulder, reaching back toward the orphanage, as though he was grasping to get back inside the concrete walls. There were no more tears from him, but low, sad moans escaped from his body.

I should have realized that this moment would not be a celebratory one for him. I should have realized that to him I was pulling him away from his comfort, from everything he knew. But I didn't. I knew what a happy day this was; I knew what he was going to. He knew only that he was being ripped away. A wave of sorrow overcame me and I ached for him.

As we rode through the city back toward my apartment, I tried to get him interested in what was going on outside the windows. But he continued only to look out the back window toward the now vanished walls of the orphanage. I tried to pull him around so he was seated frontways on my lap, but he gripped tightly to my neck and whimpered.

I called Carl and Ilse. "Jake is with me. See you at home."

Ilse yelled into the phone, "That's great! Carl and I are on our way. We have to meet him before you leave!"

We were at a dead run, pushing the taxi driver to make it back to my apartment as quickly as we possibly could. Everything was already packed, so I just needed to get in there and pick up my bags and meet Katya. Boris had hired a private car to pick us up at my apartment and drive us to Odessa.

Carl and Ilse met us at the front of the apartment building all smiles and waves and shouts of joy. "Let's see your son!"

Jake was timid and frightened and clung to me.

"It's okay, Jake. These are Mama's friends."

Carl and Ilse helped carry my bags to the car. I did one final round through the apartment to make sure I didn't forget anything. Dozens of things were still there, none of which I could take with me.

"Don't worry about this stuff, Kim," Carl said. "Give us the key and we'll make sure everything is okay until your lease runs out."

"Take whatever you want or need, you guys. You can share what you don't want with the other Peace Corps workers." I waved toward the pans and other items lying around. "I'm paid through September."

Hugs all around, then we headed down to the car, dropped everything into the trunk, greeted Katya, who had arrived, waved goodbye, and headed for Odessa. The office closed at five and we needed to get that birth certificate before then.

Four and a half hours over the worst roads in the world—it was only made worse by the fact that with every jerk, jolt, and bump Jake cringed, whimpered, and gasped. He still refused to sit anywhere except on my lap, but at least now he sat frontways and looked out the window. I was glad I had packed a car trip bag for him, filled with juice, candy, crackers, and a new toy and book to hold his attention.

I noticed that Boris was still acting uncomfortably nervous. I knew something was going on, but I couldn't tag it, and I had other things to focus on with my son now in my complete care outside of the orphanage's walls.

◆

We arrived at ZAKS, the birth certificate office, with what should have been plenty of time to get a birth certificate and be on our way.

"I can't accept this," the clerk there said as she pushed the adoption decree back across the counter. "There are eleven mistakes in this decree."

"What?" I was livid. I didn't care that I wasn't supposed to show any emotion. I'd had enough. "You and the judge's clerk spent all that time making sure there were no mistakes. How could you not have seen eleven mistakes?"

"The clerk must have printed off the wrong version. These were the mistakes I caught at the courthouse and we fixed them. We corrected these. I swear it."

"Can't you do something so she'll give us the certificate anyway?"

Boris turned and spoke to the clerk, who stubbornly shook her head and said something I couldn't understand.

"No," Boris told me. "She said she doesn't have the ability to grant our request, and that we need to come back tomorrow to talk with her boss about it."

Uneasiness settled over me. I felt the clock ticking. But what could I do? I was stuck at the mercy of the Ukrainian bureaucracy.

"We will have to wait until tomorrow, then," Boris said, averting his eyes from me. "You can stay at my house tonight."

"No," I said. The thought of spending one more minute with him made me angrier and more distraught than I already felt. I had some friends who were working in town, Adam and Isabelle Lincoln, whom Jahn and I had known prior to their leaving for Ukraine. I decided to call them and see if they could suggest a decent and inexpensive hotel we could stay at for the night.

Adam answered the phone.

"Adam, I'm here in Odessa with Jake—"

"Kim, that's wonderful!"

"Yes, but there's a glitch we need to get handled before we can go home. It looks like we're stuck here for another day. Can you recommend a hotel?"

"No, no, no. Absolutely not. You'll stay with us tonight. Have Boris bring you to our house."

Thank you, God, for taking care of us through this, I prayed on the drive over. Although I was tired and felt defeated, I was surrounded by Katya and the Lincolns. God had taken care of us.

A SIMPLE BIRTH CERTIFICATE

Katya and I rose early the next morning, Wednesday, September 2, and left Jake in the care of Isabelle and Adam. Because they had two children around the same age as Jake, he settled in and didn't seem to mind so much that we were leaving him. We met Boris at the birth certificate office.

"I'm sorry," the supervisor said. "Those mistakes on the judge's ruling have to be corrected before we can grant the birth certificate with the boy's new name on it. There's nothing else we can do." Her voice sounded final.

My phone rang. I answered it and walked outside the office. The voice on the other end was deep and mysterious. It was Viktor.

"Kim, you must get Sasha processed and out of the country. I have just received news that the prosecutor is attempting to use a law that may allow him to mail in his appeal paperwork."

"What does that mean? It was still late."

"It depends. As long as it was stamped by the post office before midnight on the due date—last Friday—the court may still accept it."

My mind started to whirl again. Our judge was saying that his ruling was final and the prosecutor hadn't filed an appeal. But now Viktor was suggesting that the prosecutor's office might have filed an appeal by mail. Because of this new information, it was even more important for us to hurry Jake's Ukrainian passport processing, but we couldn't seem to get past the first step, which was to obtain a new birth certificate with his new American name.

"This can't be happening," I said to Katya as soon as I hung up with Viktor.

"Listen," Katya said. "I'll go back to Izmail and work with the judge's secretary and assistant to correct all mistakes. I'll be back early tomorrow morning, and we should be good to go."

We dropped off Katya at the bus station, and since there was nothing left to do, I returned to Adam and Isabelle's flat.

♦

Isabelle met me at the door with news of Jake. "He's a very active little boy," she said sweetly, although I could tell she was exhausted.

Oh no. "What did he do?"

"Well, apparently he's never flushed a toilet, run water from a faucet, or seen light switches before."

He had spent the day playing with her youngest child and also flushed the toilet over and over, switched the lights on and off repeatedly, and turned the faucet on and off ad nauseam.

"Oh, Isabelle, I'm so sorry." I knew he had not experienced many of the things we take for granted, but I had no idea how deep the deprivation went.

"I didn't think you knew," she continued. "But he is a sweet little boy."

The deprivation I discovered only went deeper. He didn't know how to play with or use toys for children his own age, so we gave him toddler toys. That night, though, was the worst.

Jake and I joined the Lincolns for a meal that evening. It was obviously his first meal ever served family style. His hands went into *everything*. The entire family was patient and kind, though.

After supper, Boris called.

"I just received a call from Dominika," he started.

"The paralegal from the orphanage?"

"She told me some story that has to do with Sasha's adoption, but let me do a little checking around before we act on anything."

"What's there to act on? What did she say?"

"It's probably nothing. Don't worry, you have broken no laws by taking Sasha out of the orphan house. The judge's ruling is good. We will get you and Sasha to America as soon as possible."

And with that, he hung up.

Why can't anybody just be straight with me? I knew it would be another sleepless night, but this time I didn't even know what exactly I was worried about.

I settled Jake in to sleep. We had tried the night before having him sleep with me so that he would feel safer, but that quickly turned sour. He tossed and turned and kicked all night long. He tossed so much he even fell off the bed.

So this night we made up a nice feather pallet for him on the floor, which he liked, and he nestled right in to sleep. If only I could have done the same.

SENSORY DEPRIVATION

On Thursday, September 3, I opted to stick around the Lincolns' flat to make sure Jake didn't drive Isabelle crazy. I kept checking my phone to see if I'd missed Katya's call. By the early afternoon, I could wait no longer and called her.

"I'm on my way back to Odessa now," she said. "I hired a private car. I hope you don't mind. But I wanted to get back to Odessa as quickly as I could."

"That's fine, Katya. But why are you leaving there so late?"

"I got to the courthouse at 7:30 and just finished at noon. A lot of people kept checking and rechecking the ruling to make sure that everything was correct before they would sign off and issue final copies that were printed, stamped, and signed. Something else, though. Along with the judge's decree, I have a letter personally written by the judge stating that there was no appeal and that the court decided in your favor."

"Oh!" I exhaled loudly. "Katya, that's wonderful news. Thank you so much!"

Viktor was mistaken; Jake was truly ours.

♦

Boris, along with his wife, Vladlena, and son, Vlad, drove us back to the birth certificate office as soon as Katya arrived. Boris presented the revised documents and explained what had happened.

The worker glanced down at the name on the documents and then shook her head. "I cannot help you," she said. "This morning, we received a fax from the Izmail prosecutor's office. We must wait to issue this child's birth certificate until the appeal decision has been made."

"No, no," I said, feeling frantic. "How can this be? We have the judge's ruling. We have a letter from him! There was no appeal."

After some back-and-forth between Boris and the worker, in which the worker refused to budge, Boris finally gave up and started to walk out of the building. He looked ill.

"The prosecutor was angry about the judge ruling in our favor from the very beginning, and now he is just trying to cause more trouble."

Viktor had told me this was what he was afraid might happen and why we needed to hurry and get Jake processed.

Boris continued, "I believe he is angry you were able to process Jake out of the orphanage. This may become personal."

I believed Boris was truly concerned for me, for perhaps the first time.

♦

Back at Adam and Isabelle's house, Katya mentioned an odd conversation she'd had with Dominika while in Izmail.

"Dominika called and told me that the prosecutor's office sent men and your prosecutor over to her apartment at around midnight the other night. They demanded she get dressed quickly and accompany them to the orphan house office. Dominika said that when she arrived, she saw that the orphanage's assistant director was there also.

The men demanded they give them all of Jake's files. Dominika was very frightened. She begged me to tell you to return Jake back to the orphan house—no later than Friday."

"What? This is crazy!" I wondered if this was the same story that Dominika had told Boris.

"She said they were serious," Katya continued, "and they would come looking for you, so she said it's best for you to return Jake."

"What do you think? Does her story sound true to you?"

"The police typically come at night."

I looked at our hosts, Isabelle and Adam, and their small children. Even though I knew I was in the right, I didn't want to put them in danger.

"Listen, Isabelle, Adam, if this situation makes you nervous, we'll leave. No hard feelings. I don't want to bring this on your heads."

"Of course we're concerned," Adam said, "but we want you to stay with us. Our safety is in the Lord, not in a physical apartment. We're not going to worry about this."

"Let's try one more time at ZAKS and see what we can do to correct this," Katya suggested.

HURRY UP AND WAIT

On Friday morning, September 4, Katya, Boris, and I returned to the local birth certificate branch to try a personal appeal for help from me directly to the head of the branch.

"She's unavailable," her assistant informed us.

"When will she be available?" Katya asked her.

"She won't be. She will not see you. Go away; you have caused us enough trouble! I'm very busy now so I need you to leave. I will write a letter to the judge requesting a new letter from him when I have the time."

Boris began to talk with the woman, who looked half angry and half scared.

"She wants you to leave," he said, turning to me.

"Why?"

"Let's go outside and I will explain."

As soon as we were outside the building, I turned to him. "What did she say?"

"The prosecutor called and threatened them."

"What? How?"

"I don't know. That's all she would say. You stay out here and I will go back and find out more and try to fix this." He left me standing outside.

For more than three hours, he remained inside yelling, cajoling, pleading with them. "Where is the proof of the appeal? You have no proof," he told them. "We have an adoption decree right here. You must recognize it. You must provide us with the birth certificate. What you are doing is illegal."

I called Jahn and told him what was happening. It was early morning back home and he was getting ready for work. He became upset about the situation, but reiterated our commitment: "God has called us to this. God has asked you to be patient. Jacey and I will be fine. She's started school now, so she's doing okay. We have someplace for her to go after school before I get home. He's *our son.* It says so on the adoption decree. We are his parents. If we take him back, aren't we abandoning him? Legally he's ours, more than he's not."

His encouragement buoyed me enough to know we could continue to fight, but I was still worried. Especially because throughout this time, occasionally Boris would come outside and give me updates, but nothing promising.

I couldn't believe I was so close to taking Jake home to the States, and now this had happened. I sat on the cement doorstep crying and praying. My brain kept thinking of Scriptures about how much God cares for orphans.

Later in the afternoon, Viktor called me. "I was afraid of this happening. Where are Boris's contacts? Why hasn't he gotten you out yet? I believe the prosecutor found an old loophole about the date stamp. I called the Izmail ZAKS office myself and talked to the women, demanding them to produce the birth certificate, but they wouldn't do it. I heard about the prosecutor's threat. Whatever it was, it was serious. Those women are scared."

By five o'clock, the prosecutor had faxed the official appeal paperwork. But Boris continued to fight. I could hear him yelling, "So what if the prosecutor faxed it? Where's the official date stamp? Without it, his fax means nothing."

He stormed out of the office. "Those stupid women. They will not budge."

The prosecutor must have threatened them with losing their jobs, I thought. That would explain everything. When you live in a country that has more than 30 percent unemployment, you need to keep a job. You could lose everything.

We were stuck.

Boris dropped me off at Adam and Isabelle's place.

"Call me if and when anything happens," I said as I left the car.

For now, I would concentrate on my son and his adjustment to the outside world. I would stay in Ukraine as long as I was able. I didn't want to face it, but I knew the reality: I might have to leave Ukraine without Jake.

◆

Boris called me that night with an update about Dominika's story.

"Kim, I don't know what to believe. I heard that the prosecutor called Dominika and the assistant director over to his house Tuesday night for a dinner party, and simply asked for them to bring all the documentation to him. I still think the best thing is to take the boy back. He's been out of the orphanage now since Tuesday. And we can't get him out of the country. This is going to be a long haul, Kim. I really think it's better that you go home. You continue to fight for him from there. You can go home and be with your family. You don't even have to take him back. I will pick him up and catch the 5:30 a.m. bus out of Odessa down to Izmail. I'm sorry for coming in the middle of the night and interrupting the Lincolns. But I will pick him up, so have the boy ready."

"No. He's not going back to the orphanage."

I could tell he expected me to agree to what he was saying. He was asking for a decision: *Are you going to stay and fight for him, or are you going to go home?* And he fully expected me to say I was going home. After all, he'd had enough experience to know that no one would stay and be inconvenienced by these orphans, because that's how some families acted when they arrived. They spent a day or two, then they arranged to fly back home. They'd say, "Let us know when the court date is and we'll fly back for our second trip. We may have to stay a couple weeks then. We don't like it, but we'll do it."

"I'm not going anywhere, Boris, and Jake is not going back to the orphanage. That's not going to happen." I thought back to my conversation with Jahn earlier in the day: *"I am not abandoning this child. Every link in the chain of this boy's short life has been abandonment. He was abandoned by his mother, he was abandoned by his extended family, and he was abandoned by his countrymen. I am not going to be another link in that chain. It ends here. We are his family."*

"I don't know what to say," he stammered. "I'm—I'm surprised. I'm shocked that you are making this decision. Are you sure? This could be months. You understand?"

"Boris, there's not a single molecule in my body that wants to be here any longer. But this boy is my son and I'm not leaving without him. He's not going back to that orphanage. And if the day ever comes that he has to go back, then *I* will take him back."

The line in the sand was drawn.

◆

I went to bed knowing I wouldn't be able to sleep. I got up constantly to check on Jake and just to look at that precious child, and then lay back down and stared at the ceiling. The next day, Saturday, was our wedding anniversary. I thought I would have been home by now. I would have been enjoying a wonderful date with my husband. But I was here by myself. It only made me more miserable and homesick, if that were possible.

At some point in the early hours of the morning, I heard a car hit one of the stray dogs that wandered everywhere in Ukraine, but it didn't kill the animal. A sharp, loud yelp was followed by moans and whimpers as the dog lay on the street, several floors down, outside the window by my bed. For hours, I heard the animal cry and moan in pain, dying a slow, excruciating death.

I tightly closed my eyes, longing for the sound to stop, wanting the dog to die already, but he didn't. His whimpers permeated my soul.

I lay there as the sounds, conversations, and experiences from the last several months passed through my mind to the soundtrack of this dying dog and I felt I was descending into a sort of madness. I felt as though I was losing my mind.

"Oh God," I cried out, "please help me. Please don't let me lose control again. Please, God, please. I don't know how much more I can take."

THE CHOICE

The days following the week I got Jake from the orphanage passed by in a blur. Boris told me that since the appeal was filed, it would be twenty-one days until the new court date, so I clung to the thought that we would have the hearing, things would go in our favor, Jake would get processed, and we would both be home by the end of September.

Katya called me with news she had learned from her older brother, Maxim.

"The lead prosecutor in Izmail—*your* assistant prosecutor's boss—did not know a lot about your case or the appeal. The assistant prosecutor went over his head to the lead prosecutor's boss here in Odessa without his boss's knowledge. It turns out that your prosecutor and the top prosecutor here in Odessa both have the same political leanings. Both of them want international adoptions from Ukraine stopped."

"But why?" I asked. "That doesn't even make sense."

"Many people here believe that Ukraine should be part of the EU—"

"The EU?"

"European Union. After all, they have Romania in there. They believe Ukraine should be in the EU, because it will bring in the euro, and we know what that will do for our economy."

"Of course, it all goes back to money." I was disgusted.

"Of course. But you know one of the first things Romania did to get into the EU was to halt international adoptions."

"Wait. You're telling me they believe it is better for a Ukrainian child to grow up in this system where fifteen percent of all orphans kill themselves within a year of leaving their orphanage—that is better than, as a last resort, adopting them out to loving homes internationally?"

"Yes." Katya cleared her throat nervously. "There's more." She went on to mention the story again that the prosecutor was telling everyone about the party and Dominika being invited to it. "Maxim believes the assistant prosecutor did have the police visit her in the middle of the night and raid the orphanage files."

"That doesn't make sense," I said. "Why would he spread that story about the party, then?"

"Because you can't go around announcing you're roughing up people in the middle of the night. That would appear as...intimidation. I have some other news. I spoke with Inna at the SDA. Apparently, by law she was supposed to accompany you and Boris to the orphanage to process the paperwork and oversee your taking Jake."

"Boris never said anything about that."

"Exactly. He didn't tell her when you two were going over there, because he knew she wouldn't agree to go."

"Why? I thought she was in agreement with the adoption."

"She is. But she also knew about the notice of intent to appeal getting filed. So she wouldn't go over with you if that appeal was still hanging out there."

"That's why Boris was acting so squirrelly when he was talking with Dominika! And why he was acting nervous afterward!" It all made sense now. Dominika hadn't been asking about Katya, as I had assumed. She was asking where Inna was, and he must have given some excuse.

◆

"Why don't I have an official court date for the appeal yet, Boris? I thought it was supposed to be twenty-one days after the appeal was filed. It's now the middle of September. What's going on?"

Boris looked at me across the table at a cafeteria in Odessa. I rarely saw him anymore and when I did it was for brief bits of time with no new information.

"There is a holdup with the case. The prosecutor has filed a lawsuit against the Izmail City Council, who agreed with your adoption decree, so the lawsuit will have to be settled before the appeal date can be scheduled."

I blinked hard. What in the world was he talking about?

"You're telling me that the prosecutor is suing his own city council?"

"And he has named others as third-party participants: the SDA, the mayor..."

"This is unbelievable."

"I agree. And the prosecutor may just be getting started. The court date is scheduled for mid- to late October, so I'm going to see if I can get in and find out how it goes. This is all technicalities. He's arguing that Sasha and his brother should not have been separated, and that we didn't get the letter from the two districts in Odessa."

Which was your fault, I thought, but didn't say anything.

"He's face-saving, is that what you call it?"

"Saving face."

"Saving face. An American woman went in and won against him. Now he wants to make things difficult for everyone."

Or maybe he is pushing for time, hoping that I'll get so discouraged I'll simply return Jake and leave the country.

"So when do you think they'll schedule the appeal?"

He shrugged. "It depends. Perhaps we'll know the appeal court date by the end of October. We'll see."

I knew he was trying to put a positive spin on it. But I knew I was stuck in this country for another few months or more.

Again I felt out of control and desperate. I was by myself in this country. I was out of money. Things were going badly. I was distraught.

"Kim, try to stay positive."

I nodded, but I was thinking, *Hey, by the end of October, my hundred and eighty days are up on my visa. I've been here for six months now. I'm going to have to go get a visa. What am I going to do?*

♦

After finding out about the new lawsuits, I received another call from Viktor. "Why are you still in contact with Boris? He is causing you more problems. I have an attorney who can help you get out of the country with the boy. She is very expensive: ten thousand dollars. But she's good."

"I can't afford her, Viktor."

He sighed harshly. "I want to help you, but I can't if you're going to continue to use Boris. You need to make a choice."

I had never met Viktor. He was only ever a deep, mysterious voice on the phone and I really didn't know that much about him. Yet he told me things no one should know.

I knew Boris hadn't done everything right, and he was to blame for the majority of this mess I was in. But he was also flesh and blood. I was alone. I needed flesh and blood.

"I will need someone to help me process Jake out of the country and we've already paid Boris to do that, Viktor."

Viktor became angry. "Suit yourself. My daughter is getting married and I will be returning to the United States. I will no longer be able to help you or contact you. Good luck."

After I hung up the phone, I prayed I had chosen correctly, but I feared I had not.

A VISIT FROM HOME

I had never felt more alone. I could only share my feelings so much with the others in Ukraine. I could no longer mention specifics on Facebook, because friends had warned me about what I was posting. Whenever I talked to Jahn or friends over the phone or by Skype, I couldn't talk freely. It seemed no one wanted me saying anything by phone. No one in Ukraine would discuss anything by phone. The country had too long a history of wiretapping.

I felt angry and anxious, but mostly I felt sorry for myself. Even though I knew what I was doing was right, the stress and anxiety were really wearing on me.

"Kim, I'm worried about you," Jahn told me during one phone conversation. "Everyone is worried about you. My dad, my sister Ann, and I have talked about it, and Ann is going to visit you at the end of this month."

For the first time in a long time I felt the thrill of anticipation. Ann, Jahn's younger sister, would understand what I was going through. She had spent a year in Sri Lanka during their civil war teaching English as a second language. She knew what it was like to be under stress in a different culture.

"Plus, Dad wants to send you some money and make sure you get it, so Ann will bring that along with fall and winter clothes, since you only have summer stuff. She's also going to bring you some books in English."

I sighed with joy. "Thank you, Jahn. This is the first good news I've had in a while—especially because I need to find another place to live. Isabelle's parents are coming at the beginning of October, and they won't have room for us. We've been such a terrible burden on them. I just don't want to inconvenience them and cause them any more stress than I already have."

"Do you have any places in mind?"

"I think so. Back when I first visited Ukraine, we had lunch at a large church here that has a dormitory. I plan to leave Adam and Isabelle's flat when Ann comes, then move into the church."

Things were difficult at Adam and Isabelle's and I knew it was time to leave—but not because of them. It was just such a strain on everybody to take care of this sweet but wild child who continued to disrupt everything. And Jake was getting confused. He thought he had two moms and Adam was his dad and their kids were his sisters. How could he know any better?

By the time I would move out, Jake and I would have been there for five weeks. It was time to leave.

◆

With still no definite date set for the lawsuits, which meant still no definite date set for the appeal hearing, I grew more concerned about needing a visa. As a visitor to Ukraine, I could legally stay in the country for up to one hundred and eighty days, but after that I needed to have a visa to remain. I didn't want to add being in the country illegally to my troubles.

I figured Boris would be little help, so instead I mentioned my situation to Adam and Isabelle one night.

"That shouldn't be a problem," Adam said. "The quickest place for you to go for a Ukrainian visa is Krakow, Poland. You'd have to fly over there and get that, but let's cross that bridge when we get to it."

"Why Poland? Can't I just go to the embassy in Kiev?"

"You'd think so, but no. You have to leave the country and go to the Ukrainian embassy there to get your visa."

Yet another expense.

I asked him to look into it further for me, but deep down I was still hoping that something would happen and I would be out of the country before my hundred and eighty days were up.

◆

The timing for Ann's visit could not have been better. She, Jake, and I would stay with the Lincolns for a day, then stay at a hotel, which would get me out of Adam and Isabelle's flat and give them a week's break before her parents arrived.

Jake and I met her at the Odessa airport toward the end of September. I made a sign for Jake to hold that said, "Auntie Ann," only he held it upside down. He didn't understand what we were doing, but went along with it good-naturedly.

I was thrilled to see her, but she seemed overly concerned to see me.

"Hi. Wow, you look so different. You've lost weight," she said, hugging me. "How are you doing?"

"I feel like a willing hostage."

I filled her in on everything that had happened as we took sight-seeing tours around the town. It was a welcome break, but still stressful because she was understandably concerned and asking a lot of questions; I wanted to spend a week enjoying her company and trying as best I could to forget about what was going on.

The first night she was there, she watched me make up a pallet on the floor for Jake.

"What are you doing?"

"Jake can't sleep in bed because he falls off, so I put him on the floor."

Her face registered surprise, but she didn't say anything.

She was there for Jake's fourth birthday on September 25. We cele-brated by having a party at an indoor playland called Igreland. It was similar to a Chuck E. Cheese in atmosphere. We invited the Lincolns along with their neighbors, who had a young boy about the same age as Jake. We ate pizza and cake and sang "Happy Birthday," which he didn't understand. Everybody gave him gifts, which he didn't un-derstand. He understood that this was a party for him, but didn't understand why.

As a special treat from Ann, we took an overnight train and rode all the way across the country to the westernmost part to a beautiful city called Lviv, nicknamed the "Little Paris of Ukraine."

On the train ride to Lviv, Ann watched me pull the bedspread from my side and then take the one from her side to create a makeshift bed for Jake on the filthy floor.

"I'm not comfortable with him sleeping on the floor like that," she said, appalled.

"No, it's okay."

"But the floor is filthy."

"The bedspreads cover it. Jake is malnourished and underweight. He's four and he weighs only twenty-three pounds. If he falls off the bed he may break a bone. I'm afraid that he may be calcium- and protein-deprived."

"Well, once we get to the hotel in Lviv, he's sleeping with us."

"Okay," I agreed, but inside I chuckled because I knew it wouldn't last long.

When we arrived in Lviv I insisted on caution. Ann had kept "de Blecourt" in her name, so we couldn't sign in at hotels with either of our names. It became important not to register our passports as we traveled, as I didn't want anyone to be able to track us. When asked for a copy of our passports, I insisted we would not give them our information. I then informed them that we would be paying them in American dollars, and if they didn't want our business, we could go down the street to the next hotel, where they would accept our money. We were never denied lodging, and I could relax, even in new surroundings.

True to her word, Ann insisted that Jake sleep with us in the hotel. After enduring his thrashing, however, she grudgingly agreed that the floor pallet was the best idea.

Fortunately, we discovered that our hotel offered cribs, so we requested one so Jake could be up off the floor. He took to the crib quickly, which made me believe he hadn't been out of a crib for long. I could hear him rolling back and forth, a type of self-soothing motion for him, but I knew he couldn't fall out.

I fell in love with Lviv. It felt more like an Alps community in a Western European country like Austria or Switzerland than a town in Ukraine. It had beautiful historic buildings and distinctive green-domed churches and cobblestone streets nestled into the surrounding mountains. It felt so different from Odessa and Izmail. No prostitutes walking the streets. No drugs being used in alleyways. No street children begging. No stray dogs growling. The people were polite and even smiled. Many people spoke English and loved that we were Americans.

While we were there I thought, *Jake and I should move here. I should go back to Odessa and get our things. This place would be so much better for us. I would be in a much better frame of mind and could be a better mother to Jake if we moved here. I feel safe here.*

In fact just that June, the Ukrainian magazine *Focus* had rated Lviv as the best Ukrainian city to live in.

But then I decided no. I wanted to stay close to the people I knew whom I thought could help me. I should have decided yes.

♦

"I don't want to leave you," Ann said the day she was to leave Ukraine. She had been with me only a week, but she missed her daughter, Emma, her son, Alex, and her husband, Ken. The culture shock was difficult for her as well; even though she'd lived in Sri Lanka, she said this country was in a league all its own.

As she said the words, I thought, *My goodness, she picked up quickly on how dangerous our situation really is.*

"I'm worried about you, Kim. We all are." Her words sounded like a repeat of Jahn's. "You've changed. I don't know you anymore. You're not the exuberant, funny woman I know and love. You're pale, stressed out, and so guarded." She paused. "I'm afraid for this little boy too, and I love him already. He's so sweet and innocent. But I'm not sure you're going to get him out. I'm afraid for you, Kim."

I didn't know what to say. Her words were true. I had changed, but I didn't know how to unchange. I didn't know how to become my old self again—and I started to wonder if I ever would.

9

October 2009

MISSING SPECIAL DATES

I had known and accepted that I might be late for our twelfth wedding anniversary on September 5. However, I never imagined I would miss my daughter's ninth birthday on October 8. I called her that day, and I arranged for a present to be delivered. I could tell she wasn't herself and she missed me greatly.

As much as I put my best efforts into being a good long-distance wife and mother to Jahn and Jacey, it wasn't enough. I talked with Jahn almost daily, but since Ukraine is seven hours ahead, it was difficult to find a good time to connect for any length of time or be able to talk with Jacey. We even connected by Skype once a week, which our church helped set up for Jahn, but still it wasn't enough.

Although Jahn always tried to put a positive spin on everything, I knew he was keeping things from me to save me from worrying. But I could see sadness in his eyes. And both he and Jacey looked like they were starting to lose weight.

I felt guilty that I couldn't be there to take care of them. I prayed this ordeal would be over soon and I would be home by the end of the month.

During mid-October, my home church sent a short-term mission group over to visit and work with partner churches in Ukraine. I was able to join them when they arrived. I spent most of my time doing mission work and caring for Jake.

It felt wonderful to be able to speak English and to be among people who knew me. They were encouraging and graciously allowed me to be part of their team, as though I had come over to the country with them. It also allowed Jake and me to be able to stay in host housing with them.

While they were encouraging and concerned, I was whiny and negative. When someone would ask, "How are you holding up?" the whiny, negative part of me would emerge and I would respond, "It's so hard. I'm here feeling as if my heart has been ripped out of my chest and is laying on the ground while my husband and daughter are back home. Every molecule of my body wants to be there. But I can't leave this little boy. I can't abandon him."

That certainly left people at a loss for words. They would usually mumble, "Well, God will get you through this."

What else could they say? I knew they meant well and they were truly concerned, but I just wasn't in a place to respond well. My roommate during that trip, Robin Mulder, was an absolute gem. She seemed to understand the tension and prayed with me.

Another bright spot was that Laura Koster was part of the group. She was watching Jacey after school while Jahn was still at work, and she gave me detailed updates on her.

"Jacey really misses you," Laura told me.

It broke my heart to hear. I had already missed her first day of third grade and her birthday. I missed our after-school meetings at the kitchen table. I missed hearing about the best thing—and the worst thing—that happened each day. I missed all the little things.

I confided in her that I was afraid about how my family was doing—specifically how they were eating. I asked her to see if our Sunday school class could help out. She readily agreed and told me she would contact Laura Anthony from the class and see if she would take leadership of getting meals to my family, showing them they weren't forgotten. It put my mind at rest.

My time with them passed too quickly and I was alone again—this time without a place to stay. I packed our sparse belongings, along with the new items Ann had brought me, and Jake and I moved to a church dormitory on the other side of Odessa.

I'd visited the church once before and it seemed okay at the time. We'd had lunch there during the mission trip that I'd been on several years earlier. It had a nice playground next to it, which I knew Jake would enjoy. I prepaid for one full week, including money to have the church's cook take care of our meals, since there was no kitchen in the dorm, and stores and restaurants were not close.

When I entered the area where Jake and I would sleep, my jaw dropped. It was filthy. It hadn't been cleaned since the last travel group stayed there, and that had been months ago.

I didn't know what to do. I had already paid in full for the entire week—nonrefundable. I couldn't go back to the Lincolns'. I couldn't stay with Boris. I was stuck. I could only pray: *Lord, why do I tend to blame others and myself for what is clearly of Satan? Help me to trust in you more, rely on you fully, and truly believe that through you, all things are possible. Where I am weak, may your strength show through. When I am crumbling, may you embolden me. When I simply want to go home, help me to stay where you would have me.*

So I swallowed my pride and decided to try to make the best of it.

We would sleep there, but then spend as much time outside at the playground as possible.

During the days, Jake loved the playground. He made friends quickly and loved pretending to drive a play car around. A Jewish school was nearby, and I enjoyed watching all the people come and go, including Hasidic Jews dressed in black and wearing long curls next to their heads.

I felt overwhelmed with self-pity. I had reached a new level of culture shock.

I was feeling especially sorry for myself the day that I met Isabelle's parents when Adam and Isabelle had invited Jake and me over for dinner with them. The entire time, I had nothing good to say. I was not praising God; I was whining about where I was.

"We're praying for you, Kim," her mother said. "You know God has you. He's right here with you."

All I could think was, *Yeah, well, I wonder if you'd be saying the same thing if you were where I am. You're here for two weeks and then you get to go home. I'm stuck here.*

I was appalled by my attitude. They probably were too.

Toward the end of the week, I was stressed trying to figure out what to do and where to go next. I couldn't fathom staying another week at this place, but I didn't have the money to move anywhere else.

About midway through the week, Jake and I went to the dining hall for breakfast. A guard from the front gate was also there, getting more coffee.

He watched us while we were eating and finally said loudly to me, "Why don't you just take this boy home to the orphanage and be done with it? That's his home."

I was stunned into silence by his words that questioned why I was in his country adopting when I should be in my own country. The cook overheard and rushed to my defense.

"The church feels strongly about caring for orphans. What this woman is doing is a loving, Christian inspiration. This child needs a good Christian home to be raised in and she has graciously welcomed him into her family, just as God has done for us. You must apologize to her."

He begrudgingly did so, but it wasn't sincere.

"I'm sorry about that," she told me. "He's a new convert, so he doesn't understand about these things. It won't happen again."

"That's okay," I told her, but now I felt I had to leave.

Feeling I had nowhere else to turn, I called my father-in-law. Although I hated to do that because he had already provided so much for us, I didn't know what else to do.

"Please, get us out of here," I told him. "I'm going to need money and I'm going to need thousands. I need to get a flat, and the only area that I would feel safe is in downtown Odessa, and they are horrendously expensive. I feel like I'm losing my mind. I know the prosecutor is looking for us. There may be a reward for information about us. Please help me."

My father-in-law, Jacob, was quiet. Then with a great deal of emotion, he replied, "Whatever you need, Kim, I will make sure you have it. Don't spend the money Ann gave you; you need to keep that cash on you. You should have cash on you at all times. You go to downtown Odessa and secure yourself a safe place that's comfortable and where they speak English, where you won't stick out so much. We will make arrangements to use my credit cards to pay for it."

His generosity was overwhelming and I hated to ask him for anything else, but I knew I had to.

"There's something else. I need to go to Poland to get a visa. My time in the country legally will be up at the end of the month. If I don't have a visa, I have to worry about being in the country illegally."

"Do what you need to finish the adoption, Kim," he said.

TRAVELING TO POLAND

I made travel arrangements to go to Krakow, Poland, at the end of October to get my visa. It would be a quick trip, just long enough to secure the visa and be back within forty-eight hours.

I called Katya and asked her to come and stay with Jake while I was gone. When she arrived, she said, "Kim, my husband and I have discussed this and I want you to know. If everything fails with your adoption, we would like to try to adopt Jake. He will be with a good Ukrainian family. You know my family. I don't know how we will afford it, but I understand the government is helping Ukrainians with adoptions, so we will manage somehow."

I didn't know what to say; I was stunned.

"We both think he should be with you," she continued quickly. "He is your son. But you will not have to worry about him. If everything goes wrong, he will have to go back to the orphanage for a short time, but we will visit him every day. And we will try to adopt him."

"Thank you, Katya. If it came to that, Jahn and I would help you, financially, spiritually, all we could." *I don't know how my heart could take this*, I thought, *but I will trust you, God, if this is what you have in mind.*

It provided me such comfort to know that he would be loved and taken care of. Their sacrifice was also a very Christian thing, because Ukrainians had such suspicions of children with HIV, and it meant a lot to me to know they were willing to take him in. That's how strong her love was for Jesus, and perhaps now, for Jake.

It was a bittersweet moment for both of us.

♦

I flew out to Krakow, nervous about the tight timing of everything and about visiting yet another country by myself where I didn't speak the language. My nerves were wound tight about handling the business of getting my visa, but also I had to be extremely conscientious about money.

As soon as I arrived I checked into my hotel, which was in the historic downtown area, then headed out for an early meal. I found a great restaurant with a dazzling view of the city. I saw a beautiful cathedral from the 1400s, and carriages were passing over the cobblestone streets below as it started to snow.

For the first time in months, I began to relax. Getting away from Ukraine was a great break for me.

◆

The next morning, I headed out early to the Ukrainian consulate. I had the concierge get me a taxi to drive me there, as I wanted to be there right when they opened at 9 a.m. I arrived early and the gate wasn't open, but I knew there were people inside, so I decided to try to get in anyway.

I stepped up to the speaker, which was the worst, most antiquated fast-food type speaker I had ever seen. I pushed the button and said, "I'm here to get my visa."

A muffled voice speaking Russian replied, "Wah, wah, wah, wah, wah."

I pushed the button again. "What?"

"Wah, wah, wah, wah, wah," replied the Russian voice, now sounding more testy.

"I don't understand. I'm American," I said in my best Russian. "Ukrainian visa."

"Wah, wah, wah, wah, wah!"

I didn't know what to do and I certainly didn't want to press the button anymore. This voice was ticked off at me, and for all I knew, she would be the one who would be working with me on the visa.

Great. I've come all this way—by myself—and I can't get through the gate of the embassy!

I stopped every person who walked by me, asking them in Russian, "Do you understand English?" Finally, almost a half hour later, I found a young man who did. I pointed to the speaker. "I don't understand her. I'm an American. I need a Ukraine visa."

"Ah, okay." He pushed the button and said in Russian, "An American woman is here to get a visa."

"WAH, WAH, WAH, WAH, WAH, WAH!!!" the angry voice replied.

Whew, glad it isn't me pushing that button this time, I thought.

"Oh!" he said and turned to me. "You are at the wrong gate. This is for employees only. You must go to that gate." He pointed down the sidewalk. "Good luck."

I burst out laughing. The voice on the other side must have thought I was an idiot.

I walked down the sidewalk, found the second gate, pushed the button, and immediately the gate opened.

I entered the embassy and a young man greeted me first in Polish, which I didn't understand. Then he spoke a different language, to which I replied, "Hello."

"Ah, you speak English."

I filled out the paperwork he gave me. But when I returned it and he looked it over he said, "This is a slight problem. We are not allowed to accept payment for a Ukrainian visa here. You must go to a bank six blocks away and you must pay them there. You must get the receipt and bring it back to me here. Then you can come back about four o'clock and pick up your visa."

"You make it sound so simple, but it's not. I don't know where I'm going and I didn't see any taxis around here."

"No, you must walk."

"Where exactly am I going?"

"To this bank. Here's the address."

"No, you don't understand. I'm an American, living in Odessa, traveling to Krakow to get this visa, and you're acting like it's no big deal, that I should easily be able to find this simple address in Polish. You must draw me a detailed map so I know exactly where I'm going."

He nodded politely and drew me a crude, bare minimum of a map.

I walked back outside and prayed that I was going the right way. I was afraid I wouldn't be able to find my way back to the embassy.

God, please help me. I'm not sure where I'm going. Send someone who can direct me to where I need to go.

As I stood looking down at the map, a young, sandy blond college-aged woman with green eyes who reminded me of Jacey noticed my map in English and stopped.

"Excuse me," she said in soft, slightly broken English. "Do you speak English?"

"Yes."

"I would love to practice my English with you. Can we get a cup of coffee and talk?"

"Well, I'm on my way to a bank. I need to pay for a visa."

She looked at my map again. "I know that bank. I can walk with you there, if you'd like."

Wow, God, that was fast. Thank you!

We headed down the street toward the bank and passed a bakery. She noticed that I slowed my gait, taking in a deep whiff of the amazing aroma.

"Would you like to stop here?"

"Yes." I had left the hotel so focused on getting to the embassy that I had neglected to eat breakfast. Now I was really hungry.

I bought the most amazing baked goods and a large coffee, while she ordered a tiny espresso, and we sat down and talked.

Forty-five minutes later, I checked the time and gasped. "I really need to get to the bank."

"Of course!"

We got through the line at the bank, and she escorted me back to the embassy, thanked me, and said goodbye. I dropped off my receipt, and then with the rest of the day to wait, I decided to take a walking tour of Krakow.

The tour took me throughout the city and then to Oskar Schindler's factory. Schindler is credited with saving more than eleven hundred Jews during the Holocaust and was the focus of the Academy Award–winning movie *Schindler's List*.

It was around two o'clock and I was nervous about missing my visa—and about not having my passport with me since I had had to leave it at the embassy. Even though it was still early, I decided just to check to see if it was ready, which it was. So I picked it up and then made my way to tour Wawel Castle.

Wawel is a medieval castle that the Polish government restored into a national museum. Every king throughout Poland's history had collected something, such as tapestries or mounted animals or furniture, and the government filled the castle with them. As I walked through the rooms and looked at all the ornate and beautiful collections, I was overwhelmed by the beauty and history.

I was only there for a few hours before it closed. I was relieved my mission was completed, and soon I went back to the hotel, grabbed a quick bite, and went to bed.

That night, I had a good night's sleep. I woke up after eleven hours of sleep feeling refreshed and renewed, ate a big breakfast, and took my time getting to the airport for my 1 p.m. flight back to Odessa. The quick trip was just what I needed to give me the strength to continue the fight for my child.

SLOW MOVEMENTS

Boris woke me with a phone call.

"Things are not moving along well," he said, skipping any pleasantries. "We need answers. I need you to write a letter to the judge in Izmail and ask him where things are regarding your case. Why hasn't an appeal date been set yet?"

I still felt groggy. "Boris?"

"Write it in English, and then find a translator's office in Odessa to translate it into Ukrainian. Only Ukrainian is allowed in our courts now—a recent law change. We need to know what is happening."

"Okay. Do you have their address?"

"You can't mail it, Kim. You must take it there in person and have it checked into the courthouse, and ask for it to be filed in your case file."

"*What?*" Now I was definitely awake. "You're telling me I have to go back to the Izmail courthouse? Are you crazy? The prosecutor's office is at the front of the courthouse. I would have to walk right past his office to enter. Is this really necessary?"

"We need to let them know we are holding them to the letter of the law, Kim. They will not accept this letter from me. *You* must hand it to them and give them your passport as proof. If I go with you, it will only draw more attention."

"I can't believe what you're asking of me, Boris. I've just returned from getting my visa in Poland, and now this?"

"Oh, you got a Ukrainian visa? That is good. I was going to tell you to do that."

That day I wrote a letter to the judge, respectfully asking for an update on what was going on with our case and why there was a delay in establishing our appeals court date. Adam directed me to a translator's office in Odessa. I worked with a middle-aged woman, Rose. I was so impressed with her work and her personality that I told her I wanted her to transcribe all of my documents into English. I wanted to know every word of what had been said.

During the four-and-a-half-hour bus ride back to Izmail, I concentrated on what disguise I was going to wear as I walked past the prosecutor's office. I wore my glasses instead of contacts, and I borrowed a large Ukrainian scarf from Isabelle to cover my head. I was amazed at the difference in my appearance those few changes made.

I trembled as I walked up the courthouse steps. I kept my head down, especially as I walked through the metal detector at the entrance. I never met the eyes of the guard who observed everyone who entered. I never even stole a glance at the prosecutor's office doorway. I followed the crowd to the rear of the building. The last doorway on the left before exiting the building to the toilet area was where I guessed I had to be. The door was closed and a few people stood waiting. It appeared they might be waiting for others already inside the office.

God, I'm so unsure of where to deliver this letter. I'm so scared. Please, help me stop shaking. Help me find the correct office. Help my poor Russian to be sufficient. In Jesus' name.

As I reached for the doorknob, I heard a male voice say, "Excuse me."

I looked up and into the surprised face of Akula, the young attorney whose office was across the hall from Ilse and Carl's Peace Corps office.

"Kim? What are you doing here? You shouldn't be here," he said anxiously. He grabbed my arm and quickly walked me out the back door of the courthouse.

"What are you trying to do? Why are you here?" he asked.

I explained about Boris's idea for a letter to the judge. Akula tried his best to understand my Midwest-accented English.

"Let me see this letter." He read the entire letter, then sighed.

"Okay. I understand. But why were you going in that office? That isn't

where you need to go, Kim. That's the last office you want to go to."
He shook his head. "Come. I will take you into the court clerk's office. I
know a clerk there who can help us. Let's hope she is working today."

He took me by the arm again and led me back through the
courthouse, past the guard, past the prosecutor's office, past the
courtrooms, to the opposite side of where I had been originally. There
Akula found the clerk he was looking for and explained what needed
to be done.

I watched in amazement as I saw God use Akula that day. I wondered if I could ever fully explain to him how much his intervention
had saved me—how he had been my answer to prayer.

The letter was added to our file. I thanked Akula so many times,
he asked me to stop.

"If you need my help in the future, please just ask. I will help you,
Kim, as best I can. Come say a quick hello to Ilse and Carl. They are
worried about you. Then let's get you back to Odessa."

◆

The prosecutor lost the lawsuits. The trial was at the end of October
and Boris attended. He returned to Odessa and called to tell me how
wonderful it was that the judge found in favor of the defendants.

"But also, you would be pleased to know the wonderful things
everyone said about you and your commitment to this child. The
mayor got up and said good things. Dominika, everyone! It was very
encouraging."

"That's wonderful, Boris. So do we know when we'll get the appeal
date set?" I breathed a quick prayer that he would say the date would
be before Thanksgiving.

"Not yet. Everything depends. But it may be as early as next
month."

I was pleased with the news, but felt edgy. This didn't bode well
for our trial, I realized. *The prosecutor will be really angry now.*

"You're going to need to hire an advocate to help you through the appeal process. I know one who can help you. His name is Leonid and he owns the condo on the floor beneath mine. When we get your court date, I believe Leonid can really help you. But it's going to cost you some money."

Oh boy, here it comes.

"But here's the good thing, Kim. Leonid guarantees that if you don't win the case, you will get all your money back. I know he'll keep this promise, because he knows you and I work together—and of course I know where he lives."

"Okay. I'll meet with him."

"There's one more thing," Boris said. "I have a report the court wants you to fill out. Basically, it explains from your perspective why you feel an appeal is unnecessary. You have a chance to have your side heard. The appellate court investigator considers this information before setting a date for the appeal. They're asking you if it is really necessary to tie up the court's time. I feel we should definitely pursue this opportunity. But when you meet with Leonid, he can give you more insight."

We had an opportunity to have our case read by the judge without an appeal court hearing? That sounded great to me. Maybe we would be home before Thanksgiving.

10

November 2009

DOWNTOWN ODESSA

I found the perfect place for us to stay just off the main street in downtown Odessa. It had a washer, a stovetop, and a separate bedroom, and best of all, it was clean. Of course, it was expensive. I asked to speak to the manager to negotiate a lower monthly rate.

Mike, the man who managed the hotel, was an American who lived and worked in Odessa. He looked like he had stepped off the *Sopranos* studio set, as if he could be a tough guy you didn't want to get entangled with. He was tall and heavyset, with wavy black hair and large eyes. But when he spoke to me, I thought, *His appearance is deceiving. He seems like a teddy bear!*

I discovered this hotel was a popular place for westerners to stay when they were in town. I told him about my situation with the prosecutor.

"I'll keep my ear to the ground," he said, "but I guarantee you'll be safe here."

◆

The timing for finding the hotel was good, as a huge H1N1 scare broke out and caused the town to close down; almost every business, school, or restaurant shut its doors. One or two grocery stores remained open, but everyone had donned masks and stayed out of public as much as possible. It gave us a bit of a reprieve from the fear of being discovered.

Jake and I settled into the hotel and enjoyed peace.

I had left everything in the apartment in Izmail, thinking I was leaving the country, so I had to rebuy a few things. I wanted him off the floor and the crib in Lviv gave me the idea to get something similar for Jake to use, so I went to a large toy and baby store not far from the hotel and purchased a pack and play, which became his bed. I placed an additional mattress inside and put comforters under it to help keep him warm.

As quickly as possible I tried to establish a routine with Jake, to create a normal life for him—and for me. We ate a free breakfast every morning in the hotel's restaurant in their courtyard. Next, we had English lessons, and then would head to a large park within walking distance of the hotel so he could play outside. The park had swings, ponies, little electric cars, and a trampoline. It had old men sitting and playing chess. It had an arts market. It was like a wonderland with something new and interesting happening every moment. We would lunch out—usually an inexpensive bowl of borscht—play a bit more, and head back to the hotel.

About a week into our stay, I discovered a band pavilion in the park where the Odessa orchestra would give free concerts on summer evenings, but that now stood empty, except shortly after five o'clock, when dozens of children and their parents would show up to play in the after-work hours. To give Jake an opportunity to play with other kids his age who were better mannered than those in the orphanage, we started to go to the band pavilion early every evening. He loved it.

I thanked God for the small successes of each day.

♦

One afternoon in mid-November, Katya called and told me, "Carl and Ilse want you to call them. They have something to tell you."

I missed seeing them every day, but still tried to talk to them as much as I could, so I looked forward to the phone call.

"We just got a call from one of our Peace Corps workers in Kiev who wanted to know if we knew you," Ilse said. "Apparently, there was a report about you on the evening news there. It was your story. We're not sure they used your name, so don't be worried. But I thought you should know they were talking about you on the evening news."

How in the world would anyone in Kiev know about my story? I wondered, half impressed and half terrified.

"Was it positive or negative?"

"I guess it was positive toward you, but negative toward the Ukrainian adoption system. It sounds like they don't know where you are, so that's a good thing, I think. But still, we're worried about you."

It felt weird, but I wasn't sure what to do with the information.

"I think I'm safe here," I reassured her. "This hotel is run by an American. He's actually really nice and has been looking out for me and Jake."

"Good, but please just be safe, okay?"

"I will."

I spent a lot of time reading the books Ann had brought, but the one I treasured the most and spent the most time reading was my

Bible. That night, I picked it up and started soaking up Psalms and other passages such as those in Hebrews: "Faith is being sure of what we hope for and certain of what we do not see," and "Do not throw away your confidence; it will be richly rewarded. You need to persevere so that when you have done the will of God, you will receive what he has promised" (Hebrews 11:1, 10:35–36).

I'm trusting you, God.

Around that same time, I received uplifting news: the churches in Odessa wanted to get together and have a time of prayer for me and our adoption. I was so moved by their generosity and graciousness. I felt humbled to know that people literally all over the world cared enough about me and my family to lift us up in prayer.

While I didn't know what God had in mind for us, I knew that whatever it was would ultimately be the right thing for all of us.

TRUST BROKEN

Boris set up a time for me to meet Leonid and discuss some strategy. Although he couldn't attend the meeting since he was working with another family, he offered us his home as a place to meet. I asked Adam to go with me.

Leonid spoke no English, so Boris's wife, Vladlena, and Adam both acted as interpreters. He went through some of his thoughts and gave me his verbal résumé, a long list of his connections, and why he would be a good candidate to help us.

"What about this report I need to fill out? Boris says it's a good opportunity for me to possibly not have to deal with the appeal."

Leonid shook his head. "No, we don't need that, just let it go. Let's have them go ahead and set the appeal date."

"But wouldn't it be better if we could avoid the entire hearing?"

"Yes, but if you win, the prosecutor could appeal that report, and it would end up before the Supreme Court, which would force you to remain here for another two years. I assume you don't want that."

"No, definitely not."

"Let's pursue the appeal. You have nothing to lose. As Boris told you, if we don't win, I will refund all your money."

"How much is this going to cost me?" I finally asked.

"Four thousand dollars."

I felt the color drain from my face. Four thousand was incredibly expensive. (I knew attorneys in Ukraine who charged five hundred in Ukrainian hryvnia for a year's retainer fee.) The attorney Viktor wanted me to hire was going to charge me ten thousand, so four thousand was a deal in that respect. But the most shocking was that the day before, I had gone to a large bank in Odessa and picked up a Western Union money order—for four thousand dollars exactly.

He knew my business. Somehow, some way, he knew when I'd gotten the money, where, and how much. And if he could find that out, so could the prosecutor. He could find out where I was.

I swallowed hard and continued to stare at him.

The room grew quiet. This attorney was asking me for everything I had.

"Okay, well, I'll have to get more money because I don't have that much."

He looked at me suspiciously. "You don't have four thousand dollars?"

"No, I don't." In my mind, I didn't have that much because I knew what I had to pay for things and that money was already committed. I knew I could realistically give him only about half of it, if that much.

"Well. When do you think you can get it?"

"I don't know. Let me make some phone calls. I'll get back to you soon."

I left Boris's flat wondering if I could really trust either man— Leonid or Boris.

♦

"What do you mean he doesn't want you to file the report?" Boris asked me once he returned to Odessa. "No, no. Let's do this. It is a good opportunity. I know of someone who can write this up for us and it will only cost you twelve hundred dollars."

I couldn't believe what I was hearing. He was telling me to fork over that much money for someone to write what was, in essence, a legal brief? I felt as though I was being taken for a ride. Everyone he recommended was quoting me ridiculously high amounts of money.

"No, I think we'll follow Leonid's advice. He seems so sure of himself, and his credentials are impressive."

Boris had recommended Leonid and had wanted me to ask him this specific question. I was surprised that he was now questioning Leonid's answer. Boris said nothing else.

♦

A couple of weeks later, I presented Leonid with the four thousand dollars and I reiterated the guarantee expectation. I knew how quickly they could "forget" agreements.

"You remind Leonid that we agreed that if this case doesn't go in our favor, I get every dollar back. Tell him now."

Boris didn't want to do that. "That's insulting, Kim. We've already agreed to that."

"But I need to hear it. In Russian. With you as a witness. I want to know that we're all on the same page."

Boris apologetically explained to Leonid, adding, "She insists on hearing it again."

"Of course," Leonid said.

"And now we wait for the court date," said Boris. He and Leonid both looked satisfied.

INTO HIDING

Leonid had been working hard behind the scenes to get us a court date as quickly as possible. Finally, he let me know through Boris that our case would be reviewed before the appellate court on Tuesday, the week of our Thanksgiving. At that point, the judge would schedule the court date. We hoped it would be in early December.

I was crushed. I had never imagined I wouldn't share Thanksgiving with my family. There was movement on the case, so I hoped to get home before Christmas now. With Thanksgiving this week, Jake and I had something special to look forward to. Adam and Isabelle invited us to celebrate the American holiday with a group of Americans who worked in Odessa. The best part was that they would have traditional American food that we couldn't buy in Ukraine. It seemed crazy, but I was looking forward to eating sweet potatoes. Adam even mentioned that peanut butter would make an appearance. It was music to my ears. I was surprised by how much I missed the simple foods, such as peanuts, that I so often took for granted back home but couldn't find in this country.

Tuesday morning, I woke early, anticipating the court's ruling that day. Jake and I were dressed and ready to head downstairs to the hotel restaurant for breakfast when my phone rang.

It was David Walker, an American dentist who, along with his wife, Zoya, volunteered at the Odessa internaat number four, one of the orphanages in the Odessa area.

"Kim, I am so sorry. My wife has made a mistake. Svetlana called us asking if we knew where you were. Zoya didn't realize that she wasn't supposed to give that information out and so she told Svetlana. Svetlana is on her way to your apartment complex, and she's demanding to see her brother."

"What?" I started to panic. David and Zoya knew Jacob's sister, Svetlana, from their work with the orphanage. David had always had a soft heart for her and her situation, and we joked about what a small world it was that he knew my son's sister. Now, though, I felt danger.

"She's on her way there now. I am so sorry. Zoya feels terrible about it."

"We have to go. Now!" I hung up the phone and grabbed our coats. "Come on, Jake, we need to go quickly."

I didn't know what Svetlana's intentions were. I didn't know if she was bringing the police. Although Jake was legally my son— the adoption decree proved that, and I kept it on me at all times— because of the appeal, I didn't know if the prosecutor wanted to physically take Jake away from me and was possibly using Svetlana to get to us. Boris had warned me to stay clear of her, as he believed she could only cause trouble.

I called David back. "I've left the hotel, but now what do I do?"

"Come to our flat. You'll be safe here." He walked me through the directions to his flat. As soon as we arrived, Zoya greeted us at the door.

"I'm so sorry, Kim. I didn't realize. I never would have told Svetlana if I knew—"

"I know, Zoya. We're safe now."

Within the hour Svetlana was at David and Zoya's door, demanding answers.

I started to panic again. "Why is she *here?*"

"She's angry because she feels lied to," David said. "She wants to see you."

"No. I don't know her that well. I don't know if the prosecutor got to her. No, absolutely not. Not this way, not today. Another time. On my terms."

"Let's call Adam and see if he'll come and get you two."

Adam immediately said yes and headed over with his van. He pulled up to the door, blocking Svetlana and her friend from view, and we quickly jumped in.

We decided to spend the night at the Lincolns'. I had let my guard down and gotten comfortable enough to forget that we still had to be careful.

That evening Boris called to let me know the court had reviewed our case, but the judge had not decided on a date. He promised to do so on that Thursday—Thanksgiving.

How much more can they draw this thing out? What's the big wait for?

"Fine," I told Boris. Still I hoped they *would* decide on Thanksgiving—something for me to be thankful for, especially if the date was soon enough to get us home for Christmas.

As I lay in bed praying and strategizing what I needed to do next, my thoughts went back to Svetlana. *What if this girl isn't being used by the prosecutor? What if she just wants to meet her brother, whom she's never seen? What if she just wants to connect with the only family she has left? I don't have anything against Svetlana. She's simply a young girl who's had a tough life.*

The next morning, I told Adam and Isabelle I was going back to the hotel. "As long as I know she isn't bringing the police, and if she truly just wants to meet her brother, then it will be fine."

I decided to make arrangements to meet her, but it was going to be at my discretion—my day, my time, my place. And Jake wouldn't be with me for our meeting.

BAD GOOD NEWS

Thanksgiving Day arrived and in the afternoon Jake and I went with the Lincolns to the large gathering at one of their coworkers' apartments. About fifty people were there, including all the children. The host greeted me and then escorted Jake to a room where the children were playing and making pilgrim hats and paper turkeys.

Maybe it was because I didn't work there. Maybe it was because we were last-minute guests at the Lincolns' request. Maybe it was because it was assumed I was mixed up in some illegal adoption thing. Whatever the reason, I didn't feel welcome. Most of the people gathered there either spoke awkwardly with me or seemed to avoid me completely.

It probably didn't help that I felt on edge. The judge was supposed to schedule our hearing that day—and with each passing moment that I didn't hear word, I became more uncomfortable and anxious.

Finally at 8 p.m. Adam approached me. "Can I talk with you for a moment?" He seemed concerned.

We walked to a quiet corner of the apartment.

"Boris just called," Adam said. "They've set the appeal date."

"Why did he call you? Why didn't he call me?"

He put his hand up. "They've set the date for December 22."

All of a sudden the room grew hot and started to spin. I knew why Boris hadn't called me; he didn't want to give me bad news. The typical Ukrainian response: avoid giving bad news at all costs.

My eyes filled with tears that I quickly blinked away. "I'm going to go outside and get some air. Jake can continue to play with the other kids. I'll be back up when I'm in control." I didn't want to fall apart.

I stepped outside into the courtyard to catch my breath. *I can't have even one nice day.*

I paced and told God how unfair this situation was. After about five minutes, Adam called me on my cell phone. "Hey, we're just going to bring Jake over to your place a little later."

"Really? I'm just downstairs."

"Yeah, that's okay. We'll take him home. Why don't you go ahead and walk home and take some time to yourself. The walk will do you good."

"Thanks, Adam. I appreciate that."

He knew that every day felt like a week to me. And being here another month was a crushing blow.

December 22. I would be stuck here for at least another month—and I would not be home for Christmas.

I walked home slowly, breathing in deeply the cold night air, not really concentrating on where I was walking or what was around me. I knew Adam and Isabelle would take their time returning Jake to me to give me a chance to sort out my feelings and get my head back in the game. I wanted to cry, but the tears would no longer come.

Back in my hotel room, I sat on a chair and looked around me. I felt empty. I was tired of the continual roller coaster of emotions, riding high on hope, and then dropping through the desperate wait. I couldn't take it anymore. I *wouldn't* take it anymore.

I can't live and die on these kinds of things anymore, I realized. *It's messing with me. I need to do something else.*

By the time Adam and Isabelle dropped off Jake, I had made my decision. Whenever I become self-absorbed and depressed, the best remedy is to take myself out of the equation and focus on helping others. So I was going to find a place to volunteer my services and help those who were worse off than I.

"Will you ask Eva, your babysitter, if she'll babysit for me?" I asked. "I need to make some plans and get out of this funk."

SVETLANA AND JAKE MEET

I had David and Zoya contact Svetlana to let her know I would be willing to meet with her in the restaurant in the hotel's courtyard. I hired Mike's personal interpreter, Bogdan, to act as an interpreter for us. Then I left Jake upstairs in the room with Eva. I wanted to make sure everything was okay before I brought Jake into the situation.

Svetlana showed up alone. I noticed again how much she and Jake looked alike.

She really did just want to meet the brother she had never met.

But she seemed grateful just to have someone listen to her story. She told me about her mother.

"I think something was wrong with her mentally," she said without emotion. "A family was interested in adopting me when I was about four years old, but my grandmother didn't approve. She couldn't stand the thought of me being adopted, so she removed me from the orphanage to live with her. That family would have been a good family. I always felt I was a burden to my grandmother, that she didn't really love me. So when I got older, I started running away."

Svetlana always went back to her grandmother, until her grandmother became ill and had to be placed in a hospital, where she died. Svetlana was forced to return to the orphanage.

"I always thought living in the orphanage was difficult, but it is worse now that I have been out a while. They didn't prepare me for life on my own. I'm trying to go to school. I really want to be a chef someday."

As she spoke I noticed she coughed a lot.

"That cough doesn't sound good, Svetlana," I said, concerned. "You should get that checked."

"It's nothing. I have a cold. Listen, I know you have had some difficulty getting out of the country and I'm not sure when you are set to leave, but I would really like to meet my brother before he goes. Would that be okay?"

I looked at this beautiful young woman who'd had such a tragic life and my heart broke for her.

"Of course it's okay."

I went to our room and brought him down. Immediately, he plopped onto my lap and threw his arms around me as though he felt shy and unsure.

"Jake, this is Svetlana."

"He can call me Aunt Svetlana," she suggested.

She smiled as soon as she saw him. "He looks like me! Hello,

Sasha." She preferred to call Jake by his Ukrainian nickname. She pulled a tiny car from her purse and handed it to him. "I brought you a present."

His eyes widened as his little hand reached out to take it.

"That was so nice of you, Svetlana."

She nodded and I saw tears well in her eyes and spill over onto her cheeks. She didn't try to wipe them away.

"What is he like?" she asked.

I told her all my stories and how well he had been adjusting.

"Sasha, how old are you now?" she asked. "Have you been a good boy? What kind of toys do you like to play with?" She asked him a string of questions. He responded with one-word answers; he was more interested in playing with his car.

"I'm so glad he is happy and has a mom," she told me, still crying. "This is such a nice day. Would it be okay if I see you both again before you leave?"

"Of course, Svetlana. Anytime you want. Keep in touch with me at the number I gave you."

As she left, I wrapped my mother arms around her to say goodbye. This beautiful young woman never got to experience the love of a mother. I pulled Jake close to me and squeezed him tightly, and my heart broke again—this time for Svetlana.

♦

"So why is this adoption being held up, Kim? I wrote that letter for you a long time ago." Svetlana sat at our kitchen table munching on a hamburger I'd made for her.

I paused, wondering if I should tell her the story or not, but then decided to be open with her about it.

"The prosecutor is holding up the adoption. He's appealing it because he doesn't believe your family should be split up. The prosecutor argued that the letter you wrote wasn't enough to separate your family."

"But you aren't separating the family, Kim. Who told you that? That's already been done."

I didn't follow what she was saying. "What do you mean?"

"We have another sister, Alexandria. She was already adopted, by a Ukrainian family, I believe."

Her words hung in the air. My mouth went dry and I couldn't process what she was telling me.

"You have another sister? Jake has another sister who's already been adopted?"

"Yes. She was adopted a while ago."

So the prosecutor hadn't done his homework, and I wasn't breaking up a family after all... *if* I could trust what Svetlana was telling me.

◆

The next morning over coffee at a local coffee shop, with Svetlana's announcement still whirling around in my brain, I bumped into an aquaintance I had made living in the downtown area. Anatolli was a nice older gentleman, Ukrainian but currently living in the greater New York area. He was on an extended visit in Odessa, spending time with family. We had enjoyed occasional chats when we bumped into each other. We would sit, quietly speaking in English, and had gotten to know each other. He knew just enough about our adoption to be interested.

Anatolli was an interesting guy. He was obviously respected by virtually everyone in the downtown area, no matter where we would meet. People would interrupt us just to say hello to him and ask about his family. Other people would frequently pick up his tab. I figured he came from an important family, perhaps from former Soviet times. He seemed powerful and well connected, dressed nicely, and was always kind to Jake.

"Hello. Any news regarding your case lately?" Anatolli asked casually, stopping by my table.

"I've been given some information and I don't know what to do with it because I don't know if I can believe it or not."

"What is it? May I join you?"

"Of course. You remember the prosecutor is appealing our adoption because he said we were separating siblings. Well, get this—according to Jake's older sister, they have a fourth sibling, and she was already adopted by a Ukrainian family."

"So the family's already been separated."

"Exactly!" I said. Anatolli always caught on quickly. "But I don't know if it's true or not."

"What's the girl's name?"

"Alexandria Mazurek."

"How old is she?"

"She's between Svetlana and Nikolay, and Svetlana thinks she was born in or around 1997."

"And she was born in . . . ?"

"Here in Odessa, but Svetlana's not sure which district. She thinks it's the same one as Jake's—Malinovsky."

Anatolli nodded, listening carefully.

"I have no way to validate the info and I don't know what to do," I said.

"Well, it sounds like information for your attorney."

"Yes, of course. You're right."

He got quiet for a moment, as though he was mulling something over, then said, "Kim, do you want my help?"

I froze. All these mental puzzle pieces started whipping through my mind, flashes of images and overheard conversations of him talking about getting things done and people thanking him for his help. All of a sudden everything clicked into place. He was connected. I didn't know and couldn't prove that it was with the mafia—and I certainly wasn't going to ask him outright.

I sat quietly for a long time just looking at him before I answered.

"Under no circumstances would I ever go into debt to you," I told him straight out. "But if you'd like to help me, I would like to know whether what Svetlana told me is true or not."

"So you want my help?"

"As long as it doesn't obligate me, I would welcome any help."

"It's okay, let me see what I can find out. I would like very much to help you, my American friend."

I breathed in deeply and nodded. I hoped I'd made the right decision.

ANOTHER MOVE

A verse from the Bible kept playing over and over in my mind: "Give thanks in all circumstances, for this is God's will for you in Christ Jesus" (1 Thessalonians 5:18). God reminded me that it didn't say give thanks *for* all circumstances; it said give thanks *in* all circumstances.

I didn't have to like being stuck in Ukraine, but God's will was for me to find things to be grateful for *while* I was stuck there.

So I concentrated on the fact that Jake and I would get to see Jahn and Jacey in less than a month. Jahn was required to be at the court hearing, so he and Jacey would fly in on December 19, we'd all spend a few days together before the hearing, enjoy Christmas together, and then be on our way home—all of us, together as a family. I could be grateful for that.

I could be grateful that his boss had given him more time off in order to travel here.

I found that the list of things to be thankful for grew, even in the midst of my desperate desire to be home. And most of all, I could rest in the knowledge that I was right where the Lord wanted me to be, regardless of where I'd like to be. I prayed that my eyes and heart would be open to whatever he had in store.

At the end of November, I realized I needed to move into another flat so that once Jahn and Jacey arrived we'd have enough room to feel comfortable. I went to Mike, the hotel manager, and asked if he had a bigger place.

"No, I don't," he said. "But I rent out larger flats on behalf of a friend. They're a couple blocks away. Let me see what's going on with them and I'll get back to you."

Within a day, he reported back that the largest flat of the ones for rent was available. It rarely got rented, because people always wanted the one- or two-bedroom places. It was beautiful and spacious. It had three bedrooms and two floors and was fully furnished. The only thing it didn't have was an oven—just three burners.

"What is it with these places not having ovens?" I said aloud to myself.

The last weekend of November, Jake and I packed our suitcases and headed slowly over to the other flat. We had no moving vans or help, so I had to make multiple trips to carry our things, which ended up pulling my shoulder blades out of place, because of the weight and the number and length of trips.

Jake and I settled in and I began the work of making the place feel homey. I hoped it would take my mind off the waiting and would give me something productive to do with my time.

I went shopping and found a good deal on a convection oven, because I wanted to be able to bake. My whole focus was on making a home away from home for my family, especially since it would be more than one hundred and fifty days since I had last seen them.

I went to the Odessa bazaar and bought a small Christmas tree with tinsel and decorations.

If I couldn't be home for Christmas, then we were going to have the best, traditional, joy-filled Christmas as a family we could possibly have, here in the heart of Ukraine.

II

December 2009

A WAY OUT

One afternoon in early December, I bumped into Anatolli again. "Would you like to have coffee?" he asked. "Why don't you come back here to the coffee shop in four hours. Bring little Jake with you. No need to get a sitter. You can just walk over."

So when the time came, I bundled up Jake and headed the few blocks over to meet with Anatolli.

When we arrived a few of the employees gushed over Jake and took him to get some sweets, to "fatten you up!" I agreed but insisted on keeping him within sight.

I settled in at a table in the corner where Anatolli was seated.

"Are you unpacked and enjoying the new place?" he asked.

"Yes, thank you. I think it will be great for my husband and daughter when they join us." *How does he know I moved?*

"Good." He paused a moment and then said, "It's true. There is a fourth sibling. The file has been closed, but the prosecutor should have known about this. So you have your attorney make the prosecutor aware of this new information."

I felt sure this was finally a breakthrough, some good solid evidence that could clear us and get the adoption moving.

"Thank you, Anatolli. I really appreciate your finding this out for me."

"You know," he continued, "I have other information for you."

"You do?"

"Yes. We should just take care of all this. Let me get you all the paperwork you need."

"All...the paperwork...I need? No, Anatolli. You are very kind, but no," I said gently but firmly. "How will you ever know how God is going to get me out of this? How will you see him work if you shut him out?"

"Where is your God?"

"He's here, Anatolli, and he's got this one. God is going to deliver us. I don't know when or how—and it's certainly not soon enough for me—but he is going to deliver."

"I understand."

Okay, God, I prayed as Jake and I walked back to our apartment. *Anatolli needs to see you in action. And so do I.*

DROPPED BY OUR ADOPTION AGENCY

Throughout the months, I had tried to get a hold of our adoption agency in the United States to give updates and see if they could help me. For whatever reason, they wouldn't return my calls or would simply say, "Boris is our representative. He can help you."

But part of the problem was Boris! Finally, through Jahn, I was able to connect with Linda, the agency's executive director.

I explained the situation to her and everything leading up to and including the appeal, and I explained my misgivings about Boris. She didn't respond with anything that felt like concern or any promised assistance. As the conversation went on, I became more frustrated as I realized the agency had no intention of helping.

"To make matters worse," I continued, "I believe—although I have no proof—that the four thousand dollars I gave Leonid through Boris may end up being used as a bribe."

The agency had been very clear throughout the entire adoption process that they didn't work with people who used bribes because that went against the Hague Convention, which forbids any type of bribery among officials. If the adoption agency—or one of their representatives, even an independent contractor—were found to be involved in bribery or in violation of the Hague Convention in any way, they would have their accreditation revoked.

At my words, Linda acted unaware and would say only, "I have no idea what you're talking about," which became even more maddening to me.

I ended the hourlong conversation very upset and said, "You know, since I've been here I've been assaulted, I've been robbed, I've been stopped and questioned by the police, I've been alone...and I am still here fighting for this child. But I don't feel like you are. I don't feel like you're supporting me. I thought that's why we paid you. You should be here for me, or at least Boris should be here for me representing you. I have a problem with this situation. I have a problem with your agency; I have a problem with Boris. What are you going to do about it?"

I could tell by her sighs that she had become upset. Finally, she said, "I'll let you know."

Within two days, they stopped representing us. Linda contacted Jahn and informed him that they would no longer be able to work with us, they would refund all but twelve hundred dollars we had paid them, and the twelve hundred would go to Boris for all the extra work he had done throughout our extended stay in Ukraine. They were done.

And then they closed their entire Ukrainian adoption program.

◆

"I received a call from your adoption agency," Boris told me a day after I found out the agency had dropped us. "They forbid me to work with you anymore."

I caught my breath. He hadn't been that much help to us, but what little he had done was still better than having no facilitator at all.

"What are you going to do?" I asked tentatively.

"I do not know. I have to think about this. I would like to continue to help you, but if I do, you cannot let the agency know, because this is income for my family. Give me some time to think."

That was the last time I heard from him until the end of December.

THE WAIT FOR CHRISTMAS

I made our flat as festive as I could, and then I turned my focus to my plans from Thanksgiving night. I've discovered that when I'm stressed about my own life, I can best refocus by helping others. I found an American pastor who had moved to Odessa to work with street children there. As we talked, he encouraged me to stop by the dorm rooms they provided to the children. He also had me observe the ongoing soup kitchen they offered every afternoon. Eventually he invited me to go on a soup run, where they passed out meals to the street kids.

So while Eva babysat Jake, I helped feed and minister to those kids. It was an amazing ministry, but as I looked at all these children who had little or no family, no boundaries, no care, my heart was broken all over again. I wanted their stories told. I asked them many questions and asked if I could photograph them.

I went back to the flat and took Jake out to play to enjoy the outdoors before it turned too cold. I never wanted him to have to experience what those kids had to go through. Toward the end of November, a new restaurant for families, called Pinocchio's, had opened behind the band shell where children played after the work day. It was an indoor playland and restaurant for kids: interactive playrooms surrounded the restaurant area, and at the end was a giant room filled with balls. To play in a room for a half hour cost a few coins. The servers were all dressed as storybook characters who would also engage the children in games and role-playing.

I decided to check it out and Jake was delighted. He could play to his heart's content, and I could sit and drink a cup of tea, read one of my books from Ann, or just relax knowing Jake was safe and having a great time, inside and warm. The cost was so inexpensive I could afford it. Our trips to Pinocchio's became a routine that we followed two or three times a week.

One day after we'd been there for a few weeks, the manager came to my table. "What is the story with you and this little boy? He speaks fluent Russian and Ukrainian and broken English. And you speak broken Russian and fluent English."

Busted! I laughed. This man seemed sincerely interested, so I told him I was here adopting Jake and it was taking longer than usual.

His face grew kinder. He held up his hand to tell me to wait and he went to the kitchen. When he came back a few moments later, he was joined by most of the employees.

"My name is Scott, and this is my staff. I have told them your story and we are all moved by it. We have decided to adopt little Jake too. So he is free to go anywhere in the restaurant. He can make himself an ice cream cone or wander around. We will help watch him and take good care of him, and you can enjoy some time to relax."

I couldn't believe what they were offering me. I was overwhelmed.

From then on, they were true to their commitment. They would pick Jake up and carry him around; they would spoil him and try to fatten him up. And of course, when you give a little boy too much freedom, he takes full advantage. Jake did, and he sometimes got into trouble.

Every once in a while I would hear, "Sashaaaaaa!" or "Jaaaaaaake!" and I knew he had gotten into something he wasn't supposed to, such as waltzing into their office and playing on their computer, messing it up.

I loved it there. It was one of the few places where I could let down my guard, truly relax, and be myself. It was exactly what I needed to survive.

DELAYED

I counted the days to see Jahn and Jacey, and with each day that passed, I became more excited and nervous—excited to see them after so many months apart, nervous to make sure everything was just right, that they had a smooth time settling in, and that we got back into the routine of being a family, only now with Jake.

I used the convection oven to bake Christmas cookies. But reading Russian is a whole lot harder than speaking it. Standing in the grocery store, trying to determine if I had sugar or salt became nerve-racking.

A week before Jahn and Jacey were supposed to arrive, Jake woke up with a fever and I had a bad case of pinkeye.

Par for the course, I thought.

We stayed in and tried to keep warm and comfortable. Even with the fever, though, Jake kept asking, "Outside?"

"Inside!" I replied over and over.

As he healed, I went back to the market to stock our shelves with food for their visit. I cleaned. I prayed and read my Bible. I talked with friends and family. I did everything I could to wait patiently.

Three days before Jahn and Jacey's arrival, we got a snowstorm that dumped four inches of snow on the city and blew in gusts everywhere. Jake was thrilled by it. I admitted that it was pretty, but all I could think about was having to walk through it to get anywhere, since all I did was walk. Fortunately, Ann had brought me a new pair of tennis shoes when she visited. My boots would be coming with Jahn and Jacey—I was hoping I wouldn't need them too much.

♦

By Friday, I could barely sleep from excitement. Jahn and Jacey left Michigan on a fifteen-hour flight that would cross seven time zones and arrive in Odessa at 2 p.m. the next day.

I was worried because the roads were still a mess and I wanted to be sure to be at the airport to pick them up on time. That night a blizzard hit our area, closing the Odessa airport. On Saturday, I received an email that they had arrived safely in Warsaw, Poland, and would have to stay there, because the flight into Odessa was cancelled. Since only one flight a day traveled from Warsaw to Odessa, at the same time each day, it meant they would have to spend the night and take the flight the next day.

I started to feel worried, because our court date was set for December 22, and Jahn had to be there. If he missed the hearing, we would have to reschedule a new court date—but the courts closed down for most of January, which meant the next hearing would be scheduled for February at the earliest. And according to Leonid, we were fortunate even to get the hearing scheduled for December 22. It had cost him a favor to get us in before the court's break.

The next day came and went and no flights, which meant no Jahn and Jacey. I began praying they would arrive the next day—but it didn't look good, because it was raining and expected to freeze overnight. I felt the clock ticking.

I prayed desperately that God would intervene and allow the flight to make it to Odessa by December 21. It had to or we would miss the hearing on the twenty-second, since the flight would arrive at 1 p.m. and our hearing was scheduled for 11:30 a.m.

Jahn emailed me on December 21 to tell me the plane was scheduled to fly and was on time. I was so excited, I shouted. Isabelle and Adam drove us to the airport and we waited expectantly to see our family.

As soon as Jahn and Jacey walked into the main area, Jake's face lit up.

"Jacey!" he shouted and ran to her and threw his arms around her. Then he grabbed her hand and wouldn't let it go. He still appeared shy around Jahn.

Jahn and I hugged, then laughed as we both said, "We've all lost weight!"

Jake was so excited the rest of the evening, he barely left them alone. He chatted nonstop and took them around the flat showing them his toys.

"Okay, Jake, they're tired, let's let them get some rest."

He would nod, then go right back to chatting excitedly.

"Tomorrow's the day," I told Jahn. "I'm concerned something else will happen. I've been praying like crazy."

"It will work out," Jahn said, comforting me. "The court will rule in our favor, we'll get the adoption decree, enjoy a little time here while the paperwork is getting processed, then we'll be on our flight home."

"I hope you're right."

DECEMBER 22: THE APPEAL

We received word from Boris that he had decided to continue with the case and we would see him at the courthouse in Odessa. He would act as our official interpreter this time, however, not as our facilitator. Our side was going to have a large showing. Katya was also coming up from Izmail. Adam would be there for support. And Leonid would represent us. Eva stayed with Jake and Jacey at our flat.

We walked into the courtroom and waited. In walked a young blond woman with glasses. She put her briefcase on the table where the prosecutor would be. The prosecutor we knew was nowhere in sight.

Then another attorney walked in and settled down next to us. He introduced himself with a name we couldn't understand except that it started with G. "Leonid has another court date right now, and he felt he needed to represent them instead of you. But I am a good attorney. I am the president of the bar association here in Odessa. Leonid only gave me your file this morning, so I haven't had time to review it."

I couldn't believe what I was hearing. Our attorney had decided not to show up to our court case? And this new attorney hadn't even read our file?

Boris continued to interpret and said, "Leonid wanted to make sure he got you somebody better than him rather than the other way. And this guy is better. So you are in good hands."

"If he's read the file," I said.

Three judges—two men and one woman—walked in to begin the hearing, but the prosecutor still hadn't shown up. The lead judge looked at his file and then up toward the prosecutor. "Where is the prosecutor from Izmail who filed this appeal?"

The woman spoke. "I am from the Odessa prosecutor's office. I will be representing the case today."

The case began and our attorney, Big G, as we decided to call him, seemed to be handling everything well. The prosecutor, however, had a smug attitude and gave clipped comments.

Boris was called on to speak a few times, and our attorney filled in with a lot of questions to him. Neither Jahn nor I gave any testimony.

I kept watching the judges to see if I could gauge how they were reacting to the case. It seemed that the main judge and the other male judge were on our side. I thought they would rule in our favor. I was more worried about the female judge, who seemed to listen intently to the female prosecutor.

Finally, the hearing was over and we had to leave the courtroom while the judges deliberated our case.

We stood out in the hallway and waited for what seemed like an eternity. While we were waiting, Big G told us that he had missed an important point he would have brought up during the hearing if he had known about it, if he had had time to read our file.

"I should have mentioned that Sasha's rights were being violated by this appeal. He has a right to a family and not to be returned to the orphanage. It may have made a difference."

After more than an hour, we were escorted back into the courtroom for the decision. The main judge said the court had decided in favor of neither side. So we didn't win, but we didn't lose.

The female prosecutor smiled widely as the decision was being handed down. With a self-satisfied air, she looked as though she'd won some huge victory.

The judge looked at us and explained, "We are doing the best thing for you. You aren't going to understand this now, but this is the best decision we could make for you."

"What does that mean?" I asked after we walked back into the hallway.

"It means you must start over on the adoption," Boris said.

"They're right, I don't understand," I said, growing sicker by the minute.

Jahn couldn't talk; his face lost all color. He finally whispered, "I feel like somebody has just punched me in the gut."

"How is this decision the best for us?" I demanded. But nobody could explain why this was such a good decision. I couldn't correlate it with being a good thing for us because I kept thinking about the prosecutor's joy over it. "If it's for our benefit, why was the prosecutor so happy?"

Boris pulled out his phone and dialed Leonid. "You have to explain this to us, and by the way, you owe four thousand dollars to Kim's family." His tone was tense and biting.

Big G looked thoughtful, then finally said, "There was something to that decision. I don't understand it, but the judge really believed what he said. Let me go in and talk with him."

He was gone for about fifteen minutes, and returned looking more satisfied. "They sympathized with you in their decision. They didn't want to find for the prosecution. However, if they found in your favor, the prosecutor would just appeal it to the Supreme Court, and that would mean you would be here for another two years waiting to get on that docket—because technically the prosecution does have a foothold. Your original decision was written loosely. So the best thing they could do for you is to send you back to Izmail underneath a different judge. You'll get a new adoption decree, and you'll be out of here in a few months. You see? They really were thinking about your best interests."

But it didn't feel that way to us. I thought, *We have to start all over again? Are you kidding me?* I couldn't believe this was happening.

"So what happens now?" Jahn asked Big G.

"They will mail your file, along with their formal decision, back to Izmail and request a new judge and a new court date."

"Which won't be in January since the courts are shut down then, due to the Ukrainian holidays," I said. He agreed apologetically.

We scheduled a time to meet with Big G in two days to go over the formal written decision and to plan our next steps.

I liked Big G better than Leonid. I told Boris, "Leonid needs to give us our money back. When you can get that money back, we're good. Until then, I don't want to hear from you."

Jahn and I discussed our next steps. We needed to put together a legal team, now that we no longer had a facilitator from the agency. I wanted to go back to Izmail and hire Akula, the attorney who worked across from Carl and Ilse, because we needed a local attorney. Not only was he a friend, but he was also one of the top lawyers in the area. We also decided to retain Big G, in case we had another appeal and because he seemed to know something about adoption law. We still needed to find an attorney we could afford who specialized in international adoption.

If we were going to have to redo the whole thing, then we were going to do it on our terms.

HOLIDAYS IN UKRAINE

Christmas morning the kids got up and squealed with delight at the presents. Jake had never experienced Christmas, so he was especially thrilled.

I even made Christmas stockings and included one for Jahn without his knowledge. And he surprised me with a few presents— perfume, books, and an MP3 player. We had a nice Christmas morning even though we were still reeling from what we now termed the "punch in the gut" rather than calling it the appeal.

After all the presents were unwrapped, we got dressed and headed to a restaurant called Compote, a traditional Ukrainian restaurant that was homey, with a crackling fire and an intimate feeling of being in someone's house.

That was the first time we were carefree, happy, and could be goofy. We all put on glasses, made funny faces, and had our picture taken. Being able to laugh again as a family was the gift God gave us that day.

We realized, *It's going to be okay. We can do this. Let's just focus on the time we have together now.*

♦

Between Christmas Eve and New Year's Eve, we met twice with Big G. I loved that he seemed genuinely indignant about the way the entire case had been handled and that Jake's rights were being violated—his right to be adopted and get on with his life. He promised to spend more time researching Ukrainian adoption law in depth so we would be better prepared the next time.

At one point during one of our meetings with Big G, he became irritated at all our questions. Finally he told us, "You know, Ukrainians do not ask *how* questions. They ask only, 'Will you do this for us?' and leave the *how* to the advocate."

My problem with that, I politely replied, was that I'd already had that experience in Ukraine—and it hadn't worked out so well.

"I noticed you are charging us much more than a typical Ukrainian would be charged," I said flatly. "I believe your typical fee is five hundred hryvnia for one year's retainer, which amounts to about sixty U.S. dollars? You are charging us five hundred dollars for this one case and will only accept U.S. dollars from us. If you are going to charge us in dollars, then we expect to have our questions answered, G."

He cleared his throat and said he would do more digging.

By the end of the week when we met with him again, he seemed more confident and prepared for our barrage of questions about options and loopholes and anything else we could think of.

Jahn and I thanked Big G for his hard work and let him know that for the remainder of the year and until the middle of January, we were going to let him work without our bothering him. We would pray about the options, we informed him, but also we wanted to spend as much time together enjoying one another as a family. I knew I was going to be stuck there for another two months—at the very least—so for the next three weeks I wanted to be entirely selfish and have my family all to myself, without the stress and worry of our situation bogging us down and flinging itself into my thoughts every moment.

"I never thought we'd have to make a decision of this magnitude," I said to Jahn on the way back to our flat. "I mean, for crying out loud, it's an adoption."

Jahn nodded seriously. I saw his jaw tighten and I appreciated again how much he supported our decision for me to remain and fight. I knew he had my back—not only emotionally, but also spiritually. He and I spent so much time together praying over God's will in this situation, asking for wisdom, for discernment and clarity, and for strength to continue the battle. No matter what happened, I knew we were in this thing together.

I wasn't so sure any longer about Jacey's support, though.

From the moment I saw her beautiful face at the airport, all I wanted to do was smother her with affection. I wanted to hold and hug her and be with her. But she was angry. She'd been without a mother to comfort her and be with her for five months. She had started the new school year without me. She was involved in things at church without me. It had taken a toll on her. So although she would let me hug and love on her, I could feel the tension: she wanted my affection and was excited to be with me, but she was still struggling to handle the circumstances.

It ebbed and flowed with her. There would be times when she would crawl into my lap and say, "Mommy, I love you so much. I'm never leaving you alone." And then other times, she would push me away.

Jake only made it more difficult for her. While he adored her and followed her around like a puppy dog, he still demanded constant attention from me. I couldn't even go to the bathroom by myself. Jacey saw his needs and was unable to fully understand them, as any nine-year-old would struggle to do. So jealousy added to her anger.

I continued to do my best to shower her with affection and try to balance as much time between Jake and Jacey as I could—without leaving out Jahn, who also needed me. He'd been without a wife for those months as well. And although he was more mature and understanding, I knew my absence had been hard for him. It had been rough on me, too. I had missed my husband, my best friend, during these long months.

♦

"Kim, you and your family must come to our New Year's Eve party," Adam told me over the phone. "New Year's Eve is the ultimate holiday over here. It's Ukraine's biggest holiday, so you definitely don't want to miss it. It's like Halloween, Christmas, Fourth of July, and New Year's Eve all wrapped into one!"

"Of course we'll be there, Adam. Thanks for inviting us. Everyone will love it, I'm sure."

On New Year's Eve we headed out to do a little shopping and sightseeing before making our way to Adam and Isabelle's flat. Everywhere we went, people—kids and adults alike, but especially the children—were dressed in costumes: storybook characters, kings and queens. It was like Halloween without the scary factor.

Jacey and Jake both oohed and ahhed at everyone, until Jacey could no longer take being only a spectator and not a participant.

"I want a costume!" she whined.

We didn't have a lot of money, so Jahn and I had to get creative. We went downtown to a toy shop and found pirate hats and plastic swords, which we bought for both of the kids. Jake was delighted immediately, but Jacey just looked at my offering as though I'd lost my mind.

"You will be the musketeers, just like Barbie." Earlier that fall, Barbie had come out with a direct-to-video movie, *Barbie and the Three Musketeers*, which I knew Jacey loved, so Jacey and Jake could be musketeers.

Jacey perked up, eyes wide. "Yes!"

Thanks, Barbie, I thought and then chuckled. *Never thought I'd be saying that!*

◆

We arrived at Adam and Isabelle's in the early evening and found their flat already filled with an eclectic group of people—from their neighbors to heads of different church denominations and traditions. It was loud and bustling and wonderful. Jacey and Jake ran off to play with the other children, while we waited for the meal.

Isabelle is a wonderful cook, but she truly outdid herself with this banquet feast. We sat at a large table filled with plates overflowing with meats and traditional Ukrainian foods. We laughed, talked, and ate until we joked that our stomachs were going to explode, then we hung out and waited for midnight.

In the meantime, one of the guests suggested we all play a game based on animal sounds. The premise was that each person would be assigned a specific animal, such as a rooster or a dog or a cat. Then we would go around the circle with each person making his or her sound, then "throwing" it to someone else who had to make a sound and pass it along. The longer it went, the faster it would go.

It sounded like fun and a good way to pass the time, so we all agreed. After all, it was similar to children's games I'd played growing up. It was animal sounds; how tough could it be?

So we started the game, all of us clapping our laps twice, our hands twice, then one person made a sound that was completely foreign to us and passed it to the next person, whose sound was also completely foreign to us. The group roared with laughter at us, because we didn't know our simple animal sounds. They kept trying to teach us, but then we'd forget and say the sounds we knew, which would disrupt the game with rollicking laughter.

Finally at the end of the game, Adam explained to everyone, "Americans don't have the same animal sounds as Ukrainians do. For instance, a dog goes 'bark, bark' in America, not 'gough, gough' as we say here."

"It's almost midnight," someone said and we all gathered around the windows.

"Ukraine has the most amazing fireworks you've ever seen," Adam explained to Jahn and me. "It's like the Fourth of July on steroids."

At midnight everyone yelled, "*S Novym Godom!* Happy New Year!" and fireworks began to explode all around us. Adam and Isabelle lived on the sixteenth floor of a high-rise apartment building and had windows on every side, so we had almost an entirely uninterrupted view of the city of Odessa. We went from window to window to see different fireworks celebrations. Some were right in their neighborhood, so they exploded right outside the windows. Others were farther away. But they were all impressive and incredibly loud.

As soon as the booms started, Jake began to shake and cry. His cries grew louder until they turned into screams. I ran to find him huddled in a corner, rocking and covering his ears and screaming, "Make it stop, Mommy!"

I scooped him up and headed to the bathroom, where I shut the door and turned on the water. Then I held him close and sang little songs to comfort him and take his mind off the noises outside.

I could hear the excited shouts from the group enjoying the fireworks. I sighed. My son was still overly sensitive to loud sounds and dealing with sensory deprivation issues, and this was part of that. He and I decided to enjoy ourselves in the bathroom until the fireworks were over.

"Happy 2010," I whispered to him as he held me close and continued to sniffle whenever a loud boom would shake him. *It's already starting with a bang.*

12

January 2010

IN JACEY'S BEST INTEREST

One night as a special treat, we hired Eva to look after all the kids and Jahn and I took Adam and Isabelle for dinner at a nice restaurant as a thanks for all they had done for us.

About halfway through our relaxing and delicious meal, Adam put down his fork and looked at us tentatively.

"I've noticed some things about Jacey," he started. "She's changed. She's no longer the happy-go-lucky girl we knew, and she's been negatively affected by your absence, Kim. Obviously this is your decision, but I believe she needs to stay here with you."

Adam said everything politely and out of a deep concern, but panic immediately rose within me.

"No," I said with a note of finality. In my mind, she couldn't stay.

I was too concerned for her safety. Plus, I wasn't sure I could handle two needy kids in this culture with everything else already on my plate.

"I don't have a choice here," I said as calmly as I could. "God has asked me to be patient, and I'm trying to be patient. But I have to stay; she doesn't. It's too much to ask. And what if she gets sick? H1N1 is going around—they closed down public places for three weeks. There was no school. No restaurants were open. People walked around in masks. What if she catches the flu? What do I do then? They don't have good medicine here."

"Those are all legitimate reasons, Kim," Adam said. "Those things could happen. But ultimately Jacey needs you. She needs her mother just as much as Jake does."

"Just pray about it," Isabelle said gently. I knew what she was saying: once you become a parent, life is no longer about you—it's about what your children need. And mine needed me.

"I will," I promised. I knew Adam and Isabelle were trying to help me see the importance of keeping Jacey with me. But I couldn't see past the danger.

◆

I kept my word and prayed about it. Finally, I simply asked Jacey, "What do you need?"

Her eyes filled with tears and she said softly, "Please, Mommy. Please don't send me home without you."

Her "please" was like a knife in the heart, and I knew for the first time how bad it had been for her without me. Otherwise, why would she say that about her home, her bedroom, her friends, her school— all the things she loved? It was as though I was shipping her to someplace truly awful.

The only thing holding me back was fear, and where did fear come from? They all encouraged me to make the decision based on truth, not fear. But to me, if felt as though I was being asked to lay my Isaac on the altar. I was unwilling to do that.

God and I wrestled for a long time that night until finally I grew so weary arguing over it that I just gave in.

"God, if I'm going to keep her here, you're going to have to keep her safe. I'll do this for you and for her. But there's one place I'm not willing to go: I'm not willing to give up my daughter. This is not going to be a trade-off for me. It's not one for the other. Please, don't go there, Father, because I won't make it."

EVERYTHING CONVERGES

Jahn left Odessa in the middle of January, and I stood in the airport holding the hands of two children, watching him walk away alone. I was scared and overwhelmed.

God, if I ever needed you before, I need you now. Please show yourself to me and keep me strong.

With Jahn going home, I had to figure out what to focus on first and how to prioritize everything I was going to have to do. I held off on the homeschooling for a while, figuring Jacey needed some time to readjust to us living together in Ukraine.

Instead, I turned my focus to putting together a legal team to help me with the new court case. I knew I needed to get one more attorney for my team: someone who handled international adoption cases. I started looking on the Internet and found someone who looked promising: Andrei Sokolov, who specialized in Ukrainian international adoptions and lived in Kiev. I contacted him to see if he would be willing to take on my case as an advisor. He agreed.

Our team was in place. Akula was the main advocate who would help us through the Izmail legal system; Big G was a good attorney for any appeals that might arise again. But neither of them, as good as they were, had international adoption experience. The Kiev advocate, Andrei, did.

My next focus was on getting Jacey and Jake settled.

Jacey was wonderful for helping Jake's English. She wouldn't let him slide on anything. I would constantly hear her tell him, "It's 'the' chair. Please move *the* chair." I'd let those little things go, but she was demanding of him. "If you're going to be my brother, you need to speak the language correctly." He absorbed the language like a sponge.

She also helped him understand more fully how to play well with others. And as he became more confident, he also grew into a little stinker. He would sneak off and grab candy after I told him no. He would throw something at his sister and then fake-apologize.

One afternoon, I snuck into the bathroom and locked it so I could have a moment's peace. I heard shuffling outside the door and then Jacey yelled, "Ouch! Mom! Jake threw a slipper at me...your red one...and it really hurt." And before I could reprimand Jake, I heard him say, "Oh, I'm sorry, Jacey." I would start to get frustrated and then realize he was turning into a normal little boy who annoys his sister.

One cold afternoon, Jake kept running back and forth from the kitchen to the living room, bouncing off every closed door and hallway wall he came to, making loud car and crashing sounds. It had started to drive both Jacey and me crazy. Finally, Jacey looked at me and in a total deadpan voice said, "He's never gonna get married."

I laughed until I cried. It was just the release I needed for those stuck-in-a-small-apartment-with-two-active-children days.

♦

Laughter is the best medicine, but I never got enough of it, it seemed. When Jahn left, I felt myself go downhill psychologically, descending into depression. The weather certainly didn't help. The constant grayness matched the grayness of my mind and soul.

Adam and Isabelle were my lifelines, constantly checking up on me, showing their concern. One day, Adam called and encouraged me to move closer to where they lived, on the outskirts of Odessa. He promised he and Isabelle would start looking for a place.

I agreed, then put it out of my mind...until someone recognized me because of my red coat.

I was walking out of the grocery store when I overheard a clerk say, "Ah, the American in her red coat."

I looked down at my warm winter coat that Ann had brought me from America. Then I glanced around at everyone else: they were all in black. No colors, drab, dull. Even the fur coats were dark.

I had worked so hard to ensure that I fit in, buying their clothes, continuing to call Jake "Sasha" when we were in public, and talking only in Russian and as little as possible. I had no idea that just keeping one little thing from America would make me known. I quickly bought a long dark coat from the bazaar.

Fortunately, by the end of the month Adam called with good news: they'd found a flat on the tenth floor across the complex from them. The buildings were separated by a courtyard. And there was a small convenience store in the area that we could use to get our daily bread and other goods. An open-air bazaar was a short walk up the street.

It was time to move again. Adam offered to help and picked us up in their van and took us back to their apartment complex.

Our new home was less expensive than where I had been renting downtown. And I hoped we wouldn't need to stay there too long.

◆

"I have some unusual news that I think will affect you," Boris said over the phone. It was the first time I'd spoken to him in almost a month. "Even if the court grants you the adoption this time, you are stuck in this country, I'm afraid."

"What are you talking about, Boris?"

"The government didn't pay their printer, so the printer has cut off all requests. That means no driver's licenses, car registrations, or... passports."

"So you're telling me that even with a new adoption decree, I can't get a Ukrainian passport for Jake because the printer didn't get paid and is refusing to work?"

"Yes."

"Why don't they just pay the bill and be done with it? That seems like an easy fix."

"Well..."

"When do you think this situation will be fixed?"

"I'm not exactly sure. It could be months."

♦

One morning Andrei, my Kiev attorney, called to check in about the case, but took the conversation in a different, unexpected direction.

"You know, Kim, something just doesn't sit right with me about the women in the birth certificate office who refused to give you Sasha's birth certificate. They are fellow Ukrainians and they broke the law. It's because of people like them that the law is constantly circumvented. It's not okay with me, and I need to file a suit against them."

"You can't do that, Andrei," I said, suddenly feeling uneasy. "They'll both lose their jobs. I can't be responsible for that. The prosecutor intimidated them. Why don't you go after him? *He's* the bad guy. They're victims like me."

"No, I don't see it that way. They allowed him to intimidate them. They should have stood up to him and done their jobs, and they didn't. You were in the right. You had all the documentation. That was a fully valid, legal adoption decree. It should never have been turned down by that birth certificate office."

"He would have just stopped me someplace else."

"No, I don't agree."

"Andrei, please don't file the suit. You can't do it on my behalf; you don't have my permission."

"I understand your concerns, Kim. I hope you understand mine."

♦

Laughter continued to be hard to find. At night, I lay in bed unable to sleep and worried about how we were going to pay for everything, and how I was going to handle everything. It seemed fear paralyzed me and kept mounting. I began to wonder where God was.

The next day, I heard that a friend, Amber Clark, had begun a Bring Jake Home fund and Facebook page. She'd felt impressed to pray for our situation and felt as though God was encouraging others to donate funds for our necessities. I couldn't believe it. God had shown up again.

For some reason, though, I was unable to lift out of the heaviness that covered my mind, and although I saw good and encouraging things happening, I couldn't break away from the fear and worry. I still panicked over something happening to Jacey, or that the prosecutor would try something new and send police to take Jake from me, or that I would get kicked out of the country and have to leave Jake.

Each dreary day would pass with too little sun, with kids who were whiny and cold and didn't understand about safety precautions or their mom's fears, too little heat, not enough money, desperately missing Jahn, and days without sleep. The best help came from so many people sending me encouraging messages and prayers over Skype, Facebook, or email. I clung to those messages and desperately prayed to get quickly to the looking-back part of this experience, hoping to find some joy and laughter.

NO LEGAL RIGHT

Toward the end of January, Akula began to meet with me every week, giving me updates and strategizing our next moves. He had to come to me because I couldn't risk being seen in Izmail.

We met in the restaurant where Jahn and I had taken Adam and Isabelle. As we ate our lunch, Akula said matter-of-factly, "You know, you really have no further legal right to keep the boy."

"That's not true, Akula. Andrei said, according to Ukrainian law, they have to send a legal request for his return to our home in Holland, Michigan. The prosecutor hasn't done that. I refuse to break any laws, but I'm not returning him to the orphanage unless I'm forced to. The prosecutor has to follow Ukrainian law, Akula. And legally, nobody has ever asked for his return."

Akula only shrugged.

"If I keep the initial decree with me, will anybody question that?"

"Probably nobody will know. You should probably still carry it, but..."

But this is something else for me to worry about

Within two days of my meeting with Akula, I received a call from Boris.

"I wanted to let you know that pressure is building around here for the court to demand Jake's return to the orphanage."

"You don't understand, Boris. The prosecutor isn't following the law on this. You know what was happening to him there, how the kids picked on him, his bite marks, wounds, the lack of nourishment. How would Jake ever trust me again? I won't break the law, Boris, but I'm not taking him back unless I absolutely have to. He's just a baby!"

I called Akula to discuss a few other alternatives, but none were great. They included returning Jake to the orphanage temporarily, which I firmly refused, knowing that "temporarily" meant something different to them. I opted to keep him, stay hidden, and trust God to prevail and hide us.

♦

Within a few more days, I received a phone call from Akula with good news: we were being fast-tracked. The courts had resumed session after their long January break and our case had already been assigned a new judge and we'd been given a pretrial conference date of February 11.

I wasn't sure what to think, as things didn't normally happen fast like that, but I was determined to keep my eyes on God and what he could do, not man.

13

February 2010

ANOTHER LAWSUIT

During my now weekly meeting with Akula, he dropped another
bombshell on me.

"The February 11 court date has been dropped."

"Why?"

"There's another lawsuit. You will need to retain me for both of
the suits. The adoption and this new lawsuit."

He pulled out my file and opened it. "Do you remember the lawsuit the prosecutor filed against the Izmail City Council, which failed
last October?"

"Of course," I said. How could I forget?

"It appears now he is naming individuals and suing everybody sep-
arately. He is going to sue them one at a time. The first person he has

named is Inna from the Izmail SDA. This means each of these cases must be decided before the judge can go on to handle the adoption decree. But I have already spoken to the judge on your behalf."

"But that's how many different cases? It would take forever before the judge could rule on the adoption case."

"Yes."

I knew where this was going. The prosecutor knew that I wasn't going to simply give up and leave without Jake, so he was going to draw everything out. He had probably deduced that we had dated paperwork at the embassy, which allowed us only a year. If the dead-line ran out, I would be forced to leave the country and begin the entire adoption process at square one from back home, which was *really* square one since our adoption agency had dropped us.

I looked at Akula. He was my attorney, and he was going to ask for more money. I sighed heavily.

"Okay, how much is this going to cost?"

"Two thousand six hundred to retain me overall. This includes both suits."

I put my head in my hands and rubbed my forehead. I couldn't possibly go back again to my father-in-law and ask for more money. He had already been beyond generous.

I began to tear up.

"Kim, crying is not going to help anything."

I glanced around the restaurant, which was empty. I realized this was the first time I had teared up in months.

Well, at least I know I still can, I thought.

"This is what I'm going to do," he said. "I will see if I can speak with the judge about this and we'll figure out how we're going to han-dle it. We're going to have to have a pretrial on this one. That's when the judge will determine how he's going to handle this...situation."

"Can you please get it as soon as possible? It's February already! I *have* to be out of here by July."

"I'll see what I can do."

That night, I reread a message my mom had sent me the previous week. She had been reading promises from God and came upon Isaiah 54:17 from The Message translation: "Any accuser who takes you to court will be dismissed as a liar. This is what God's servants can expect. I'll see to it that everything works out for the best. God's Decree." I claimed that promise to be true for us.

Then I went onto Facebook and asked my friends there to take a moment and call our congressman's office about our situation. I asked them simply to let him know they were concerned and praying about our plight, and ask for his help. The clock was ticking.

FEARS REALIZED

The winter grew more harsh and Odessa was hit with a terrible cold spell for a week. We had Soviet heating, so there was no thermostat. We got what we got.

We had an oil heater we plugged into the wall in the bedroom. It sparked and caused a large black ring around the outlet, which stopped working. That was the only outlet other than one on the other side of the room, which I needed for the phone and the computer. I had to move the heater into the hall, but the warmth couldn't reach the bedroom. We could see our breath.

I already dreaded nighttime, because it was when I lay wide awake unable to sleep. But now I had new reasons to dread it: my children and I faced bone-chilling cold. I had to put both kids to bed in layers of sweats, sweatshirts, and stocking caps on their heads. With Jake's low body fat, I was concerned he was going to suffer from hypothermia. I had never been that cold.

Jacey slept in bed with me, and I had to bring Jake into bed, because I saw his lips turn purple. I slept between them, figuring

I wasn't going to sleep anyway between the insomnia and Jake's thrashing. But there was no reason for Jacey not to sleep.

I lay there quietly pushing my breath out and realized how the rest of the world lives. I would never imagine going to bed fully dressed with a hat on just to try to stay warm. We had only so many blankets. We had no other heat options. Towels, coats piled on top of us—we used anything we could to keep warm.

That was the worst week. I didn't think I could get any more seriously depressed. But somehow I managed.

The following week, I noticed that Jacey wasn't acting right. She complained about not feeling well, and when I felt her forehead, she was burning up.

Oh no. Not this. Not Jacey.

I experienced constant fear that I would lose them both, and that fear kept me in the darkness that had lived with me from the moment Jahn left. I couldn't sleep. There were days on end when I couldn't eat. I was so scared. And now Jacey was sick.

The fever refused to break and soon she developed a secondary double ear infection. I was beside myself with worry. I remembered an American doctor practicing in Odessa who had helped Jake when he had that eye infection, so I called her and explained the situation. She asked Jacey's weight and age and then figured out what medication and dosage she should take.

"It's important not to give her more than this amount," she said. "They don't make children's medication over here, only adult dosage levels, so you want to make sure you don't give her an overdose."

I ran to the drugstore and picked it up without a prescription, along with some chocolate pudding and anything else I could think of to get Jacey to eat. She was unable to swallow the huge pills, so I crushed them and disguised them in the pudding, which tasted dreadful.

At the first little mouthful, she spat it out and whined.

"Jacey, I know it tastes terrible, but you have to take this. You're a sick little girl; this will make you better."

"No! I won't take it. I don't care!"

I was beside myself. Finally I thought about putting the entire pill into one teaspoon of pudding, but then she had the rest of the pudding to eat that would get rid of the taste.

I tried again, but she refused even to do that. She clamped her lips shut anytime I tried to get near her with the medicine.

I tried to reason with her. I tried to pry open her mouth. I tried to beg and plead with her. I tried to bribe her. Nothing worked.

As a last resort I pulled out a large wooden serving spoon and threatened to hit the top of her leg.

"Open your mouth, Jacey."

"Hmmm-mmm," she hummed through closed lips.

I threatened again, explaining why it was important to take the medicine.

She didn't care, but her eyes filled with tears. So did mine.

"Jacey! You must take this medicine!"

"Why are you doing this to me, Mommy?" she cried. "Why are you being so mean to me?"

How could I possibly explain to her that the nightmare I feared would happen was coming true and I was terrified that I was going to lose her? She was whiny, wouldn't take the medicine, and wasn't making things easier.

"I know you don't want to do this, Jacey, and I know you think I'm being totally unreasonable right now. But you don't understand. It's because I love you. If I could take it for you, I would."

She finally took the medicine and ate the rest of the pudding. She complained about it, but she took it.

"Thank you, Jacey. I know you aren't going to like this, but you have to take this medicine three times a day for ten days."

Afterward, I went into my room, shut the door, and cried out to God for her complete healing.

TRYING TO GET A RHYTHM

Because I had no control over anything, and the waiting and depression were closing in on me, I decided to do the best I could to get into a routine. I started homeschooling Jacey and trying to make up for lost time. I worked with the private Christian school she attended back home. They sent me the curriculum and we worked via the Internet. Fortunately, Jahn had brought most of her books with them because Jacey was behind and not doing well in her studies. The books we didn't have, Jahn picked up from the school and shipped to us once he got back home.

Our money situation continued to hold my most focused attention. We were broke. The Bring Jake Home fund got us through. Donations from friends, family, and generous anonymous donors would show up just as I spent our last dollar on a loaf of bread. And while I praised God for his kindness and provision, I felt guilty being forced to rely on other people, knowing we could never repay everyone for the amazing ways they had saved me and my family.

In the midst of the darkness of my soul, there were other bright spots. I continued to meet with Akula, who finally gave me some "good" news. Apparently our congressman, Pete Hoekstra, had contacted a high Ukrainian official about the case, and I began to get word that other officials were discussing our case. We now had a pretrial set for March 10. God only knew when the actual trial would be.

Jake's half sister, Svetlana, continued to be a light in our lives. She visited us frequently, hanging out and sometimes spending the night. We adored her, and Jake quickly warmed up to her after his initial timid meeting with her. She was always eager to play with Jacey and Jake. And she seemed to enjoy hanging out with us. She loved learning about America, so Jacey took the liberty of filling her in on the important things, such as television shows.

My heart broke for her that she'd been robbed of having a carefree, joyful childhood. She was a beautiful, smart young woman, and I wanted to help her as much as I could. I prayed constantly for God to shed light on what would be best for her situation. And he provided through my mother and my father-in-law.

They were touched by hearing Svetlana's story, so both of them independently sent money earmarked for Svetlana, which I took and bought her clothes, shoes, and a heavy winter coat. In the dead of winter, she would show up at our flat in a lightweight fall jacket and tennis shoes.

"Where are your boots?"

She would shrug. "I don't have any."

But she was most excited about receiving a suitcase, which she'd always wanted.

"I don't ever go anywhere, but...just in case," she said.

The most worrisome thing about Svetlana, though, was her cough. It was a deep, rattling, persistent cough.

"You should get that checked, Svetlana," I told her again when I noticed she'd coughed and then quietly wiped something from her mouth.

"It's nothing," she replied nonchalantly. "I'm getting over a cold, that's all."

But it worried me. I had grown attached to this young woman and had now added her health issues to my ever-increasing worry list. I knew that tuberculosis was common in Ukraine, especially in orphanages, where poverty and malnutrition were rampant. I only hoped she was right and it was left over from a cold and nothing more serious—or contagious.

She knew I was working with a team of attorneys for the case, and one day she insisted on going with me to visit them.

"If my letter didn't work the first time," she explained, "then I'll simply rewrite it so the prosecutor can't argue with it."

I appreciated her willingness to help out. So the next time I went to visit Big G and Boris, I included her.

♦

Toward the end of February, I received an email from Karen Brink, a strong intercessory prayer warrior who, along with her husband, Don, had committed to praying for us. She wrote that she couldn't explain it, but recently I had been weighing heavily on her heart— much more so than normal. She awoke at 3 a.m. one night praying for me and for the heaviness to lift. After she finished praying, she turned on the television to a religious broadcasting station. Pastor Charles Stanley was on, preaching a series on the life and trials of Old Testament Joseph.

"I think this is an answer to that prayer, Kim," she wrote. "Stanley is preaching on everything Joseph had to go through until he finally got to the point where God could use him. I think you really need to get that series and listen to it. You can pull it up from his website."

I thanked her and downloaded the series onto my computer to listen to. With every word Charles Stanley said, I felt myself finally being pulled back from the darkest depression. I had felt like I was on some sort of brink, on the edge, and Satan had such a hold, because I felt so alone and so overwhelmed. The sermon series brought my mind back to the right spiritual perspective. He gave me the strength I needed to keep pursuing the goal.

After I finished that series, I thought about how often God uses people to encourage others—from Karen, who listened to God's voice and obeyed him at 3 a.m., to Charles Stanley, who spoke the truth from God's Word, not knowing who would be touched, but obeying God's call to preach. It reminded me again of how important it is to be obedient when God calls us to something—even when that something doesn't necessarily make sense. Rather than asking, "Why, God?" we need to say simply, "Yes, God. Here I am. Use me." And as helpless and weak as I was, I still longed for him to use me—however he would choose.

14

March 2010

ANDREI'S LAWSUIT

I began taking all my legal documents to Rose, the translator in Odessa, for her to translate into English. I wanted to know what had been said, and didn't trust that Boris was giving me the full translation. Rose adored Jake and grew attached to him, and we quickly became friends.

One day while I was visiting her at her office, she told me about a friend of hers who worked in city administration. "My friend wants to invite us over for dinner, you and me. Can you get a sitter and come? It will be just us girls."

"Yes, I'll go." I thought it would be a nice opportunity to further our acquaintance and possibly make another friend. So a few nights later we headed to her friend's apartment for a home-cooked, delicious Ukrainian meal.

While we were eating, our host mentioned she'd gotten word that there was going to be a hearing that involved my case and the birth certificate office.

Oh no, I realized. Andrei did file a lawsuit, even after I asked him not to pursue it.

"I'm going to attend this trial and find out what's going on," the woman continued. "Let's get together afterward and I'll fill you in."

I felt nauseated.

♦

I dropped off more paperwork for Rose to translate and she told me that her friend had attended the trial just as she said.

"What did she find out?" I asked, almost wishing not to know.

"She has invited us back to her flat for dinner."

So again Rose and I went to the woman's house, and over another amazing Ukrainian home-cooked meal, the woman gave us the details I feared most.

"Those two women lost their jobs...because of what they did to you."

I called Andrei the next day.

"Are you satisfied, Andrei? Those two women were fired."

"Kim, those two women needed to lose their jobs. Where do you think you have to go back to get the birth certificate? Did you really think they were going to give you the certificate the second time? Don't you understand?"

My mind cleared and I did understand. I knew why he had pursued the lawsuit: it was on my behalf, to pave the way.

"But they're just going to put in somebody else. How do I know they won't do the same thing?" I asked.

"We'll worry about that later. But I had to get them out of there."

MARCH 10: REAL TROUBLE BREWS

I hired a private car, and Jake and I headed back to Izmail for the pretrial. I left Jacey with the Lincolns, but needed to take Jake with me, since he had now become too much of a handful. I didn't want us to be more of a burden on the Lincolns than we had already become.

I arranged to stay with Carl and Ilse, so we went to their flat and enjoyed our time together.

The morning of March 10, Katya came to their flat to watch Jake. I was justifiably nervous about someone finding out Jake was back in town for fear they would tell the authorities, who might take him back to the orphanage. Katya, I could trust.

We were in the same courtroom and sat in the same place as during the first adoption hearing. The prosecutor, still looking annoyed (although this time his hair was cut and he appeared more presentable), sat at the same table across from us and still focused on anything but looking at us.

"If everything goes smoothly, the judge will set the trial for two weeks from this pretrial," Akula explained. "So we would get a trial date for sometime around March 24."

"So then if the judge rules in our favor, we could leave in April?" I asked.

"Yes, technically," he said.

A new judge entered the room and sat at the front, glanced through a few papers, then looked at the prosecutor. "This is a pretrial hearing for the adoption of—"

"Excuse me, Your Honor," the prosecutor cut in, "but we cannot proceed with this pretrial hearing since we have a lawsuit pending, which needs to be handled before the actual adoption."

The judge's eyes narrowed slightly. "Those are personal lawsuits that have no bearing on this adoption case right now. What's more important is the decision about this adoption decree. The other cases may or may not even need to be pursued based on my findings in this particular case."

The prosecutor went pale, then quickly turned a shade of pink. His jaw muscle twitched and he inhaled sharply.

The judge looked at the prosecutor, almost daring him to question his statement. But the prosecutor said no more, so the judge continued, asking Akula a few questions, then the prosecutor.

"It appears straightforward with all the paperwork. So I will go ahead and set the trial date." He shuffled through his calendar. "Let's set the date for... March 30."

The prosecutor slammed down a paper. "Your Honor," he said, barely able to contain his tone, "technically, the trial should be set within two weeks. That date is into the third week."

"I realize that," the judge said. "My docket is full and I can't fit it in, so we'll set it for the following week, on March 30."

"We have no problems with that date, Your Honor," Akula said quickly.

"Good," the judge said. "March 30." He rose and exited. As soon as he was gone, the prosecutor pushed back his chair so hard it fell over, and he stormed out of the courtroom. All his paperwork and his briefcase remained on the table.

"Where's he going?" I asked.

"I don't know." Akula frowned and wore a look that said, *Whatever he's doing can't be good.* He silently placed his papers in his briefcase and closed it, then stood and said, "I'll be back. I want to see where he went."

I didn't know whether to be excited about finally getting a trial date set or scared about whatever the prosecutor was planning next. After about five minutes Akula returned wearing a worried look.

"He's over at the police station, Kim, and I don't like the looks of this. Let's go back to my office and wait to see what we can find out."

Akula and I sat in his office waiting anxiously. Carl and Ilse stopped by from their office across the hall to await any news. About an hour later, Akula's phone rang.

His eyebrows furrowed nervously as he listened to the voice on the other end. He spoke just a few words, then hung up.

"You need to get out of town. Now," he said. "The prosecutor put out a warrant for Jake's return. That means you'll be arrested if Jake is found in your company. I'll get a copy of the warrant, but you need to get out of here."

I didn't have enough money to hire another private car or take a cab. We'd planned on taking a bus back, which I couldn't do since the bus didn't leave for hours.

"There's the private minibus across from our flat," Carl reminded me as we left Akula's office. "It leaves more often, but we'll have to hurry since I think it might be leaving soon." None of us mentioned to Akula that Jake was back at their flat waiting for me to pick him up.

"This is kind of exciting," Ilse said. "It's like one of those spy movies." I could tell she was trying to make things lighter. If we were caught, they would take Jake back—but they could also take me to jail for having him, and it would also put Carl and Ilse in danger since Jake was at their apartment.

We got Jake and headed to the bus stop just as people were boarding. Something nudged me to fake our names on the tickets.

"I hate to ask this," I said to Carl and Ilse. "You know I haven't used my name here since any of the trouble started. Would it be okay if Jake and I used your names to purchase the bus tickets?"

"Of course," Ilse said immediately and quickly handled the ticket situation.

I had taken the minibus before, so I knew the routine. On the regular bus, you could just buy your ticket without giving a name or making a reservation. But on the minibus you had to give a name for your reservation. Then somewhere along the route, about

halfway to your destination, the bus would pull off to the side of
the road where a car sat waiting. Someone from that other vehicle
would board the bus and check names from the roster. If there were
any empty seats the driver might pick up another customer along
the way.

Jake and I boarded the minibus and got settled into seats about
halfway back. The bus pulled away from the curb and had driven
about five minutes when all of a sudden a police car pulled in front
of it, forcing it to stop.

This had never happened before, so I feared it had something to
do with us and the warrant. Instinctively, I pushed Jake's head down.
"Stay down. Everything is okay," I whispered to him in Russian, taking no chances with translation.

Jake saw the urgency on my face and nodded.

I pulled my coat hood up and covered as much of my head and face
as I could, then I kept my head down.

An officer walked to the driver's side of the bus and pushed his
head through the open window and looked at all the passengers.
He started to yell at the driver and demanded to see the roster. He
checked every line.

*God, protect us. You brought us this far. Don't let him come on the bus.
Don't let him discover us.*

I was trying to calm my breathing when it hit me: we'd put those
tickets in Carl's and Ilse's names at the last minute. There was no
Kim or Jake de Blecourt listed on that roster.

Finally, the officer allowed the bus to go. When I was sure we were
out of sight of the police car, I gently lifted Jake up and brought him
onto my lap.

"We're okay," I whispered. *Thank you, God.*

I rubbed my hand over Jake's now thicker and shiny head of hair
that had been thin and brittle when he was in the orphanage. I
looked down at his tiny hands and gently ran my fingers over his fin-

gernails. They were now strong where once they had been so thin I could peel them away like an onion.

The orphanage's care versus my care. But you want to send him back, I thought toward the prosecutor. *Not because of what's best for him. You couldn't care less about this little boy. You want to send him back because you're so arrogant and cruel. You want to win at all costs.* "But I won't let you," I whispered aloud. "My God will not let you win."

♦

It was close to midnight and I was finally getting ready for bed. I knew I wouldn't sleep that night—I'd basically stopped sleeping fully ever since I decided to allow Jacey to stay with me—but I still went through the motions of putting on my pajamas and lying in bed. I was heading toward my bedroom when my phone rang.

Who in the world is calling me at this time of night?

"Kim." It was Akula. "I have a copy of the warrant. It's a national warrant. I'm going to petition the judge to remove it, but until he signs it, don't leave your apartment for any reason. Consider yourself under house arrest. I don't want you going anywhere. This is serious, Kim. Do you understand me?"

I swallowed hard. "Ye—" I choked. "Yes."

"Good. Do not leave." And he hung up.

I went back into the living room and fell onto the couch.

Twenty days to stay completely hidden. I knew I could handle that, but what was I supposed to tell Jacey and Jake? Spring was finally here and they wanted to be outside in the sunshine, playing and running and enjoying the warmth that had finally arrived. How could I keep them cooped up in this tiny apartment for twenty days? And what if the police found us? They would take Jake away from me, from our family. They would drag him away and force him back to that loveless place. And what about Jacey? What would she do when I got hauled off to a Ukrainian jail?

More and more questions came, but no answers. I sat up most of the night allowing every worst-case scenario to play out in my brain, bombarding me with horrors I had never imagined before. I prayed for relief, for some peace, but none came.

♦

The following morning, I explained as much as I could to Jake and Jacey without sharing so much as to make them afraid or anxious.

"We have to be very careful, because some bad people may be looking for us," I said. "That means for the rest of this month, we have to stay inside. We can't go out and play. I know this will be difficult for you both, but you have to promise to help Mommy out and be good about it. Okay?"

They must have sensed my seriousness, because neither of them argued with me.

I breathed out heavily. Nineteen days to go. *God, please don't let us be found.*

Barely three days passed before I realized I needed to let someone official know what was happening. I pulled out the American embassy business card I'd received and connected with a marine guard on duty at the consulate.

"I'm an American citizen in Ukraine," I explained. "A warrant has been put out for the return of my adopted son."

He took down all my information and told me someone would call me back shortly.

Half an hour later, John Armstrong, the deputy consul general of the U.S. embassy in Kiev, called.

"I'm not sure they're going to be able to find you," he said after I'd told him my story. "But when they do find Jake, they will arrest you. I need to get some other people involved in this. Let me call you back."

Within the hour he called again.

"I need to get your information," he said. He took down my passport information, my address, the correct spelling of my name, my date of birth. "Do you have your visa so that you're legally in this country, since you've been here past the hundred and eighty days?"

"Yes."

"Okay, I'll get back with you."

The third time he called, he told me how to act once I got arrested. "If you are found, you are going to be arrested, you understand that. By law, we are able to see you within seventy-two hours of the arrest. Just hold on, because we will come. If they offer anything to eat or drink, make sure you take it. No matter how bad the water or food tastes, drink and eat if you can. Whatever sickness you can get from that is better than the alternative of not eating or drinking."

I tried to absorb everything he was saying, but I was consumed with thoughts of Jacey.

"My daughter is with me," I finally blurted out. "What happens to her once I'm arrested?"

The phone went dead silent, then he said, "You have an *American* child in Ukraine? We have no rules for that. We have *never* had an instance where a single parent had a child with her in Ukraine and then got arrested. I have to think this through," he said after a moment. "Okay, this is what has to happen. She has to know. You have to explain everything to her and she has to have a place to run. Tell her where to run and she has to stay there when you're arrested. Do you know someone who lives nearby?"

"We know a family."

"That's your plan. When they come for you, it will probably be at night. She will be disoriented. Don't let her fight them, don't let her do anything. You tell her to run to that family. Does she know how to get there?"

"Yes."

He took down her name, birth date, and passport number and then hung up.

Not long after that call, someone else contacted me. I didn't catch his name, but he sounded higher up in authority than John Armstrong.

"Kim, I'm just calling to let you know we're aware of your situation. We have checked out your details and it's true. There is a warrant out for your son. You need to stay in your apartment. If they stay at the door and don't barge in, don't invite them in. But know that they may break down the door. We have no idea how they will react in this situation. But you cannot be out in public under any circumstances, because in public they can just take him. It's better if you stay inside." He was very matter-of-fact in his explanation. "We're very sorry for what you're going through. We understand this has been a very long haul for you. This is the first time I'm hearing about this situation, but I'm glad I'm hearing about it now."

"I understand, and I appreciate any help you can give."

Just when I didn't think life could get tougher, it did.

THE BREAKING POINT

Everyone was feeling stir crazy. For two weeks, we stayed in the apartment. Isabelle and Adam would bring us things or we would go out quickly at night to the nearby convenience store in our apartment complex. We never lingered and we never stayed out for long stretches of time, and, worst of all for the kids, we never went to the playground—even the one just outside of our complex.

Our days were filled with claustrophobic, suffocating closeness in our apartment. Everyone got on everyone else's nerves. Jake's high energy had him literally bouncing off every wall. And Jacey hated her schoolwork and not having any friends around.

The nights were the longest. All night long, I listened to the elevator going up and down in the center of our building. Each time I wondered, *Is this the time they come for us?*

Around March 23, Akula called with an update about the petition we had been waiting for the judge to sign.

"He won't sign it until the court date," he told me. "He feels his signature alone will not be enough to stop the prosecutor. He wants the petition read in open court and ruled on, then signed by him and the two jurors. That makes it a much stronger document."

"That means we're still stuck here until March 30," I said, feeling resigned and frustrated. "I appreciate the thought that went behind his decision, and I get it. But not going out of the apartment, not letting my kids play in the sunshine, is making us all edgy."

"I understand, Kim, but it's best not to risk it. Stay put."

That afternoon, feeling at my limit of tolerance and sleep deprivation and having yelled at them one too many times for finding my last nerve, I told the kids to watch a DVD cartoon while I scrounged in the kitchen to fix something for us to eat. They turned the cartoon up to full volume, which drove me crazy. I chose to shut the door between the living room and kitchen. The longer the cartoon played, the happier they sounded.

I'm so sick of this! I thought. *Since Jake left the orphanage last September, I have never been asked officially to return him. And now this prosecutor thinks he has the right to file a warrant and force him back? Well, until they follow their own laws and write me a letter requesting that he be returned, I won't take him back to that place that gave him nightmares. I won't do it.*

I pulled out some food and was going to grab a pot when I saw a huge cockroach crawl across the floor.

I'd suspected cockroaches in that place—I'd lived with them before in Ukraine. But this one was fat and huge and boldly strutted across the floor in broad daylight, and I flipped out. I kicked the wall and beat the counters and shouted.

"Where are you, God? You got me here and you told me to be patient, and now...where are you?"

It was the first time I had released my building anger. I was so angry at the situation and at God. I couldn't understand why he was allowing this to happen. I couldn't control myself anymore. I slid to the floor. The agonizing months of pent-up anxiety, pain, heartache, fear, and confusion all came pouring out of me, and I lost self-control. I had tried to be obedient and patient. I'd tried to be a nice Christian woman not questioning or getting upset or blaming God. But I couldn't hold it back anymore. All my frustration spewed out of me and went directly onto God. I was gut-wrenchingly honest with him and told him everything I was feeling and how disappointed I was. I didn't edit myself or try to be proper or sweet or soft-spoken. I wanted to know where he was because I hadn't seen him for quite a while.

As I spent myself with my words, demanding to know where God was, he showed up. A calmness spread over me like a blanket and I regained my composure. I felt him whisper into my soul.

It's okay. I'm here. I have never left you. And I never told you you couldn't go outside. Take your children and go outside and play and shop. Resume your life. What are you afraid of?

All of a sudden I realized God was right; he had been there all along. I'd just chosen not to see him. I'd chosen to forget that just because I didn't see him working didn't mean he wasn't. He was there on the bus with us when the police stopped us. He was in the courtroom. He was with Jacey when she was ill. He had never left us.

I stood and took a deep breath.

Thank you, I whispered sincerely. *Please, forgive me.*

I washed my face in the kitchen sink, walked out to the kids, and turned off the DVD.

"Okay, you two, grab your coats. Come on, we're going outside to play."

"But you said we couldn't," Jacey said.

"We're going outside? Yay! Let's go!" Jake yelled and hopped off the couch.

I was done being held up in that apartment. We were going to go about our business—not flaunting ourselves, but not hiding either.

The sunshine felt wonderful, and to hear my children laughing as they played was the best gift I'd received in a long time.

MARCH 30: BACK TO IZMAIL

Jahn returned to Odessa on the twenty-ninth, a day before the trial, since he was required to be present. I had never been so excited to see him. I had missed him terribly. I wanted our time together to be worth every moment we'd spent apart. It lifted my spirits just to have him with me, flesh and blood, whom I could touch and hold and cuddle up to at night. Although I knew he would have to fly home right after the trial, I hoped the next separation would be only a few weeks. Then we would be home together, all of us, as a family.

We both were cautiously optimistic that this time around would stick and we wouldn't have to remain for another appeal. But we both knew anything was possible, and the clock was still ticking. When Jahn had returned to the United States the first time, he'd signed papers in the embassy regarding the adoption. Those signed and dated papers became a countdown. We had one year from the date of those documents to finalize the adoption. If it didn't get finalized, the documentation would be null and void and we would be required to return to the States without Jake and begin the entire process again stateside.

Neither of us could imagine that was God's will for us or for Jake, but I had finally learned to trust that God was in control and that he had us here for a reason. He would never waste anything, but all things—even this experience—would be used for his ultimate glory.

We left Jacey and Jake with Isabelle and Adam—having given Jake strict orders to behave and obey Isabelle or else—and we headed back to Izmail for what I prayed would be the last time. Svetlana joined us, insisting that she appear in court because "I want the judge to know I have seen Sasha and you together and I know he is in a good family. I want to let the judge know, too, that you took me to meet my other brother—and you didn't have to do that."

God had allowed me the opportunity to introduce all three Mazurek children to each other in February. It seemed so wrong to me that they had never met. And it felt like the least I could do if I wasn't to be so fortunate as to adopt them all.

On the drive to Izmail, Jahn said, "Oh, I almost forgot. This week I got a call from a Maxwell."

"Maxwell?" Maxwell was a friend from my theater days, before I was married. I'd recently reconnected with him and several other theater friends through Facebook and they were following my Ukraine experience. "What did he want?"

"He was in Italy on vacation and met an American there named Tom Thompson, who's a director of a small orphanage in Chisinau, Moldova. Apparently, Tom used to help with adoptions in Russia, then he worked in an orphanage here in Ukraine, before finally becoming an orphanage director in Moldova. When Maxwell learned that Moldova borders Ukraine, he told Tom about our situation. And then he put Tom on the phone—he called from Italy!"

"What?"

"Yeah, so I tried to summarize the past year for this guy, who completely got what I was telling him and the seriousness of our situation, because he's worked in these post-Soviet places with orphanages and adoptions. I told Tom about Adam and gave him Adam's contact information. He said he was going to get in touch with him. I also told him to Facebook friend you, so you might get a friend request from him."

"Okay, good to know. He may give us some good insight, which hopefully we won't need anymore after tomorrow!"

"True."

The morning of the trial, Jahn and I prayed that God's will would be done above all else, we placed the entire day in his hands, and then we headed back to the courthouse. I was concerned about the warrant, but hoped that no one would come after me since Jake wasn't with me.

It felt as though everyone I had met during this experience was at the courthouse: Katya, Inna, Dominika, Svetlana, Carl, Ilse, Boris, Akula.

We went into the courtroom and waited to begin. Our side of the gallery was filled with witnesses and supporters; no one was on the other side, not even the prosecutor.

That's odd. I wonder where he is.

Akula glanced at his watch and back over to the prosecutor's side, then he shook his head.

I could feel the tension rising as our group started to complain about the prosecutor's lateness.

Boris told me, "We can't have this trial if the prosecutor isn't here."

"You've got to be kidding me," I said, now getting flustered myself. "Jahn flew all the way from the United States. This *can't* be happening."

"I'll be right back," Akula said, rising from his seat. "I'm going to the prosecutor's office to find out what is happening."

We kept waiting and watching the clock and the door. No prosecutor. Finally Akula stepped back in with a disgusted look on his face.

"He's not here," he said. "He's not in town at all. So I told them they have to send someone to the courtroom to represent their side. The judge sent notice of this date and the prosecutor didn't ask for an exception, so somebody needs to get over here. Nobody will come."

"What does that mean?" I asked.

Akula shrugged. "It could mean nothing. It could mean the judge will postpone the hearing. It depends..."

"But where do you think the prosecutor is? He was so aggressive about this case. It doesn't make sense for him not to show up."

He shrugged again. "Maybe he went somewhere. He was cleaned up the last time we saw him here. Maybe he's on his honeymoon."

I remembered the last time I saw the prosecutor. He'd had his hair cut and looked sharp. Maybe Akula was right. And that would make sense for his level of anger toward the judge, which had spewed out on me and Jake with the warrant as... retribution?

The hearing was set to begin and the same judge from the pretrial entered and sat down.

"Where is the prosecutor?" he said, looking unsurprised by his absence.

Akula said, "He's not here, Your Honor. I've already gone over to his office and explained, but nobody wants to come over."

"Did they send a recusal slip?"

Boris began to interpret everything for me, and was actually doing a good job this time around. I looked at him and smiled. He simply nodded back.

"No, I have no record of one, Your Honor."

The judge sent a court clerk to make sure there was no request for a movement of date from the prosecutor.

The clerk returned and said, "Nothing has been filed."

The judge said, "Well, he had notice of it and he's not here. Let's proceed."

Inna and Dominika gasped audibly, clearly not anticipating this decision.

The judge ignored their outburst and moved forward, calling on each person to identify himself or herself and the connection to the case, then deciding whether or not they should remain in the courtroom.

Jahn and I could stay, along with Boris, Inna, Dominika, and Akula. Carl, Ilse, Svetlana, and Katya had to leave.

When the judge dismissed Svetlana, she stormed out. As Jake's sister she felt she had a right to remain in the room and hear everything that was going on.

"Are there no representatives here from the two Odessa district birth certificate offices, representing Sasha's and Nikolay's birthplaces?"

"No, Your Honor," Akula said. "And we received no letter from them either about their refusal to separate the boys."

"Why is that important?" I whispered to Boris.

"By them waiving their right to have a representative here, it null and voids any dissent against the separation issue."

"So by them not showing up—"

"It's a good thing. It takes care of the loophole the prosecutor was using about them not wanting to separate the boys."

"Oh." One challenge down.

With most of the room now cleared, the judge called each person forward to testify. And each question seemed long and drawn out, with follow-up question after follow-up question.

"He's certainly being thorough, isn't he?" Jahn whispered.

"He doesn't want to give any opportunity for the prosecutor to come back and argue against the way he did things," Boris explained.

Inna's testimony went by. Dominika's testimony was next. Everything seemed to be proceeding as it should.

The judge allowed Svetlana back into the room to tell her story. She had calmed down and seemed pleased that they were allowing her to give her testimony and share what she'd seen and experienced with our family. I was so proud of the way she handled herself during the questioning, and I was glad they'd given her the opportunity to speak, since it was important to her.

Akula came next. He brought with him a photo of our family all dressed in matching long-sleeved blue shirts and smiling for the camera. He presented it proudly to the judge and the two jurists.

"This is a family," he said, pointing to the photo. "Look, they are a family." He wanted it introduced as evidence to have it added to our court file. He was very insistent that they look at it and include it in the case.

As the judge and jurists passed it among themselves, I could see them smile and nod slightly. One of the jurists even looked at me and winked.

They approved! It seemed obvious they liked what they saw.

"If it please the court," Akula said next. "Kimberly de Blecourt would like to speak."

The judge, who had been taking notes throughout the course of the trial, barely glanced up but gave a quick nod.

Akula turned and motioned for me to begin.

I took a deep breath and rose.

"Your Honor. This child is a wonder. Since I have known him, I have discovered such an amazing little person, filled with potential and joy and love. He deserves a chance at a full life with a family that loves him, that longs to be part of his world.

"This is a child who nobody wanted. His mother abandoned him at birth. His father is unknown. He has no extended family who can raise him and care for him. None of his countrymen will adopt him. But I'm here. I will love him. I will be his mother."

The judge stopped writing and began to listen intently.

"My stay here over the last year has proven my commitment to this boy. I love this child. And he has grown to love me. I believe with everything within me that I have been called to be his mother.

"My husband and I want this child in our family. And we're so committed to him that if his brother's adoption with the other American family falls through, we will adopt him too. I will come back to Ukraine to adopt him. I will go through all of this all over again, because these children deserve to be loved and part of a family. They have value and worth. My family is pleading with you to approve our adoption request once and for all. Please, allow us to go home."

I paused, then slowly sat back down. I had pled our case the best I could.

I squeezed Jahn's hand. He glanced at me and smiled.

"Nice job," he said softly.

Thank you, God.

It was a longer trial than any of the other ones because of how extensively the judge went through each piece of evidence and testimony. But the longer it went, the better I felt. The prosecutor wasn't there to argue against anything, and the judge was clearly making sure there would be no grounds for appeal.

By the end of the hearing, we were escorted out of the room to wait on the judge's and jurists' decision.

"If the length of that hearing is any indication, we may be out here waiting for quite a while," I said to Jahn. So we found some seats and settled in.

Less than fifteen minutes later, though, the door opened and the clerk told us they were ready for us. Everyone looked at one another wide-eyed and surprised. This was the shortest wait we'd had.

I started to get nervous. Was that a good sign? I was sure they liked us and were on our side, but had I been mistaken? Would they decide to put it off until the prosecutor could be there?

We walked in and took the same seats.

The judge looked at Jahn and me and said, "This court finds for Jahn and Kimberly de Blecourt. The adoption is cleared to go through on all counts with the blessing of this court and Ukraine."

He continued, "I want to apologize to you on behalf of Ukraine for any troubles you may have incurred. And I want to make it very clear that my office will personally oversee that every border control office and every police station throughout the country of Ukraine will receive notice that the warrant for Jake's return has been rescinded."

God showed up once again.

♦

"Okay, Akula, what now?" As soon as the hearing was over I started to grill him.

"You still have to wait the ten days for an appeal motion to be filed, if one will be filed."

"The prosecutor didn't show up, so can he still appeal?"

"Yes, he can still appeal even though he wasn't here. I don't know on what grounds he could appeal, but yes, technically, he can."

I knew the prosecutor well enough to know we couldn't rest easy. We weren't home free yet.

Now the real wait began...again. Ten days watching the clock tick by, waiting to hear word one way or the other. I looked at Jahn.

"God brought us this far," he said matter-of-factly. "He'll see it through until we're all together in America."

"Yes, I believe he will," I said.

15

April 2010

TEN-DAY COUNTDOWN

Easter was fast approaching and we had so much to celebrate: our deliverance in more than one way and our Savior's resurrection. It was the first holiday nobody had to entice me to be excited over. Jahn, the kids, and I went to a large grocery store in Odessa and bought food for Easter dinner, a traditional Ukrainian Easter cake, and plenty of eggs to decorate. Fortunately, preparing for Easter helped pass the time while we waited to hear about the possible appeal.

Jahn packed and headed home. I hated to see him leave—mostly, I hated that he was leaving without us. But we both knew that God was taking care of the details and we would see each other soon, preferably that month. The prosecutor had four more days to file his notice of appeal, and we continued to pray that God's will would be done in the process.

I received a Facebook friend request from Tom Thompson, who had met my friend Maxwell in Italy. He mentioned he'd also connected with Adam, and asked that we keep him apprised of our situation and that he would be willing to help in any way he could. Although I appreciated his offer, I wasn't sure how he would be able to help. So I tucked away his name and continued with my day-to-day business of waiting.

With each day that passed, either I contacted Akula or he contacted me for updates—and each day it remained quiet on the Izmail prosecutor front. I boldly prayed for the prosecutor's hands and feet to be bound and that no appeal would be filed. Yet I still had moments of insomnia when I would lie awake with my mind racing.

Svetlana moved with a friend into a new apartment and wanted us to visit. I readily agreed, knowing it would mean so much to her, but would also take my mind off the prosecutor and his intentions. I did my best to appear calm to everyone, yet I kept wondering, *Are we finally going home?*

We had a wonderful visit with the girls, although I noticed Svetlana's cough persisted, and I begged her to get it checked out.

"I will, I will," she said, I think mostly to make me stop nagging her about it.

Before we left, Svetlana asked if she could see us again before we left.

"Of course!"

Of everyone in Ukraine I was going to miss, she would be the one I knew I would miss most. I had grown to love her as my own.

◆

Day ten arrived—a Friday. That evening, I phoned Akula to see if he'd heard anything through the Ukrainian grapevine.

"Nobody has even seen him. He hasn't been to his office. No word. No sign. Nothing."

"Good," I said. "Let's pray it stays that way."

"You will need to come back to Izmail Monday morning to pick up the official decree and documentation, and then you can begin the process of securing Sasha's birth certificate and passport."

"You don't have to tell me that twice!" I laughed. I felt giddy, but a sense of disbelief fell over me. After everything that had happened, it was hard to imagine we were about to start the final process to bring Jake home.

COMMEMORATING THE DEAD

My entire goal now became to make as many connections as I could to get us processed through the system and home as quickly as possible.

Because of Andrei's lawsuit, I hoped the birth certificate office wasn't going to give me a hassle with Jake's document, so I put that concern out of my mind.

Next, I contacted the American embassy's Adoption Unit in Kiev and forwarded everything they would need to get Jake's passport work started—a passport photo, an initial copy of the adoption decree, and other information. That meant that instead of a two-day appointment at the embassy, we would only need to be there for one day.

Now I had to consider the problem with Jake's passport. The government printer still hadn't been paid for their work, so the holdup on passports was an ongoing problem. I had heard of other American adoptive parents who were finding ways to get old red-covered passports, so I decided to check that out with the Odessa passport office.

Boris went with me to talk with the woman in charge there. When she heard our situation, she said bluntly, "We have not had those red-covered passports for five years. As far as I know they are not available anywhere in Ukraine, and I *know* they're not available here."

She could not give us any further information, so we left.

"We have to find somebody who has a connection to get one of the red passports," Boris told me.

"I don't know," I said. "If she says they don't have any, they don't have any. Maybe some other district has one."

I wonder how God's going to clear this passport mess.

During that weekend of running around trying to work ahead to get things ready to leave, I heard news of an American mom who returned her adopted son to Russia. She put the seven-year-old on a plane by himself back to Moscow with a note that said he was violent, had psychopathic tendencies, and she no longer wished to parent him. I couldn't imagine making that decision. Here I was getting ready to take my son home with us, not leaving him alone for barely a moment, and this mom put her child on a plane alone with a note. But I also understood her frustration somewhat, especially her feeling of having been lied to. I prayed for them both that night.

On Sunday morning Jacey, Jake, and I took a bus to Izmail and spent the day and night with Carl and Ilse. It was a relaxing, joy-filled time. But it was bittersweet. They had become dear friends, my lifeline in so many ways, and I was going to miss them. They would remain in Ukraine for another year before their term with the Peace Corps was finished and they would return home. I thanked God again for providing good friends I could trust.

"You know, Kim," Ilse told me that evening, "you have a different relationship with God. Through this entire experience, you've never wavered in your faith in him. I can't imagine going through what you've had to endure, but I've been moved by watching you."

I was touched by her words and didn't know what to say. Finally, I just hugged her. "Thank you, Ilse. You're a dear friend. God has been so good to me by sending you and Carl into my life. I couldn't have survived this without you two."

◆

Bright and early the next morning, our whole gang went to Akula's office, excited that we were going to pick up the official decree. He still hadn't seen the prosecutor and wasn't sure where he was, so he recommended that he go to the courthouse and pick up the decree himself while the kids and I hang out in his office.

Behind his office building we found a dilapidated swing set and teeter-totter, so I took Jake and Jacey out to play. When Akula returned, he found me there and motioned me back up to his office. I could tell by his expression he was tense.

"What's going on?"

"Well, the decree is finalized and uncontested, and the judge has signed it, along with one of the jurists. But...you understand this is second Easter, right?"

In Ukraine they have Easter, but then the following week they celebrate second Easter. I wasn't sure what that had to do with our situation.

"On second Easter, or *Providna*, you eat a meal with your dead relatives at their gravestone. It's tradition." He paused, apparently so I could take it all in.

"And?"

"The other jurist is away visiting the little village in which he was born. He is having a meal with his parents."

"His...*dead* parents?"

"Yes. It means we cannot pick up the decree today because he must sign it and he is not here."

"You have to get him in here."

"He will be back tomorrow. We will pick it up then."

"You don't understand. We need to get this decree; we need to get out of here!"

"It will be okay," he assured me. "Don't worry. We will get it tomorrow."

On Tuesday, we returned to Akula's office bright and early and repeated the same procedure: we waited while Akula walked to the courthouse to retrieve the decree. Again he returned empty-handed. This time instead of looking tense, he looked surprised.

"The jurist isn't back yet," he announced.

I felt my anger bubble up. I called Boris.

"What's going on here, Boris?" I told him what was happening.

"What? You don't have the decree yet? I thought you were back in Odessa. I thought you were calling me to go with you to the birth certificate office. Put Akula on the phone."

I handed the phone to Akula and listened to him speak rapidly in Ukrainian, of which I didn't understand much. All I knew was that the conversation was heated. I could hear Boris yelling over the phone and Akula spitting words back. Finally, Akula handed me the phone and walked out of the room.

"Boris?" I wasn't sure if he was still on the line or had hung up.

"I told him you will gladly pay for a taxi to go out to the village, pick up the jurist, and bring him back in so he can sign that decree. He can then either take it as a free taxi ride or you will pay to return him to the village if he needs to finish his feasting. And you agree to this, right?"

"Yes."

"You make sure Akula does it."

"Okay, yeah, good, Boris." I hung up and found Akula and said, "So are we going to call that taxi?"

"We don't need to do this! He's going to be back."

"Akula, I'm agreeing with Boris on this one. Call a taxi. You know where he is; you told me the name of the town. Send it out there. Get him in here to sign this decree. I want to be in Odessa before the birth certificate office closes *tonight*."

"Okay," he said, but I could tell he wasn't happy about it. He walked out of the conference room and closed the door behind him.

I walked to the conference table, sat down, and began to smack my head over and over against the table out of sheer frustration.

"Mom, what are you doing?" Jacey ran to my side. "Stop that, Mom!"

"I'm okay, I'm just *really* frustrated." I stopped and looked at her. The image of me hitting my head repeatedly caused us to start laughing at how ridiculous it was.

An hour and a half later, Akula came back into the conference room. "The jurist is here. He just arrived at the courthouse."

By 2 p.m. we had the signed decree. March 30, 2010, was listed as the official adoption day. Jake was now legally ours—again.

◆

Although I knew we had little chance of making it back to Odessa before 5 p.m. when the birth certificate office closed, I decided to try anyway. I hired a cab, we said our goodbyes, and we were on our way.

Somewhere between Izmail and Odessa, we hit a terrible traffic jam, in which we just sat. It felt more like we were in a parking lot.

Finally, I told the driver, "It's okay, we're not going to make it. Just drop us off at our flat." I gave him the address.

It took us more than six hours to get back to Odessa.

That night, I started to pack slowly. I went through our belongings and made decisions about what we were going to take home and what we were going to leave behind.

I called Isabelle to let her know we were going to give her and her kids some things, and then I filled her in on all that had transpired.

"We've got the decree, but the prosecutor may try to stop us again at the birth certificate office tomorrow. Isabelle," I said hesitantly—I hated putting this request on her—"you may have to clean up some stuff in this apartment. I have a feeling that we may have to leave in a hurry. I can't explain it, I just have a nagging feeling about it."

"I understand. What do you want me to do with all the leftover stuff?"

We briefly discussed what should go to whom. After I hung up with Isabelle, I called Svetlana and arranged to visit her the next day to say goodbye.

Later that evening, Boris called me.

"Kim." He sounded weary. "I just found out the prosecutor has reappeared and he has checked out your file from the courthouse."

"I wish I could say I'm surprised."

The clock started ticking loudly again.

ANOTHER APPEAL THREAT

On Wednesday morning, I met Bogdan, Mike's interpreter, at the birth certificate office. Boris was unable to make it because he was with another family. So I hired Bogdan. Boris's wife, Vladlena, wanted to help out, so she met us there as well.

When we walked into the office, we discovered that the woman behind the desk was a temporary worker. Bogdan explained the situation.

"I know who you are," she said, looking directly at me. "Your prosecutor has called. He says he's going to file an appeal."

"No, he can't. The ten days have passed. He missed the deadline and didn't file his letter."

"Well, he said he was filing. So we have to wait to see if it will be accepted."

"What?"

Vladlena spoke up. "She's right. The courthouse can still decide to accept it—even if it's late."

"Wait a minute. Nobody ever told me that could be a possibility! What's the whole ten-day thing for if he can just waltz in and file whenever he feels like it?" I was so angry I was shaking. I looked at the clerk. "So you're telling us you aren't going to give us Sasha's birth certificate?"

"Right."

"Okay, look, I need to get out of here for a while," I said. "I'm going to go meet Svetlana."

"Let's all take a break and meet back here at 1:30," Vladlena suggested.

I picked up Svetlana and took her shopping, all the while trying to remain cool, but Svetlana kept looking at me suspiciously.

"Is something wrong?"

"I think this may be the last time I see you. I may be able to get Jake out of the country and take him home with me, but I'm still not sure yet. And I have to be back at the birth certificate office by 1:30."

She glanced at her watch. "You should probably get going."

"Yes." I hugged her tightly and held on for a few moments. "I hate leaving you here."

"Thank you for buying all this stuff for my new apartment. I really appreciate it."

"It's my pleasure, Svetlana. You just make sure you take care of yourself, okay? And get that cough checked out!"

"I will! I promise. Bye!"

I started to walk away and turned for one last look. I waved. I wanted to remember her beautiful face and lovely eyes. She was so happy, and she smiled brightly at me. Then I turned and left. I wondered if I would ever see her again.

I met the others at the office and tried to talk to the clerk again. She still wouldn't process the new birth certificate. So we let her know we weren't leaving until she helped us.

"Listen," she said, "I'm just a temp here right now. I found out this morning I didn't get this job. Someone else got it and is scheduled to start Monday. Plus, I'm pregnant and I have a doctor's appointment this afternoon, so I'm closing the office early. I really don't know what to do about your situation. I have to see if the prosecutor from Izmail is going to fax what he says he has. I told him it has to be officially stamped by the court. I will give you your new birth certificate tomorrow morning. Just come back here and if there's nothing on the fax machine, I will take care of it. You come a little early and I'll take care of you first."

I could tell she was trying to be nice, but we were all beside ourselves.

"So that's that. No birth certificate, and possibly another appeal. What *is* it with that guy?" I walked out of the office. "Okay, so I guess we meet here tomorrow morning and pray he doesn't fax anything over."

◆

After another night of no sleep, I had trouble functioning Thursday morning. I tried to get the kids dressed and fed, but everything was going wrong, and I just couldn't force myself to move faster. But before I left the flat, I grabbed a gift for the clerk I had set aside for her the previous night: a Russian-English Bible for children. Akula had told me before that Ukrainians love to have their books inscribed, so I wrote, "To your precious unborn child. This is my gift to you. May you both be blessed."

Adam joined me, and by the time we arrived at the birth certificate office, we were five minutes past its opening. Bogdan was already there.

"Is there a fax?" I said.

"No fax," Bogdan said. "She's putting together Jacob's new birth certificate now."

She brought everything over to us, then stopped and thought for a moment. "Let me give you a certificate of adoption as well, so there's no question that this is everything."

She pushed everything over to us to inspect. Bogdan read through it all and didn't find any problems. So we paid her, and before we left, I pulled out the little Bible and asked Bogdan to tell the woman how sorry I was for upsetting her the previous day and this was my gift of thanks. I opened the front cover and asked him to read the inscription to her as well.

As Bogdan translated my words to her, she started to cry.

"Thank you," she said and held the Bible tenderly against her.

Thank you, God, for impressing this last-minute thought on my heart.

GOD'S HAND MOVES SWIFTLY

Bogdan, Vladlena, Adam, and I left the birth certificate office and now were on a timed paper chase. We had to run with the birth certificate to get Jake's new tax identification number. We arrived at that office just as the woman we needed to talk to was walking out to her car for an early lunch.

Fortunately, Vladlena knew her and hopped out of Adam's van with the envelope of documents. She talked with her for a few moments and presented the envelope to the woman, who took it and told her she would take care of everything after she returned from lunch. We would need to return after that.

Vladlena got back into the van, and while we were deciding what to do for lunch, I received a call from Mikhail, Nikolay's adoptive parents' facilitator. I had reached out to him earlier during my time in Ukraine, but he was unable to help me because he felt it would be a conflict of interest. I wondered why he was calling me now.

"Kim, I understand you got your birth certificate." *Here we go again with information in this country!*

"How did you know that?"

"Never mind. Listen, I feel bad for what has transpired and that I was unable to help you more. I can help you now, but I don't know if you have the money, because I know you are broke. But I want to make this available to you. Do you want a red passport?"

I didn't fully grasp what he was asking. "I'm sorry, what?"

"I have connections there in Odessa. I can get you a red passport."

"When?"

"You can have it later this afternoon, if you'd like."

I mentally processed his statement. The wait to get a blue passport was ten to twelve days—and that was *if* you could get it because the country was still having printer problems.

"Yes! Thank you, Mikhail."

I turned to Adam. "You're not going to believe this. God just cleared up the passport problem." By 4 p.m., we had Jake's passport and his new tax identification number.

"I can't believe it. I've never seen anything like this before," he said. Then suddenly he stopped and looked at me wide-eyed. "Kim, you have to pack! We can get you tickets for the train to take you to Kiev tonight. You'll get there in the morning and can go straight to the embassy, get Jake's health checkup and his visa, and you can leave tomorrow night for the States."

I couldn't believe what had just happened. In less than twenty-four hours, I had Jake's new birth certificate, new tax ID number, and Ukrainian passport.

"When God's ready for you to leave, he parts the waters!" I said and laughed as we started to run.

IN KIEV

Adam and I stopped at the train station to purchase tickets for the overnight train to Kiev and discovered that the train wouldn't be running that night because they would be working on the tracks.

The only train going to Kiev was leaving at 8 p.m.—leaving less than two hours for me to pack up everything, say our goodbyes, and be on our way.

Adam dropped me off at my building and went to his apartment to get the kids. Soon Jacey and Jake were back and excited, along with the entire Lincoln clan. Adam grabbed the suitcases and took them to his van, with all of us following behind.

At the train station, a crowd was already bustling around, getting situated in their cabins. Adam helped carry our luggage onto the train and into our first-class cabin.

"Here." Isabelle pushed a bag into my hands. "This will take care of you." I glanced inside. She had packed food for our supper, a snack, and breakfast.

"Oh, Isabelle, thank you for this."

Isabelle gave a tight-lipped smile and her lower lip started to quiver. Then she started to cry.

The conductor's voice came over the loudspeaker announcing the train would soon be pulling away from the station.

"Well, we should go," Adam said. We all hugged goodbye.

Isabelle hugged us too, but couldn't say anything anymore.

Boom, boom, boom! We all jumped.

Outside, Boris was banging on our window and held up his finger to say, "Wait!" Then he disappeared. The next thing I knew he was standing at our door inside the train.

"Boris!"

He threw his arms around me. "I am so happy!" He pulled back from me, and I could see tears in his eyes. "I am so happy for you!"

"I thought you were out of town with another family."

"I just got back! I wasn't going to miss saying goodbye to you!"

He hugged the kids and kept saying, "I'm so happy, I'm so happy!"

Finally, the conductor made another announcement.

Boris said, "I must go—or else I'll end up going to Kiev with you!" He laughed. "You are a good family. You will have a good life, Sasha." And with that he left.

◆

The next morning, we arrived in Kiev. The sky was heavily overcast and gritty-looking. We got off the train wielding our luggage and met up with Alla again.

"Hello!" she said in perfect English, grabbing one of the suitcases. "Follow me."

When we got to her friend's car, I stopped short. It was an economy-sized car.

Three adults, two kids, and four suitcases. Her friend's eyes opened wide when he saw us coming. He walked to the trunk and opened it.

"We'll squeeze it all in somehow," Alla said. I could tell she didn't believe her own words. "Let's go to our flat first so we can drop off all your bags, then we can head over to the American embassy."

We arrived at her parents' flat and struggled to get all our luggage to their door.

"I love your apartment," Jacey said, remembering our previous visit so many months before.

"Thank you."

Alla's mother came into the room to greet us. Alla said, "Mom, I have another quick appointment I have to run to. Would you be able to escort Kim to the American embassy?"

"Of course."

"That's okay, Alla," I said. "We can make it there."

She shook her head immediately. "No. I don't want you to be alone here."

"Ah," I said, understanding her concern. "You know about the prosecutor checking out our file."

"Yes. We just need to make sure he doesn't try anything and that we have you covered in case you need to get away quickly. Boris and I think his strategy will be to try to stop you at border control, because that's the last thing he can do."

That made sense. The prosecutor could put out word to border control that we couldn't leave because another appeal had been filed.

"Who knows what connections he has here," Alla continued. "We need to keep you all safe."

FINAL PROCESSING

We arrived at the American embassy a half hour before it officially opened. We were hoping to be first in line, but discovered several other people ahead of us for visas and other issues. We were the only ones awaiting an adoption. Once the embassy opened, we waited another half hour or so for a doctor to give Jake a health checkup. The doctor cleared Jake's way for a U.S. visa.

After I paid for Jake's medical exam, the clerk informed me that we had to go back to the visa area to fill out more paperwork and have a final interview. Since we knew it would be a little while before the medical work was processed and submitted over there, we decided to take an early lunch and then go back to the flat to drop off Alla's mom, meet Alla, and pick up our luggage.

After lunch, we arrived at the visa office, signed in, and waited among several other adoptive families and their facilitators. By this time, Alla had returned and joined us in the waiting room.

Another clerk called my name and escorted me to a little room with a window between us.

"So you're adopting Jacob?" the woman asked.

"Yes."

"It looks like all your paperwork and everything is here." She passed me a clipboard and said, "Fill out these papers. When Jacob's visa is complete, the duty officer will call you."

I returned to the waiting area and found a quiet place to sit. Jacey and Jake were around the corner in a children's waiting area playing with the toys and games the embassy had provided.

As I worked my way through the paperwork, I saw Jahn's signature at the bottom of several of the forms. He had signed and dated these when he left Ukraine the first time, nine months earlier: July 17, 2009. It was surreal as I signed my name below his.

We thought we'd waited a long time in July!

I turned in the paperwork and went back to my seat. There was a couple with their young adopted daughter about Jacey's age and their facilitator sitting against one wall, and a family with several children and a facilitator across from them. I sat alone, since Alla had stayed with the kids in the other room. Everyone made polite small talk ("Where did you get your child?" "How old?" "Do you have other children?"), and then the facilitator with the larger family looked at me and said, "So who was your facilitator?"

"Boris Romanov."

He froze. "Izmail?"

"Yes."

He spoke slowly, incredulously. "Are you the American woman who's been here since last year?"

Everyone fell silent and stared at me.

"Uh-huh."

"I can't believe I'm meeting you."

I guess our adoption had become even more well-known than I had imagined.

The clerk called my name and I followed her to a window with a speaker. She swore me in as Jake's adoptive parent, that I would care for him and act on his best behalf. Then she handed me Jake's Ukrainian passport with his U.S. visa pasted inside, along with a sealed envelope that had all of his immigration paperwork. She informed me that I was not to open the envelope under any circumstances and that once I arrived at the first U.S. airport we touched down in, I was to take the envelope to their immigration office and hand it over to them.

I thanked her and excitedly went out to the waiting room to get Jake and Jacey so that we could leave. By now it was about 3:30, so we headed to the airport, which took us about forty-five minutes, because we hit the beginning of rush-hour traffic and the airport was on the outskirts of the city.

As we passed monuments and landmarks, I silently said goodbye to Kiev and Ukraine. *I'm going home.*

EYJAFJALLAJÖKULL

On the way to the airport, we decided the driver would drop me off so I could get our boarding passes, and Jake and Jacey would stay with Alla in the car.

As we neared the airport entrance, I noticed something seemed wrong. Cars were backed up along the side of the road. We wound our way until we got to the main entrance, and I saw people loitering everywhere. Suitcases were piled on top of one another like pancakes, making giant towers.

What in the world? I thought. "What's going on?"

Alla looked worried. "I don't know, but you need to get inside and get your tickets. It's almost 4:30. Then come back out and get us."

I walked through the entrance and could barely find a place to step. Every bench or chair was taken, and people were standing or sitting over every inch of the floor. Some gathered in a circle playing cards. I saw one group drinking from a bottle of vodka; others were reading or sleeping, or were crying and on the phone having frustrated conversations. It was like a giant human circus.

Toward the center of the lobby, I saw two televisions elevated above the crowd with a large throng gathered around them. A small band of people was winding their way toward the TVs, so I followed them.

I remembered that a Polish air force plane had crashed in Russia earlier that week, killing everyone on board. Many people from high up in the government were on that plane, including the Polish president and his wife, the former president, military officers, and fifteen members of the Polish parliament.

Perhaps all the people in the airport were headed to the funeral and the television had already begun funeral coverage, I assumed. Since Kiev is the capital of Ukraine, a neighbor of Poland, perhaps these people either had family there or were officials going to pay their respects.

I got close enough to the televisions to see that all of them were showing photos of a smoking, billowing volcano. One of the stations had closed captioning in English running across the bottom of the screen. A volcano, Eyjafjallajökull, had erupted in Iceland. The ash and smoke were causing all planes to be grounded across Europe, including in Kiev.

"*You have got to be kidding me!*" I said too loudly in English.

The crowd around me all turned and stared.

I stood in disbelief for a few moments until it hit me: *Departures. Where are the departures?* I frantically scanned the room looking for the departures screens, and, finding them on the other side of the televisions, I started rushing through the crowd, this time like a football player trying to make it to the end zone.

Cancelled.

Cancelled.

Cancelled.

The same word sat next to each flight number all the way down the screens. Only three flights were delayed—one of them was ours.

I have to get Alla, I realized.

It took more than five minutes to get back to the front entrance, since I had to get back through the crowds.

I cannot believe this is happening, God. Seriously, I don't understand.

I finally got outside and couldn't find the car. I had forgotten to note where they'd let me off and couldn't remember what the car even looked like, other than that it was small.

"Kim!" Alla yelled out of the car while the driver honked.

I ran over and explained the situation.

Alla was incredulous and nervous. "Okay, let's get everyone into the airport. I'll stay with the kids and the luggage, and you go to the ticket counter and find out what's going on."

We pulled out all the luggage and began slowly to carry it into the airport.

God, please open a space for us, I silently prayed.

Off in a corner I noticed an empty space, so I yelled to Alla and we headed that way. Then I went to the ticket counter to see about the status of our delayed flight.

At the counter the flight board said our flight was delayed until 8:30. I handed the KLM employee my reservation sheet.

"I'm sorry, we're not ticketing for that flight."

"But it says it's delayed."

"Yes, but I don't think it's going to fly today."

I manuevered back to our seats.

"Did you get the tickets?" Alla said.

"No, the woman said they weren't giving any tickets, because the flight probably wasn't going to go today."

"But it says delayed, not cancelled. They have to give you your tickets."

"I'm just telling you what she told me."

She looked at me as though I'd probably gotten something wrong in the translation. "Give me the reservation sheet and I'll check into it."

Off she went.

"Alla, is everything okay?" I said when she returned more than an hour later.

"No. They're listing it as delayed, which means you have to stay here, but the woman told me the flight isn't leaving tonight. If they cancel it, several other flights were cancelled before yours, which means those people get priority on seats and you will have to stand by. You're lucky, though: your flight hasn't been cancelled, only de-layed, so you may not have to be in the standby group."

"What do we do?"

"I don't know. I need to call Boris." She pulled out her phone and turned away from me. I could tell she hadn't told me the whole sit-uation. She turned back to me and held out the phone. "Boris wants to talk to you."

"What are you doing? You have to get that boy out of the coun-try!" he said.

"Boris, what am I supposed to do? They've shut down air traffic. I don't have control over a volcano!"

"Kim, I can tell you this. You cannot be in the country come eight o'clock Monday morning, do you understand?"

"Clearly!"

"Okay, okay, we will just wait. Don't do anything, Kim."

I told Alla to go home. I knew she probably had other plans and we would be safe enough staying in the airport. But she refused.

"I promised Boris I wouldn't leave, and I won't."

At 8:30, the time on the departure board changed to "delayed to 10:30."

I groaned. I was exhausted by the stress and by trying to keep the kids entertained. Tempers flared and lots of bad behavior was on display among the passengers, so I tried to shield my kids by having them pull out the DVD player and watch movies. One woman in particular caught my attention. She held a beautiful white wedding gown in a see-through garment bag and cried while a young man sat beside her trying to console her. We were all trying desperately to get out of Kiev and go someplace else, and we were all stuck against our will.

By ten o'clock, I knew we weren't going anywhere, so I suggested that we try to find a hotel room. I knew it would probably be impossible since most of the people in the airport had taken their luggage and headed out.

At 10:30, the departures board announced that the flight was delayed until 1:15 the following day, Saturday, so Alla said we were to stay with her family at their flat.

When we arrived, her mother met us with little sandwiches and hot tea. The smell of baking cakes filled the flat. But I wasn't hungry. I realized I hadn't bathed for three days. I just wanted to take a shower and lie down—although I knew sleep would not be my companion again that night.

I stood in their wonderful, clean shower with hot water beating down on me and I tried to cry. I wanted to release all the pent-up frustration and fear. But no tears came.

I put on a clean set of clothes that I would sleep in and wear the next day, then headed to the kitchen for a hot cup of tea. I gathered up Jacey and Jake and got them bathed and put in bed. They fell asleep right away, while I lay wide awake.

As I listened to the children's steady breathing and laid staring at the ceiling, a song from one of the *VeggieTales* videos that the kids had watched in the airport popped into my mind. The song was from the scene when Daniel was in the lions' den and an angel appeared. With a pure, sweet voice the angel sang, "Don't cry, Daniel. Fear not, Daniel. You are not alone. There is one who is watching you . . ."

As I replayed that song with the angel singing, my breathing slowed and I felt a sense of peace wash over me. I finally fell asleep for a few hours.

RETURN TO ODESSA

I awoke after four hours of solid sleep and began talking to God. I poured out my fears and doubts. Although I knew he had brought us so far and had kept us safe, I was still scared that somehow I wasn't going to get Jake out of the country.

I know you're going to show up in a big way. I want to believe that, but I just can't see how. They're predicting flights are going to be grounded for at least a couple of days. How are we going to fly home? I've already paid for the tickets. Our money for tickets is gone.

At eleven o'clock, Alla's father took Alla and us to the airport.

One o'clock came and went and the flight was bumped to 5:30, but still not cancelled. Then it was bumped to 8:30, then to 10:30.

At ten o'clock Saturday night, after a long day spent in the airport with the potential of spending another full day there on Sunday, I called Adam and explained the situation.

"At 10:30, I know they're going to delay it again until tomorrow," I told him. "I don't think that plane is going to fly. The BBC channel here at the airport is saying that twenty countries have closed their airspace and they don't know when flights are going to start up again. I feel like I'm waiting too long. Can you think of anything we can do?"

"Kim, we know Jake can't be on this side of the border come Monday morning, so we're going to have to drive you over the border and not fly you. If the plane doesn't fly at 10:30 tonight, you need to catch the overnight train back to Odessa—"

"That's the prosecutor's oblast, Adam. I can't take him back there."

"Listen, we have to do this. I will find a driver, and if I can't find one, *I* will drive you over the border. You have to get across that border Sunday. We can't wait for the planes."

I sighed heavily. "Okay. But all of our money is tied up in those airline tickets."

"If the flight doesn't go tonight, you have Alla get in writing from the airline that the flight was cancelled. Expedia will get you your money back."

At 10:30, just as I predicted, the flight was delayed to 1:15 Sunday afternoon. I told Alla to do as Adam suggested.

"I don't know if this is the right thing to do, Kim. Boris is going to be mad at me."

"I'll deal with Boris," I told her. "We just need to get out of here."

We got the letter written and signed by the airline employee, then Alla's dad arrived and rushed us to the train station. We purchased our tickets and boarded, securing some of the last first-class spots, and within minutes the train pulled out of the station.

Because we had rushed so much and all the adults were anxious, the kids picked up on that and became upset, whiny, and agitated, plus they were hungry because we hadn't eaten in a long time. But I had no food; all I had was water.

"I don't have any snacks for us, so let's just drink some water and try to go to sleep," I said, trying to make the best of the situation. "But guess what? You don't have to brush your teeth tonight! How about that? And tomorrow we're going on an adventure!"

I tried to pull myself out of the worry and focus on mothering my children.

About an hour into the train ride, Adam called with the news that he had found a driver willing to take us across the border.

"His name is Sasha. He is a Christian, and a good husband and father. We will pick you up at the train station and he will drive you into Moldova at the border crossing between Odessa and Izmail."

I wasn't happy about this news. I didn't know this man, didn't

know how well Adam even knew this man, and wondered how trust-
worthy he would be.

"Kim, when you meet him, you are going to feel safe with him. I
promise."

I gritted my teeth, but said okay.

◆

The next morning as we pulled into the station, Adam and another
man, who I assumed was Sasha, spotted us in the windows. Adam
waved. I caught only a quick glimpse of the other man, but he was
large and muscular. As soon as the train stopped, they boarded and
met us at our cabin to help us collect our luggage.

"Kim, I want you to meet Sasha," Adam said.

My neck bent backward as I looked up at this very tall man. He
was thirtysomething, slim and blond, with a crew cut. His steely
blue eyes frightened me at first, but then he smiled briefly, which
made him look pleasant and gentler, and put me at ease. As soon
as his smile faded, however, his jaw muscles clenched and he looked
scary and overly serious.

He reminds me a little of that Russian Ivan Drago—Dolph Lundgren—
who boxed Rocky Balboa, I thought.

He stuck out his hand for me to shake. "Hello," he said in a
friendly voice. "I take you across border today."

He greeted Jacey and then gently rested his broad hands on Jake's
shoulders. At that moment, I knew my friends had chosen wisely.
I could trust Sasha. I was betting my life and, more important, the
lives of my children on it.

We piled everything into Sasha's gray sedan, which was only
slightly larger than Alla's friend's economy-sized vehicle, and headed
toward Adam and Isabelle's flat to drop Adam off. On the way, Adam
let us know that Isabelle was baking some breakfast and snack items
for us to eat on the way.

"Also, I spoke with Tom Thompson last night. He's offered for you to stay with him at the orphanage until you can catch a flight home. So Sasha is going to drive you to Chisinau to meet Tom."

A little tingle passed over me. God had paved the way for our escape by having Maxwell go to Italy and meet Tom there and then introduce Tom to Jahn and me. God knew the kids and I would need a safe place to stay when we left Ukraine.

While Adam went to his apartment to grab the food, Sasha suggested that we run into the convenience store to pick up extra water and anything else we might need because he didn't want to stop during the drive. We had a long way to go that day to get to Chisinau, the capital city of Moldova, about a four- to five-hour drive from Odessa—if we didn't have any trouble passing through border control.

THE ARREST

I knew this road well, as I took it every time I went between Odessa and Izmail. A part of Moldova juts into Ukraine and across the only main highway between the two cities. So with each trip, I entered and quickly left Moldova. But this time we would turn onto a different road, go through border control, and remain in Moldova.

My mind raced in a thousand different directions, mostly playing out worst-case scenarios of the prosecutor paying someone at the border control to take Jake from me. Sasha tried to keep up with some light conversation, I assume to take my mind off what we were facing, or maybe to take his own mind off it. I didn't respond; I couldn't. I no longer had it in me to make small talk. I just wanted out of this country and the nightmare that had become my life.

He told me his story of coming to faith in Jesus, that he had been a Christian for eighteen years. He told me about his wife and children. And then he said, "I am a competitive kick-boxer. I have won many awards. Today was another competition that I gave up so I could drive you across the border."

That got my attention.

"Oh, I'm sorry. It was a kickboxing competition?"

"No, today was the knife-fighting competition."

"How do you have a knife-fighting competition and have any competitors left for the next one?"

"No, no. They are hard rubber knives. You get points for hitting people in certain key places. Believe me, it's a popular competition. You get trophies."

Adam got the right guy to get us across the border!

◆

When we arrived at the border, we pulled off to the side and parked in front of the border control office. Sasha insisted we remain in the car and that he take our passports into the office to explain everything. I was uncomfortable with that idea, wondering why we couldn't simply show our passports to the guard and have him check us through. But Sasha explained that we might have difficulty since Jake was leaving the country permanently.

After about a half hour, Sasha returned and informed me that I would have to leave the car and join him in the building—without my children. I refused.

He then informed me it wasn't up for discussion. I would get out of the car and I would walk into that building and leave Jacey and Jake in the car alone.

I could hear my heart pounding in my ears and I began to shake. Something was definitely wrong. I shot up a desperate prayer, tried to put on a calm demeanor as I told my kids I would be right back and that I loved them, and then I walked with Sasha into the building.

♦

"My name is Kimberly de Blecourt," I explained to the officer in the main office. "I understand there may be a problem with my passport."

A look of disgust flashed through the officer's eyes. Then he laughed a hollow, wretched laugh.

"You have been misinformed, Mrs. de Blecourt. There is no *problem*." He sneered. "*You* are under arrest."

My knees threatened to buckle. I grasped the edge of a desk to steady myself. One of the young guards swiftly turned away and then came up to me from behind. I thought he was bringing handcuffs to escort me away and I began to hyperventilate. Instead, he bumped something against the back of my knees and I realized he was offering me a stool to sit on.

While I tried to calm myself and get my breathing back under control, I determined not to cry, no matter what they did or said to me. I would stay strong. I had to for fear I would completely fall apart.

Okay, I can deal with this, I thought frantically. *But what about my kids? Who's going to take care of them?*

I looked at Sasha and said, "What about my children?"

He didn't say anything, but pushed back his shoulders and stepped closer to the head officer. For a moment, I thought he was going to land a punch. Instead, Sasha began to speak calmly and softly in rapid Russian that I could no longer understand because my mind was spinning.

The only thing I could grasp was their tones. Sasha spoke calmly and respectfully, and the lead officer responded with curt, harsh words that grew louder with each exchange.

Finally, they both paused for several long seconds and simply stared at each other. Then Sasha spoke slightly louder and more aggressively than before. He said something and held up a finger, then said something else and held up a second finger, and continued until he had ticked off three fingers, as he made his three requests known.

It was the officer's turn to be silent. Eyes narrowed, he was obviously considering Sasha's words carefully. Finally, without a word, he nodded sharply, turned on his heel, and exited the room.

Sasha turned to me and said, "Excuse me, I have to go out to the car and get all my identification papers."

"Sasha, what are you doing?" A Ukrainian never gives up his identification information willingly.

"I told them I would take personal responsibility for you. In exchange for your release, they will copy my identification information. They will arrest you on paper, but not take you into custody. They wanted me to pay for your release, but I told the officer that I'm going to take all those papers and present them to the officer's commander in Odessa to see if he has a problem with your passport. If he does, then I will pay whatever fine is owed to him. I will be right back; I just need to go out to the car."

"Will you please tell the children that I am okay? Please don't say anything about my arrest."

"I will speak to the children. Don't worry, and *don't move* off that stool."

He left the room with the second guard following behind.

I was left alone with the youngest guard who had provided the stool. I could tell by his face that he felt sorry for me. He moved behind a desk, pulled out a bunch of forms, and started to fill them out.

No one bothered to tell me what exactly I was being arrested for. I assumed it was because the warrant for Jake's return had not been pulled from this office. Sasha had told me they'd mentioned there was a problem with my passport, but I didn't know what that meant.

Eventually, the guard reached across the desk and picked up my passport, opened it, and copied my information onto the forms. He was filling out my arrest paperwork. My whole body started to shake and I got overheated and started to sweat. I swallowed hard and tried not to move, as Sasha had instructed.

Sasha reentered with his information and dropped it onto the desk in front of the guard. The guard began to copy down all of that information nonchalantly as though this type of thing happened every day.

Finally, the guard pushed the paperwork toward me.

"You need to sign here and here," Sasha explained as he pointed out each line that required my signature.

The guard pulled out the carbon copies and handed them to Sasha, who folded them and kept them with him. Nobody looked or spoke to me, and nobody offered me a copy of the arrest paperwork.

"We are free to go," Sasha said.

I wasn't sure my legs would allow me to leave the stool. Yet I forced myself to stand. I wasn't clear on everything that had taken place, but I sensed that we were getting back into Sasha's car and leaving Ukraine. Or at least I prayed that was the case. I couldn't imagine turning the car around and heading back to Odessa. I didn't think my nerves could handle that.

ESCAPE TO MOLDOVA

"Nobody say anything until we cross the border," Sasha said as soon as we got back into his car. Everyone remained silent.

The border gate rose and we drove past the guards. Instead of going straight, which would have taken us back into Ukraine toward Izmail, Sasha turned right and pulled onto a dirt road. We had entered a border zone between Ukraine and Moldova.

This route had been a matter of discussion between Sasha, Adam, and our contact in Moldova, Tom. Their discussion revolved around the best route to use to drive us into Moldova: the longer route directly into Moldova, the route we had chosen, or the shorter route through Transnistria, a small, unrecognized state nestled between the Dniester River and the eastern Moldovan border to Ukraine. Time was of the essence; we needed to get Jake across the border, yet they were concerned about this autonomous region inside the Republic of Moldova. Transnistria was occupied by Russian peacekeeping forces, allegedly guarding a large Soviet ammunition depot still residing in Cobasna, on Transnistria-controlled territory. They were not welcoming to international travelers.

As we drove, I thought about the sacrifice this man had just made for me. He had risked everything to get me across the border: he had given the Ukrainian authorities his identification information. Ukrainians never give that up. They don't want anybody to know their identities or to be on anybody's list. They don't want their cell phones tagged. They are suspicious of everything, because they understand the government's control.

We continued to ride silently on that dirt road for quite a while until we pulled onto a paved road again. Sasha turned right and pulled in front of a little brick building that looked like an old small-town American post office.

"I need to get out again," he said as he turned off the car. "I have to go inside and get permission for you to officially enter Moldova. I'm not expecting any problems here, but I want you to stay in the car. I will handle everything."

Within fifteen minutes he exited the building, got into the car, and handed me our passports.

"All is done," he said. He pulled out his GPS, plugged it in, and turned it on. Nothing happened. He turned it on again. Still nothing. He unplugged it, replugged it, and turned it on. It wasn't working.

"I don't believe this," he said, disgusted, as he placed his GPS back into its case. "Moldova. It is such a backward country. Of all countries they want to send you to, they pick *Moldova*. They don't even have maps for GPS. Nobody in this country has bothered to map out the roads. What a terrible country."

"Are we in Moldova?" Jacey asked. "It looks just like Ukraine!"

Sasha stiffened. He started the car and backed it out quickly. "I suppose we will find our way without GPS."

I looked out my side window and tried not to laugh.

The ride was long and we were all silent. Every once in a while, we would pass a sign that appeared to say we were headed toward Chisinau. Sasha's eyebrows furrowed with each sign, and I got the feeling he had never been to the capital city.

We finally came to a town and he suggested that we stop to stretch our legs and get some lunch.

"That sign says pizza." He pointed to a little restaurant. "Let's get pizza."

We went to the pizzeria, and over lunch, Sasha told me why I had been arrested.

"You were arrested for being in the country illegally," he said.

"That's not possible. I had my visa. They could see it was pasted into my passport."

"Yes, but it wasn't registered with the government. So they arrested you for failure to register your visa."

"That can't be." When I returned from Poland with my visa, I had gone to the OVIR, or immigration, office in Odessa to log it. I went alone and presented my visa and passport. They explained something to me in Russian, which included that I was supposed to leave the building, but the rest of what they said I didn't really understand. So when I left I had thought everything was taken care of and I was legal again. Apparently I was supposed to do something else or go to a different office and have the visa stamped and registered. So what I thought was registered and finished wasn't.

"I should have taken someone with me to the OVIR office," I said. The only bright spot in the arrest was that it was because of a language barrier mistake and not anything to do with Jake or the prosecutor.

"You shouldn't have been arrested at all," Sasha said. "It was ridiculous and that is what I told them. But if they stand by their decision and I pay a fine for this, they may not allow you back into the country for five years. You may be blacklisted."

◆

As we approached Chisinau, we called Tom for directions. He led us to a large parking lot in the middle of the city where we were the only car. Within moments, an unmarked white van with tinted windows pulled up beside us.

Sasha got out of the car and waved, but no one got out of the van.

This is weird, I thought. *What's going on?*

After a few more minutes, the back of the van opened and a young man with dark complexion and hair got out and approached Sasha.

This man clearly looked Eastern European. I was looking for an American.

"Stay here," I told the kids and got out of the car. "Where's Tom?" I said to Sasha. "I'm not comfortable with this."

"It's okay," Sasha reassured me. "This man, Viku, works with Tom."

The van's back door reopened and a young boy about Jacey's age or a little older hopped out and started talking with Viku. Viku then looked into the back of our car, around our mammoth green suitcase, and caught sight of the children.

"There are the children!" he said. His face brightened and he waved back at the van.

Everyone was being cautious. It seemed as though they were checking on us to make sure we were who they were expecting, and we were checking on them to make sure they were who *we* were expecting.

"Thank you," Viku said to Sasha and shook his hand. "We have it from here."

Sasha turned to me. "Are you okay with this? I think they are all right, but I won't leave if you aren't completely comfortable."

"I don't know. Tom mentioned a right-hand man and his name might have been Viku, but I don't remember."

Viku encouraged us to take our luggage out of Sasha's car and go with him. I was tired of being handed off to strangers, not knowing whom to trust, being forced to hope that they had my kids' and my best interests in mind.

As we pulled out the luggage and said goodbye to Sasha, a black SUV pulled up and out came Tom, who greeted me warmly.

"Let's get you and the kids to a safe place," he said.

With Viku following in the white van, Tom drove us to a westernized hotel situated next to a Moldovan police station.

"If anyone comes after you, they're not going to come to a place next to a police station," he said. "They're going to think you're hiding, and who would hide next to a police station?"

The hotel room had a refrigerator, so Tom drove us across a busy highway to a large supermarket. "We'll get you some food and then let you get settled in. I'll check on you once a day. It looks like you may be here for a while since the planes are still grounded."

Tom instantly put me at ease. Maybe it was because he was so kind or maybe because he was an American, I'm not sure, but I felt safe with him. I felt I could trust him.

Later that evening, two boys from the orphanage, Tony and Vasyl, came and played with Jacey and Jake while Tom talked with me and asked how I was doing. I felt confused and exhausted and still not completely at ease. I began questioning my overall mental health at this point. The toll of my time in Eastern Europe was becoming apparent even to me.

After a while he left, but he encouraged me not to leave the hotel. "Just stay here and lock your door. Call Adam and let him know you made it okay. There's nothing to worry about. You'll be fine. You are safe."

I slept through the entire night for the first time in months.

◆

The next morning, Tom came to visit and brought with him news that the airlines were selling tickets again and it looked as though we'd be able to leave the following week. I tried to contact Expedia to get refunded for the plane tickets, but they were inundated and the refund wasn't going to come anytime soon. Unfortunately, those tickets had taken our credit card to the maximum limit, so we had no more money to buy new tickets.

"Does Adam have a credit card?" he asked.

"I don't know."

"Let's call and find out."

Adam had a credit card he kept for emergencies and it had no charges on it.

"This is an emergency," Tom told Adam. "Can we use your card to buy the plane tickets to get Kim and the kids home?"

Adam agreed.

So Tom, who was also like a travel agent extraordinaire, contacted Expedia for me to see what he could do. We found out that the volcano's eruption and ash cloud had created the highest level of air travel disruption since World War II. So I would be lucky to get home anytime soon. While he was on the phone with Expedia, he watched the flights online fill quickly. Tuesday filled, then Wednesday, and he became angry with the Expedia representative. Finally, he was able to get us tickets for Thursday from Chisinau to Istanbul, on the other side of the Black Sea. But we would have to stay in Istanbul until Sunday, when we could finally fly to America. Three more days in Moldova, and then another three days in Turkey.

God, are we never going to get home? I prayed. *And how are we going to pay for this? I hardly have any money!* I could just see us stuck in Moldova or Turkey because of lack of funds.

I didn't know what I was going to do, but I knew the kids didn't need to know about that burden.

After we got the airline tickets squared away, Tom sat down to talk with me.

"Sorry about the weirdness of the way we picked you up," he said. "But I had to make sure you weren't being followed."

"Yeah, it was a little weird, meeting in that empty parking lot and everything."

"When Adam called and told me your situation, I didn't know who might be tagging along behind you. I've been in a number of serious situations in Russia, Ukraine, and here in Moldova, and it's made me extremely cautious. So when I knew you were coming, I devised a plan. I called Ukraine's Ministry of Foreign Affairs and Ukraine's State Border Guard Services, who are linked with the SBU—the Security Service of Ukraine, previously known as the KGB. I verified that your names were not in their database. Their system showed no arrest warrants to bar your exit. We expected the Ukraine-Moldova border crossing to possibly refuse your exit, given the behavior of the prosecutor, who is from eastern Ukraine, a region famous for corruption. If your prosecutor had the connections, the border guards could have held you long enough to give him enough time to come and arrest you himself. This all did seem bold for a Ukraine prosecutor—but based on our experience, realistic. Our policy is never to pay bribes, so our lawyer was standing by to have a word with the Ukrainian border officer in command and strongly present the truth regarding your status. If this failed, then other friends would attempt to escort you through Transnistria to Chisinau."

I was impressed; he had definitely thought this through quickly.

"I knew as soon as you crossed the border, but I still needed to be sure nobody had followed you."

"Wait, how did you know that?"

Tom simply smiled and continued, "I asked several police friends to sit in the café beside the parking lot—coffee on me—and keep an eye out for anything suspicious. Then I asked my sports director, Viku, who is president of a national martial arts organization, to arrange for team members, comprised of orphans and athletes, to have a strong presence around our meeting point. Once Viku confirmed you were who you said and nobody was tailing you, we figured everything was okay. But you aren't out of the woods yet. I don't know this prosecutor who's been after you or who he's connected to—but I do know the system, and I know you can't trust he won't try something here. By now he'll know that you're in this country, so..."

"So more hiding."

"I'm sorry. But listen, if you need to run out to the grocery or anything, I'll take you."

More hiding, more fear, more worry. I thought back to being under house arrest when the prosecutor issued the warrant and how God freed me from that worry, so I decided that if God had kept us safe in Ukraine, he would keep us safe in Moldova.

That night over dinner, I told the kids, "Guess what? We're on vacation!"

"Huh?" Jacey looked at me as though I'd lost my mind.

"Yep, we have a week off. Tomorrow, we're going to go over to that big mall across the highway and just have fun. We're going to buy you some little presents for your backpacks and you can play with them when we're finally on the plane going home."

Jake had no idea what vacation meant, but Jacey did and her eyes lit up.

That night, I did our laundry and hung everything out to dry so our clothes would be ready for us to wear the next day—the first day of our "vacation."

♦

Tuesday, I awoke refreshed after another full night of sleep. We walked across several busy intersections and finally got to the mall, which turned out to be a children's mall. Every store catered to children.

I added a few things to the bag my sister-in-law Ann had started for Jake, and I created a similar bag for Jacey. They were filled with little things to hold their attention during the long flight home.

We even eked out enough money to go for ice cream with Tom and several boys from his orphanage.

On Wednesday, we returned to the mall and walked around, then came back to our room, and I repacked more thoughtfully for the trip.

Via email, a producer from our local Fox news station in Michigan contacted me. "Would you be willing to be interviewed about your being stranded in a foreign country due to the volcano?"

It was my first interview by Skype. It felt so strange to be talking about the volcano and not our adoption journey. So at about 3 a.m. Moldova time, I was interviewed live. Yet another first in our adoption journey.

A part of me still couldn't quite believe we would be leaving the next day. Surely, something or someone would detain us again.

ANOTHER STOP

Our flight was scheduled to leave for Istanbul in the afternoon, so Tom picked us up and took us to the Chisinau airport a little after 1 p.m. At the ticket counter, everything went well—we secured our boarding passes—until the airline employee weighed our luggage. The mammoth green suitcase was overweight.

"This is overweight for this particular flight. You're going to need to pay extra for it to go as is." The price he quoted was exorbitant.

"Hold on a moment," Tom said and walked away. I saw him pull out a sheet of paper, scribble something on it, and return.

What is he doing? I thought. The employee was busy taking care of some other things and didn't pay any attention.

Tom returned to the counter and said, "Here it is. See, this gives her permission for this luggage. She was supposed to leave from a plane in Kiev, which allows this luggage weight, but they redirected her here, and now she's leaving from here to Istanbul and she's taking that flight to Chicago. So you should give her a pass on the fee."

I tried not to show my surprise and play along, although I had no idea how this was going to work with the employee.

The man glanced at the paper, looked back down at the scale, then nodded. He typed something into the computer, pulled out a sticker, affixed it to the luggage, and dropped everything on the conveyor belt.

I nearly fell over.

"I travel a lot," was all Tom said. We were cleared to go to our gate. We said our goodbyes and he positioned himself where he could make sure we got through security and border control. We made it through everything without a hitch and I glanced back to see if he was still there. He was, and he waved.

◆

On the plane, I put Jacey and Jake by the window seats and I took the aisle seat. Across the aisle sat a fiftysomething blond pilot who was catching a flight to Istanbul, because he had to fly a plane from there the next day. He looked and sounded to be American.

During the short flight, we struck up a conversation. He asked about my husband and I told him Jahn was already back in the States. He looked surprised.

"You mean you're traveling alone with two children into Turkey? Has no one told you anything?"

I wasn't sure how to answer.

"You can't go into Istanbul by yourself."

"But I am."

"You don't understand. You aren't safe as an American woman in this country. It's a Muslim country and they're not especially friendly to Americans—particularly women."

I could tell he was sincerely concerned.

"Please promise me you'll go straight to your hotel and stay there until your flight leaves."

"I had no idea. Thank you for telling me and for your concern. No offense, but you don't understand what I've already been through. And God has looked out for me through everything, so I'm sure he has it covered in Turkey as well."

"See? That's something you can't say in Turkey. You can't talk about God." He launched into a laundry list of all the things I couldn't do or say. Then he grew quiet. "At least it's cleared up from the volcano and it's a beautiful day."

"Yes, I'm glad of that."

When the plane landed, he helped me get our bags out of the overhead compartment and his final words to me were, "Stay in your hotel room."

I hadn't been afraid until that moment. *God, here's another situation I need you to show up in.*

Fortunately, a lot of people spoke English, so it was easy for us to make our way to our hotel, which was in the heart of the tourist district. Everywhere we walked, people touched my children, tousling Jake's hair, patting Jacey's cheeks, and saying some word in Arabic that I didn't understand.

Finally, at the hotel registration desk I said, "People keep saying something to me and I don't know what it is."

"Oh! They're telling you congratulations," the desk clerk told me.

"For what?"

He looked at me surprised. "Don't you know? Tomorrow is our Children's Day Festival. It's a national holiday here in Turkey and it will last all through the weekend. People come in from all over the world to help celebrate."

"Well, we've arrived just in time, then, haven't we?"

"Yes! And when are you leaving?"

"Sunday."

"You'll be here for the whole thing. You and your children will love it."

God showed up.

♦

Our hotel room was wonderfully clean. We fell onto the bed and sank into the mattress.

"Mom, this is the softest bed ever," Jacey cooed.

"I know," I said, ready to go to sleep right then.

We ate a light supper and went to bed, ready to explore Istanbul's tourist district, enjoy the festivities, and swim in the hotel pool on our "vacation."

The next morning, while it was still dark, a singsongy Arabic voice blared into our hotel room, apparently from a loudspeaker right outside the hotel window.

I jerked awake.

What in the world?

I sat up disoriented, while the kids somehow continued to sleep. It took me a moment before I realized it was the call for Muslim prayers. I plopped back onto my pillows and covered my head, grateful I could pray whenever I wanted. Now I just wanted to go back to sleep.

A few hours later I finally rose and took a long, hot shower in the most beautiful bathroom—it was covered in marble and gold. I noticed for the first time that I felt I was on vacation, too. I checked my email and saw that Adam had sent me a note about some friends he and Isabelle had in Istanbul who had agreed to pick us up Saturday to show us around.

Even though I was supposed to be fearful and extra cautious about being alone with my children in Turkey, I felt no fear. For the first time in months, I paid attention to myself and my appearance. I styled my hair and put on a little makeup; I felt good.

God protected us through a warrant; he protected us next to a police station; he would protect us in this Muslim country. So I got the kids up and ready and headed downstairs for breakfast, and then out to explore Istanbul.

On every corner was a baklava stand selling dozens of different kinds of fresh baklava from pistachio to chocolate to cherry. It reminded me of all the different fudge shops in American tourist towns. Many stands also offered sweet corn on a stick, which smelled wonderful. All the shops were opening and the shop owners were preparing for the day, pulling out their awnings and presenting their wares strategically outside.

We window-shopped through this wonderful mixture of post-Soviet, Greek, and Muslim cultures. There were beautiful glasses and coffee cups and dishware, Turkish rugs, and sleek women's apparel. Everywhere we went, the people greeted us joyfully, congratulating us on Children's Day. Jacey and Jake loved it because they got little gifts, coins, or snacks in most of the shops.

I noticed throughout the day that the blaring loudspeakers would call people to their prayers and everything stopped while the people knelt and prayed. I prayed too for the country and its people, who had yet to meet the Christ who loves them desperately.

We met Adam's friends on Saturday afternoon and they took us through other districts of the city. We saw historical sights, palaces, and the oldest buildings still standing. The culture and atmosphere were amazing to take in, but after a while I thought it might be best to return to the hotel, so I suggested that their kids could join Jacey and Jake in the hotel swimming pool, which excited everybody.

That night, I breathed in deeply and told God how much I appreciated everything he had done on our behalf. Hindsight is twenty-twenty, and as I thought back over the year, I saw God's hand clearly moving over and over and over.

You sure do love this boy that I now call my own, don't you? I prayed. *Thank you that you loved him so much, you moved people all over the world to bless him.*

GOING HOME

Sunday morning, the call to prayer woke me again, but this time I didn't mind. We were going home! I couldn't get to the airport fast enough. We boarded and I announced that Jake and Jacey could now open their goodie bags and play with their new toys. Although it was a long flight from Istanbul to Chicago, I rejoiced the entire way, and several times considered asking the pilot if he could fly any faster!

We landed in Chicago to storms, which meant that our flight to Grand Rapids was delayed. Of course it would be delayed, I thought. Why make anything smooth at this point?

When we finished with the U.S. immigration office in O'Hare Airport, we rushed our luggage to the check-in counter for our short flight to Grand Rapids, Michigan. There was a long line, so I asked an airline representative if we could move to the front of the line as our flight was being boarded.

"You may make your plane, but I doubt your luggage will."

I stepped up to the counter and placed our large green suitcase on the scale. A middle-aged African American clerk looked over her glasses at me and asked for my identification.

"You're not going to make this flight," she said.

"Please, put our suitcase through. We'll go back to the airport to get it when it comes in, but my children and I are going to be on the last flight into Grand Rapids."

"You're not going to make it and there's no way this suitcase will make it until sometime tomorrow."

I smiled. "I know you don't have any idea of what we've been through over the last year, but I just know we're going to make that plane. Please, just put the suitcase through."

At that moment, an announcement came over the speaker: our flight to Grand Rapids had been delayed for one hour.

The clerk looked over her glasses at me again. "Who are you?" she asked suspiciously.

I smiled and pointed up. She nodded her head, as if in agreement, and checked our large green suitcase for home.

Finally we were able to board our last plane, and after a short flight across Lake Michigan, we landed in Grand Rapids. Part of me thought it was a dream and I was going to wake up in my flat in Ukraine. And although I was excited to be home, I knew I had changed. I was exhausted, mentally worn down, and much more serious.

As soon as we walked into the airport terminal, we heard cheers and yells from a crowd of our friends, family, and news crews. Jahn ran forward and grabbed me in a tight embrace. I looked at all these beautiful faces, people who had sacrificed so much for this moment.

They all had tears running down their faces. But my eyes were dry as a desert; I had no more tears in me. I just wanted to go home and sleep. I knew I should be more excited—and part of me was—but another part, a deeper part, had shriveled up through the experience. I attempted a bright smile and thanked everyone for coming.

It felt surreal. After eleven months, I was finally home—with our son, Jake. I had survived. Because of God's goodness, Jahn and I had accomplished what we'd set out to do and we were blessed to be able to bring a wonderful little boy into our family.

I looked down at our son, who appeared ready to cry from his over-tiredness. *God has great plans for you, little one.*

I placed my arm around both Jacey and Jake and looked at my husband.

"Come on. It's time to go home."

Epilogue

We experienced a rough transition once we were home.

I was thrilled to be in my own bed, to have my clothes in a closet and not cluttered in a suitcase, to watch television programs in English, and to drink water from the tap. But I couldn't turn off my brain and still felt anxious and numb all at the same time. I was fearful of driving and I suffered from debilitating nightmares.

The jovial, quick-to-laugh person I had been was replaced with a serious, suspicious person who was always on the lookout for a fight.

I was angry—especially at Jahn. My logical, rational side knew the truth of our situation, but it didn't matter that we'd decided for him to be at home. My thoughts would accuse him: *Where were you? Why did you leave me there? Why did you make me go through that alone?* I knew that wasn't really how I felt, but those thoughts would break into my mind and stick. Fortunately, the anger toward him didn't last too long, I think because he handled me right.

Jahn took off the kid gloves and was straightforward: "You're out of bounds here. What you're saying doesn't make sense. You're picking a fight where there's no fight, Kim."

I gave Jahn permission to tell me when something was a legitimate fight and when I shouldn't go there, because I couldn't recognize the line anymore. It was all blurred to me.

I struggled over other emotions as well. It took about a month before I could start crying again—and then I didn't stop. I couldn't go anywhere and talk about what had happened in Ukraine without breaking down.

I think that part of me took so long to recover because I felt as though I was still in Ukraine. It took months to feel as though I was truly safe and home, that no one was going to come and try to take Jake away or hurt us.

I was holding in a year's worth of the stress and traumatic experiences, and they finally started to come out when I got home. I would wake in the middle of the night in a cold sweat, sure that the commander of the police force had found us and was going to arrest me. I would roll over in bed, expecting to see the police.

I also began to experience auditory hallucinations, hearing children cry.

"Who's crying?"

"Kim, nobody is crying," Jahn would tell me over and over.

Finally, Jahn became so concerned, he encouraged me to seek therapy. When I was finally able to visit a counselor, I was diagnosed with post-traumatic stress disorder and referred to another counselor who specialized in its treatment. With that counselor's help, using EMDR (eye movement desensitization and reprocessing), I was able to get to the root of the issues.

I didn't receive real relief, however, until I relived the incident where the woman hit me over the head during the first couple of weeks I was in Ukraine. It was a surprise to discover I had lived with PTSD the entire time I was in Ukraine, because that incident, along with the stress of it, had gotten physical. I was assaulted, and that's what prevented my brain from processing things in a healthy manner.

I've come a long way, and can now sleep a full night, although I still occasionally struggle with anxiety from the experience. Oddly enough, it returned when I began to work seriously on this book. But I pray that it's only a temporary experience and that my mind is flooded instead with all the reminders of how God delivered us.

As for Jake's transition, at first he was especially shy of all the attention and fearful over things we take for granted—such as grass. He had never seen it before and was afraid to step on it or even touch it. He clung to me or Jacey constantly. But with each day, he became more confident and comfortable in his new home. Jahn and Jake have bonded slowly, but have enjoyed going fishing together and doing other guy things. Jake loves helping his daddy.

Jacey was delighted to return to her school and friends and singing. She has responded to the role of older sibling well and her little brother loves to sit on her lap and be cuddled. She's taught him how to throw a football and how to play other games. They have truly become siblings—to the point where they can now annoy and pick on each other without end.

◆

So many things happened during my time in Ukraine that I couldn't possibly tell them all. Some are private memories: some good, treasures for me and my family only; some painful; some neither good nor bad, but remaining private for safety reasons. This book includes the major points I felt most important to tell God's miraculous story.

God's story is still being created in my continued relationship with Jake's half sister Svetlana. We've stayed in contact, and after my constant nagging she went to the doctor and was diagnosed with tuberculosis. She is in need of serious medical care. I promised I would be by her side. I know God will make a way, even when none is visible to us, because he loves her as much as he loves Jake. Ultimately, I would love to see her make a life filled with love, joy, and health.

This book details my journey with God and my eventual calling to be His hands and feet to the oprhaned in the world. The world grew incredibly small for me through my travels and I no longer feel comfortable sitting on our sofa while so many children suffer. I have been instilled with a heart of longing to serve Him by serving His children—all His children. I cannot remain still. And so an advocate for orphans and their right to a family has been born. My involvement with a local post-adoption support group, a local foster care outreach, and my international work with Food for Orphans (foodfororphans.com) has begun. I have no idea where my continued journey with God will lead me. I only know that God continues to call; I continue to follow.

And now the fight continues for *all* orphans and children who need families who will love and care for them—until they too can all go *home*.

Acknowledgments

In the prologue of this book, I stated that while this is a de Blecourt journey, ultimately it's God's story and for his glory. But a story is never written alone, just as a symphony is never played with only one instrument. Many people weave into our story and I couldn't possibly name every one—nor can I name the many in Ukraine who played a significant role but whose identities I am unable to share for fear of retribution against them. So to those whose real names I can't list, you know who you are. Thank you. God knows your names and has special blessings planned for you throughout eternity, because you dared to care for one of the least of these.

For the people whose names and identities I can share:

Jacob de Blecourt, an amazing father-in-law who sacrificed financially for us to bring Jake into our family. Our son couldn't possibly have a better namesake.

My parents, Judy and Jim Elhart, and Rodney and Ann Seeds, for encouraging us, praying for us, and believing in us from day one. Your phone calls meant more than you can ever know.

Ann de Blecourt Waker, sister-in-law extraordinaire, for your support and love—and for visiting us and bringing much-needed items to Ukraine!

My brother, John Seeds, for your spirit-filled emails to me when I was in the depths of despair.

Donald and Karen Brink, our spiritual mentors and fellow Gideons. Thank you for your prayers in the middle of the night, your encouragement and direction, and for spoiling us through your love and pot roast.

Don and Linda Wilson, for the tear-filled nights of prayer with Jahn, for mopping up our flooded basement, and for your continued friendship and love.

Carl and Ilse Whisner, outstanding Peace Corps workers and the best friends to have when you're stuck in a country alone.

Our pastor, Dean Parham, and our church family at Immanuel Church, Holland, Michigan. You gave to us through your encouragement, prayers, and finances. You are an amazing group of believers. You prayed us home.

Our Immanuel Church Small Group, Dave and Cari Uitdeflesch, Rich and Deb Muyskens, and Pete and Sally Mulder. Thank you for your constant coverage in prayer, your thoughtful scriptural studies, and your encouragement during our long journey.

Jahn's Wednesday Morning Breakfast partners, Rick Walker and Brent Campbell. Your listening ears, broad shoulders, and understanding hearts allowed Jahn to express his fear, frustration, and faith on a weekly basis.

The University of Minnesota Department of Pediatrics, International Adoption Medicine Program and Clinic, for your valued assistance while we were in Ukraine.

Tim and Sandi Bastiaanse, for always having a place at their table for Jahn while he was home alone, for helping to decorate our new son's room so it was ready for his arrival, and for offering the laughter only best friends can provide.

Amber Clark, for arranging a prayer walk for our family, and for sharing your contacts, your love of the written word, and our Father's heart for the orphan.

Tammi Dryden, our photographer and friend. May your adoption story be a sweet one. I cannot wait to see your entire family together at last.

Marc and Laura Anthony and the Direction Adult Sunday School class, who always started their fellowship with, "Jahn, give us an update on Kim," and who arranged meals for my family while I was away. Thank you for your continued care.

Laura Koster, who took care of Jacey until her dad came home from work each day. Thank you for being "Mom" when I couldn't be. John Koster, for the love, attention, and "wrestling" with Jake during the mission trip. And a thank-you, Landon Koster, for the daily after-school craft times Jacey so loved.

Andrea Sybesma, who initially traveled with us to Ukraine to aid in filming our apotion. Your friendship, assistance, and heart for adoption made dark days brighter. May you find your place in advocacy for orphans soon.

Dave and Erin Buckley (and Dylan, Jaron, and Austin), for your many home-cooked meals for my family while I was away, all the clothing and toys for Jake, and your date nights and family outings with us. We love you.

Jon Daniel and Jenna Campau, who gave of themselves through fellowship, spiritual journaling, and financial contributions beyond belief. Thank you for your obedience to God. May your family continue to be blessed.

Bruce Visser and Dale Visser, for supporting our decision to adopt, even when it meant Jahn's absence during the busiest time for construction in Michigan.

The staff at Visser Brothers, Inc., for your prayers and concern, and for picking up the slack in Jahn's absence.

Shelly Beach, who helped shape the initial chapters of this book and wrote a killer proposal that landed a contract. Thank you for your continued encouragement.

Wanda Sanchez, whose gifts and skills as a publicist have helped me refine my vision and expand my reach, and infuse me with confidence.

West Michigan Word Weavers, for your belief in our story from day one and for your ongoing assistance as the journey continues.

Bob Crough of Canine Antics and his family, Lindsey, Madison, and Dayna, for puppy care beyond the call of duty. Your kindness enabled us to keep our beloved Buddy.

Calvary Schools of Holland and Mrs. Nancy Leach for their extraordinary efforts to help Jacey finish third grade from abroad, assisting me to guide her, and for their prayers and concern on our behalf.

David Sanford, for his initial advice and expertise on how to put together the idea for this book. You and Renee are wonderful adoption advocates.

Tina Jacobson of B&B Media Group, for believing in this project while it was yet happening, for your initial pro bono work, and for the long-distance phone conversations to Ukraine.

Steve Laube, my agent, for catching the vision and encouraging me to hold out for the right publisher who would also catch the vision and passion for this project. I couldn't have done it without you, Steve.

Ginger Kolbaba, for your hours of interviewing to squeeze God's story out of a woman reliving the hardest moments of her life. Thank you for sharing your dedicated talent and for putting words to God's story. You rock!

Joey Paul and the team at FaithWords, for your commitment to God's story, for being willing to let him shine in and through this book, and for your unparalleled support throughout the publishing process.

Jahn, the love of my life and the best father to our wonderful children, for your unbelievable support, encouragement, and strength throughout life's journey.

Jacey, my precious daughter, who fills our life with joy and song.

Jake, my sweet Sasha, who brings the wonder of discovery to our lives.

My Facebook and email friends. During those long, arduous months in Ukraine when I thought I was losing my mind and wondering where God was in the midst of the darkness, he continually showed up in your thoughtful messages.

My heavenly Father, who never abandons, you were always working behind the scenes. Lord, how I love and praise you, my teacher, my rock, my shield, my deliverer, the master of my life. May you forever be glorified.